The Bunny Lover's

Complete Guide To

House
Rabbits

The Ultimate Handbook for
Successfully Living Indoors with a Pet Rabbit

By:
The Bunny Guy

Edited by:
Rani Vaughn

To my Mom, who will always be missed.

First Edition

ISBN-10: 0985003200
ISBN-13: 978-0-9850032-0-3

Director Properties, LLC
603 Seagaze Dr., Suite 320
Oceanside, CA 92054

Table of Contents

Acknowledgments

I first want to thank my family who taught me how to love, especially my mom who passed away while I was writing this book. She always seemed to understand my passion for bunnies, even when it seemed a little weird or over the top. I will always miss her.

My wife, Denise, deserves recognition for her dedication and loyalty to her passion for all animals. She instilled in me the notion that most misery amongst animal species is caused by humans and therefore only humans can help alleviate it.

All of my pets have always been considered part of the family, and each and every bunny that I have had has contributed to this book with what they have given me. The one thing that you can always count on is if you give love to your pet, you will certainly receive something in return.

A thousand thanks must also go to the San Diego House Rabbit Society volunteers. They directly and indirectly taught me almost everything I know about rabbits and helped lead me to be a voice for lagomorphs everywhere. I know I was blessed to live in a place with such an amazing, active chapter of this important rabbit-centric organization.

There must also be gratitude expressed to all the rabbit-rescue volunteers everywhere who have discovered that they can make a difference, one bunny at a time. I hold in the highest esteem the many thousands who have supported their local chapter of the House Rabbit Society or other rabbit-rescue organizations. You are all heroes in my book. Your work will eventually help make things better for all rabbits in the future.

Chapter 1:
Why a Book About Rabbits?

People frequently refer to me as "The Bunny Guy," but I was not always an expert with rabbits. It is surprising how many rabbit owners know very little about their charges, but I, too, was totally ignorant about how to properly care for bunnies, even as I had my first several as pets. When I realized that I was part of the large majority of rabbit owners who loved their rabbits but who did not really know how to properly care for them, I decided to go on a mission.

My quest became to learn all that I could about rabbits, and to share that knowledge with as many other bunny lovers as possible. I began by volunteering at an animal shelter and attending classes given by my local House Rabbit Society chapter, San Diego House Rabbit Society (SDHRS; www.sandiegorabbits.org), so that I could obtain as much hands-on instruction as possible. I also applied to become an educator for SDHRS, and began talking to hundreds of folks about proper house rabbit care and welfare.

How to care for and interact with a house rabbit is not intuitive, especially if you were raised with cats or dogs. Everything from feeding to housing to petting your bunny has very little in common with how you may have cared for and played with other types of pets. Most of the information about how to do all these things in regard to house rabbits has not been readily available in the past. Also, many of the things I have read online or been told by a vet were not completely true or factual; there are just so many myths and misunderstandings about house rabbits.

It is not because rabbit owners out there intend to be cruel or to mistreat their pets, but I discovered from my own experiences that it is mostly due to ignorance that four out of five pet bunnies do not receive the proper care in regard to their diets, living conditions, exercise, and interaction. I completely understand how this can happen, since I made all of the common mistakes myself in my first years living with rabbits.

Rabbits cleverly do unexpected things, such as Scotty, who likes to climb this tree during exercise time at the shelter.

This is why I decided that I needed to share all of the knowledge I have accumulated about rabbits with you, and to tell my story about how I came to be known as "The Bunny Guy." I hope you will learn many new things from this book, and will come back to it again and again for reference. There is so much to learn about bunnies that it is really an ongoing process; even veterinarians who specialize in treating rabbits are constantly learning new things about lagomorphs (that's the scientific name for rabbits).

There are so many popular misconceptions held by the public about rabbits, such as they make great pets for children—and nothing could be further from the truth. Much of what the general public knows about rabbit care and feeding comes from the days when rabbits were farm animals kept in small hutches or cages out in a barn or backyard, and has nothing to do with how companion rabbits need to be cared for. Rabbits are a very misunderstood pet, and are in fact the third most-euthanized animal in all shelters across the United States.

Through working with my local Humane Societies and educating people about lagomorphs, I have seen a tendency for the public to consider rabbits "disposable" pets. For example, if someone brings a rabbit home and things just don't work out (such as the rabbit displays destructive behavior or fails to become litter-box trained), the person will often get rid of him, and then just go out and spend another $30 to bring home another rabbit, thinking it will be a different situation. It's not uncommon to see unwanted pet rabbits set free so that they can run and roam with their "buddies in the wild" (I have actually heard this said). This is as unconscionable as doing the same thing to a cat or dog, and actually worse, since rabbits are prey animals who literally do not have any buddies out there in the wild and are often the targets of attacks by other animals—including cats and dogs.

Every rabbit has a completely individual personality. Just like with other pets, you will never find two bunnies who like exactly the same things or behave exactly the same way. That in itself is testament to how complex and interesting these animals are. If you learn how to speak your rabbit's "language" and interact with your long-eared friend, you will swiftly see, and appreciate, how unique each one is. I hope that this book will give you some

understanding of how to give the right signals to your rabbit, and to correctly interpret the ones your bunny is giving you, so that you will be able to successfully communicate with each other and become lifelong pals.

Befriending a house rabbit is about trust and communication. When your rabbit learns to trust you, you will be amazed how he will communicate and share every part of his life with you.

So, in short, the main purpose of this book is to dispel all of the myths about house rabbits and to provide you with all the information you need to properly feed, house, communicate with, and care for your unusual—but incredibly special—pet. I will also expose bunnies for the

Rabbits are playful and interactive pets.

wonderful, dynamic companions they are who will provide you with countless hours of laughter and tons of love. You truly have not lived until you have seen a bunny dance or been kissed all over your face by your loving bun. My hope is that, through education and preparation you, like so many others, will become a "bunny slave" for life, as I have been since finding my first rabbit several years ago and bringing her home.

Another goal is for this to be the one rabbit book that you will read cover to cover, but also use as a reference manual on an as-needed basis. If you've never had a house rabbit, I suggest that you read Chapters 1-12 first: These are the most critical ones that you should be familiar with before bringing home your companion bunny. If you are reading this book and you already have a bunny in your home, then you'll probably want to read the entire book right away, as you are likely to learn many things and might want to make some immediate changes to your existing rabbit routine.

Another reason I decided to write this book is because there is a limited number of good books available about house rabbits, and I felt that one written in layman's terms by an expert rabbit lover would be very useful for those who are on the same path that I have been on. Through this book, I aspire to make a connection with you, since everything here is heartfelt and my own true stories and experiences.

I begin this book with me finding my first bunny and end with how you can become part of the force that changes the future for all rabbits everywhere. I will be brutally honest by sharing all of my own mistakes in hopes that you may learn from them and not have to go through finding out about them all the hard way, like I did.

If you are starting out at square one and know very little about rabbits, you have a wonderful, rewarding experience ahead of you. As with all learning, only perseverance keeps you going until the end. When you have a tough issue that is perplexing you, then get this book out and refer to it. Most likely, someone has gone through what you are experiencing. Be wary of things you might read on the Internet, because I have found a large portion of things written about rabbits

there is not totally true or to be trusted. Some of the untrue stuff I have read was even written by veterinarians, so you must always be cautious when researching house rabbits online.

I have found my best resource for learning to be the many House Rabbit Society websites. They are all run by rabbit experts who often know more than many vets when it comes to rabbit issues, especially if the vets are not rabbit specialists. You can visit the national House Rabbit Society's website at [www.rabbit.org], and also locate the HRS chapter nearest you on their site.

It is also useful to develop a network of bunny friends and mentors. You can do this online at fun bunny-centric sites and at your nearest House Rabbit Society chapter by becoming a member. If there is not a local HRS chapter close to you, then you might consider starting a casual, regular social meeting where other bunny lovers can get together with you. These are easy to start and a lot of fun for both you and your bunny.

I wish you and your house rabbits all the best, and I hope that this book provides you with answers to all of your rabbit-related questions.

See the **Resources** section at the end of this book for a list of websites that are house-rabbit related.

NOTE: This book refers to rabbits in the gender-specific "he" instead of using the impersonal "it." Every time I mention "he," you should know that gender can be either male or female, and unless I specifically say I am referring to male rabbits, all references apply to both sexes.

Summary

- How to care for and interact with a house rabbit is not intuitive.

- There are many popular misconceptions held by the public about rabbits.

- Every rabbit has a completely individual personality.

- Befriending a house rabbit is about trust and communication.

- My best sources for learning about rabbits are the many House Rabbit Society websites.

- It is always useful to develop a network of bunny friends and mentors.

A group of friends enjoy a picnic at the park with their bunnies.
That's me on the right with Lucy and Denise (with the ponytail) is holding Ricky.

Chapter 2:
How I Became "The Bunny Guy"

Long before I was "The Bunny Guy," I was just like most people and knew very little about rabbits. My adventure learning about them has been a journey, just like yours will most likely be. When I look back at where I started and how far I have come, it is easy to understand why most people need a book like this before they ever bring their first rabbit home. As I have said before, many things about bunnies are not intuitive, and I made many of the same mistakes that I have been coaching people about for years. In order to have a healthy, happy bunny, you will want to avoid these same mistakes.

My first memories of encounters with rabbits are not until I was a teenager. Several of my neighbors had rabbits living in backyard hutches that I would see while visiting friends. Any handling or petting of these rabbits was completely out of the question, since they all displayed intense aggression typical of caged buns; you might withdraw a stump if you put your hand inside any of their cages expecting to rub their ears. These were not friendly, cuddly pets. I am pretty sure that none of them were spayed or neutered.

I grew up with our family always having a pet dog and never experienced any time with a rabbit until about 20 years ago. My parents had just moved to a retirement community and had asked me to pick up some stuff they had left in the backyard with my big truck. When I moved some panels, out hopped a tiny white bunny with very long fur. I was very surprised when she allowed me to walk over and pick her up. I thought that some little old lady who lived in the neighborhood (since it was an over-55

community) must have lost her because she was so tame.

After placing ads in the local paper and all around the area, my wife and I realized that we now had our first pet bunny. For lack of a better name, "Miss Bunners" joined our dog, cats, and goldfish as a family member. I did not know any better and built her a cage with chicken wire (horror!) and some pieces of old wood that I had lying around. What I knew about rabbits could be described in one word: nothing.

We visited Miss Bunners several times daily in the backyard by the pool, and we were always amazed by how she would jump out of her cage into our arms when we opened the door. Looking back now, she was such a sweet little girl who never complained about our not knowing any better than to house her in her backyard cage. She was, and still is, the only albino, Mini lop-eared Angora that I have ever seen. She required almost-daily brushing, and we spoiled her with lots and lots of treats (again because we did not know any better; see **Chapter 9** for information about how to properly feed your rabbit).

Miss Bunners would become very cross and let us know how disappointed she was if we missed one scheduled treat time. Her treat of choice was Lorna Doone® cookies, which is probably the worst possible treat we could have ever given her. It is hard to say how old little Miss Bunners was when we found her, but she was doomed to have a short life by living outside and being fed nothing but pellets and sweet human food. She lived with us just over four years before we found her passed away in her cage one day.

I did not know that she had died early. I had asked some friends who had a rabbit before how long rabbits could live, and they told me six years at the most (not true). This led me to believe that Miss Bunners' passing was normal and to be expected. Little did I know that I had done all the wrong things and most likely was the cause for her leaving us so soon. It would be years before I would become aware of this.

Our second rabbit was rescued from a very small wooden hutch in my sister's backyard. Her daughter had gotten the rabbit a year or two earlier and, now in high school, no longer had time for him. He had become very difficult and aggressive, so my sister did not argue when my wife informed us all that she wanted to take the bunny home with us so that he would not continue to be neglected.

It had been a little over a year since we had lost Miss Bunners, and we missed having a loving, friendly bun as part of our family menagerie of critters. Still totally ignorant of how to house and care for a rabbit, we hired a handyman to build a huge rabbit condo in the pool area. It was extremely roomy and was built to last, but it had a wire bottom because we still had never heard of a rabbit being trained to use a litter box. The huge cage was built with a hopper to feed the new guy unlimited pellets—just like the vet had told us to do.

Of course, now I know that these were all wrong things to do, and that rabbits should never be given unlimited pellets once they are beyond six months old, because it can shorten their lives by half from giving them too much food. Still, like all good parents, we wanted to give this bunny a better house and life than our previous rabbit was given, even though we still did not have a clue how to do it properly. Having our dog-and-cat vet give us the wrong advice did not help us, either.

We named the new guy Mr. Bunners, of course, since he was a boy. The first time we put him on our patio so he could hop around, we noticed a huge problem. He was aggressively circling and attacking my wife by grabbing hold of her leg and mounting her. At first it was funny, because he only did it to her and never did it to me. The humorous aspect quickly evaporated and we suddenly learned the number-one rule of having a pet bunny: Unspayed or un-neutered rabbits are not good pets.

I will devote a whole chapter to this subject later in the book (**Chapter 8**), and needless to say, our little guy had neuter surgery that very week. Luckily for him, he survived the surgery, because we made another huge mistake by taking him to our cat-and-dog vet, who would eventually oversee his death several years later. We now know that you should only take your bunny to an experienced rabbit vet (also known as an "exotics" vet). Let me say that again: Rabbits are delicate little critters who require special veterinary knowledge and expertise in order to be properly medically treated. Part of having a pet bunny is having an experienced rabbit/exotics vet available for whenever you might need him or her. Finding one should be done before you ever bring a bunny home. You can locate a rabbit/exotics veterinarian by visiting your local House Rabbit Society website.

Mr. Bunners is the rabbit who taught me that bunnies should live indoors with their humans. Even though he had this huge condo out in the backyard, I felt guilty because he put up such a fuss when I went to catch him to put him back in the condo at night. He clearly did not want to go in there and would let me know it. This bunny was very aggressive from the day we brought him home and he never hesitated to make it clear when he disapproved of something by using his teeth. I had nicknamed him "The Chomper."

After about a year of him clearly telling me that he was upset about sleeping outside in his condo, I had this bright idea to buy a child's playpen so that Mr. Bunners could spend his nights in the house. We had no idea there was such a thing as an X-pen that was made for this purpose. We still had never heard of a house rabbit and neither had any of our friends. Most of them thought we were a bit strange because we now had a bunny living indoors with us.

It would be years before we learned about litter-box training, so Mr. Bunners had his own set of towels that would be changed daily to keep his abode clean. Looking back at his pictures now, I can see that he was overweight and not very healthy, but we did not know it at the time. Like all bunnies, he had a sweet tooth and loved to beg for treats. He was already chubby from an all-pellet diet when we brought him home, and he got heavier over time from all of his favorite treats. I thought I was being caring by giving him what he wanted. I could not have been more wrong.

This was the beginning of my daily interaction with a rabbit indoors. It is totally different from when you go outside to visit your bunny. When you socialize with a rabbit indoors, you are relating to a companion animal, and there is a huge difference. Indoors, a bunny is part of the family, whereas outdoors he simply is not. It is my personal feeling that outdoor bunnies are nothing more than livestock, because true pets must live indoors in order for you and your family to be able to experience the joys of their company. If he is living alone outdoors, then you have a frustrated and lonely rabbit.

One day, Mr. Bunners appeared very lethargic, which was not normal. He was sprawled out in a funny way and it looked like he was having trouble breathing. We have always been rather in tune with our pets, so we noticed it right

away and once again took him to our cat-and-dog vet that we loved.

We were asked to leave Mr. Bunners at the vet's office, and told that they would call when they knew what his problem was. Later, we got a phone call from the vet saying that they were going to do some kind of procedure to help him, and that as soon as they turned on the clippers to shave him, the sound gave him a heart attack. They said that he died of fright. Whether it was true or not, it haunted us.

Me, aka "The Bunny Guy," with Ricky, Lucy, and Star on my lap.

After that experience, we swore we would never leave another bunny at the vet all alone like that. I felt that if I had been there, maybe Mr. Bunners would not have been so scared and died. I had no clue that the reason he was at the vet in the first place was a result of the poor diet and care the little Chomper had received from us.

13

Don't get me wrong: We dote over all of our animals and spend thousands each year on vet bills, medicine, and food. We have always called them our "kids," since our real children have long moved away from home. It was not because of neglect that our bunnies' lives were shortened. It was 100 percent pure ignorance. We were loving our bunnies to death.

My wife and I took Mr. Bunners' passing very hard and the grief was severe. At first we blamed the vet, and then we blamed ourselves. Mr. Bunners took his place in the row of boxes containing the ashes of all our past pets on top of the piano. It would be six months before we felt we were ready to adopt a new bunny.

Mr. Bunners was very overweight living outside in a wire bottom cage.

Since bringing Mr. Bunners home and learning from him that bunnies really need to live inside the house, I had heard of our local chapter of the House Rabbit Society. I went onto the Internet and sought them out. I saw that they had bunnies who were up for adoption, so I filled out a several-page adoption questionnaire. I was a bit shocked to hear that I was being denied an adoption because our previous bun had lived in an outdoor cage.

The bunny foster mom told me that I needed to get a book about house rabbits and read it completely. I bought the only book I could find on the subject and read it two times. When I returned to try to adopt again, we were introduced to two wonderful buns. One was a lovely, large, lop-eared girl named Maribelle and the other was a smaller, all-black Havana girl bun named Pamela. It truly was a hard decision, since we wanted to take both of them home.

We watched as they both played in a Cottontail Cottage, and both seemed a little shy to me. Maribelle was a little more shy than Pamela, so we decided to adopt Pamela right then and there. She rode home with us in her carrier to live in a big, new rabbit condo that we had bought for her. (We like this style of rabbit abode because it looks like a piece of furniture and does not appear as if it belongs in the backyard like plastic or metal cages do; read **Chapter 10** for more information about housing your rabbit.)

Pamela turned out to be painfully shy and, again in our ignorance, we never picked her up or held her since she made it very clear that she was not into that. We thought that we were doing the right thing by not handling her if she did not want to be handled. If I had it to do over again, I would never have taken this approach, because I have learned that part of the socialization of a bunny is him learning to be handled for grooming and, of course, petting.

Most rabbits are not born enjoying being picked up and, as a matter of fact, it is an instinct for them to fear it. For most wild rabbits, if they are leaving the ground, they are about to get eaten, so it is natural for a bunny not to want to be picked up. It is through trust and learning that a bunny can bond with his humans and tolerate it. Some end up doing this better than others, and some will actually ask for it. Just remember that if you simply never handle your bunny, he never learns to accept it at all.

Even though I had read the book about house rabbits several times and was referring to it when we had rabbit questions, I continued to give our new bunny improper care. Pammy (as we nicknamed her) had learned to beg for treats and we always gave in when we saw her cute poses that she would do to get whatever she wanted. Popcorn, peanuts, and lots of other stuff that she should have never gotten to eat were regularly given to her and, over time, they took their toll. Most people just do not understand how devastating it is to a rabbit's long-term health to have a diet like this.

One day we awoke to Pammy not wanting her usual treats, and we became even more alarmed when she had no interest in her evening salad. We kept trying to coax her into eating, instead of taking her directly to the vet. When a bunny stops eating or pooping, he needs to go to the vet *now*, not in a couple of days.

By the time we realized that we had an emergency on our hands, it was the weekend and our choice of rabbit vets had become very limited. My wife remembered that when we had adopted Pamela, we had been given a coupon for an exam by a local rabbit vet. In light of our last experience with a non-rabbit vet, we decided that we needed to see one with rabbit experience.

When we brought Pammy in to the vet, it was the first time we had ever picked her up or taken her anywhere in the four years that we had her. I am sure this made the whole event way more traumatic than it needed to be.

Our first red flag that day was that the vet suggested, after a series of X-rays and tests, we do exploratory surgery to find the problem. I had read enough on the Web to know that this was

Pamela liked to look out the window from on top of her Cottontail Cottage.

not a good choice and that the survival rate for this kind of surgery was not very high.

We were sent home and told to give Pammy fluids under her skin and to force-feed her with a syringe several times a day with liquid food. For ten days, we would have to catch this rabbit—who had never been caught by us in years—and one of us would have to hold her down while the other forced her to swallow this stuff that looked like something from the movie *The Exorcist*.

I think Pamela knew we were trying to save her life, and it brings tears to my eyes now to think that I was actually enjoying the intimate contact with her, doing the fluids and food. I was becoming excited to think that, after she got well, I would be able to have more touching contact with her. In those last two weeks, we became closer and more in tune with Pamela than we had ever been before. She began doing several things that were new and exciting, and we were positive that she was going to come out of this crisis a new-and-improved bunny.

After ten days with barely any poops and little eating, we brought her back to the vet. From everything we had read and heard, she should not have survived that long without pooping or eating, so we still had hope she would eventually get better. We were still against the exploratory surgery, and so a barium procedure was suggested. I had received one of these myself and felt that it was a much more benign and safe thing to try.

We had promised Pammy that we would not leave her at the vet like we had done with Mr. Bunners, but the vet convinced us that this was necessary. We had the vet promise to do the procedure herself and, with reservations, we left the office. We were shocked an hour later to get the distressing phone call for us to come and pick her up.

A vet technician had forced a tube that was too large into her throat and had punctured her lung cavity. The vet did not realize this and then proceeded to pump the barium into Pamela's lungs instead of her stomach. This mistake was 100-percent fatal, and we were told there was nothing that they could do.

We were in a panic and retrieved Pammy as quickly as we could to take her to a veterinary emergency room, where they opened her up and tried to remove as much of the barium as possible. We knew the chances of success were going to be slim, but we were very encouraged when Pammy awoke from the surgery and recognized us. I am crying as I write this now, remembering how I was so hopeful that our precious little girl would make it.

Pammy slept quietly through the night and then had a seizure early the next morning and died. I was inconsolable when I got the call from the hospital. My wife and I cried non-stop for days. Every time we thought about her, we would both break down into sobs. It just seemed so unfair that she was robbed of the last years of her life, especially when I had such high hopes of an even closer relationship with her after she recovered.

One of the best things I did after Pammy died was to have a necropsy done. The vet told me that she had very severe fatty liver disease, but it would be six months before I would learn what that really meant. I had a lot of anger at the vet who I felt had botched the barium procedure, and I took no responsibility at all myself for what had happened to my little bunny girl.

In our grief, my wife and I decided to go to work at our local Humane Society to help other rabbits and to take our minds off our loss. We had asked the San Diego House Rabbit Society if they needed any new volunteers and they had directed us to fill in for a while at the shelter, where we could learn about and help the bunnies. We started going in one day a week together, cleaning the rabbit cages and socializing with the buns.

To learn even more, I started taking advantage of the monthly educational classes given by our House Rabbit Society chapter to the public. In this learning process, it suddenly dawned on me that the reason Pamela had fatty liver disease in the first place was because of me. Even though I had read the book and could not have loved her any more, I had overfed her with foods that she should have never had to the point that she got sick and died.

That was a terrible revelation, and it made me aware that the number-one reason bunnies out there were not living the long lives they deserved was because of the lack of knowledge of their owners. This sent me out on my mission of first fully educating myself and then sharing this knowledge with as many people as I possibly can in hopes that, someday, how to properly care for house rabbits will be common knowledge, just like it is for dogs and cats.

After a couple months volunteering at the Humane Society with the buns, my wife and I adopted a sweet pair of bunnies that we ended up bonding together. Ricky is a little black Havana boy who reminded me so much of our precious Pamela, and Lucy is a large, lovable New Zealand White girl.

For Lucy, meeting Ricky was love at first sight, but Ricky was a lot more difficult to convince that they should live together. It took six weeks of intensive interactions to finally get the two bonded, but now they happily do everything together.

I quickly realized that they would never be anything like my previous bunny Pammy. I would always miss the way she used to come and cuddle up next to me on the floor and how she would nip at my toes under the blanket to tell me that she wanted to do that. Now, at this point in my journey, I know that every single bunny is special and has his own unique personality. No bunny can ever be like your last one, and each one is as different from another as humans are.

It has now been a couple of years since Ricky and Lucy joined our family, and they are the happiest, healthiest bunnies I have ever had. Ricky will come when he is called, and both of them will jump into my lap for a healthy bunny treat. They never get sweets, fruit, or unhealthy treats. They both work as "spokesbunnies" for our local House Rabbit Society, and have learned to tolerate long car rides and interact with lots of people.

A couple of months after bringing Ricky and Lucy home, we got a phone call from the chapter manager of the San Diego House Rabbit Society asking if we could foster a very sick bun for the weekend. We picked her up from the shelter and ferried her to several vets. She had been attacked by an animal and one of her eyes was hanging out and very infected.

That weekend of fostering turned into three months of vet visits and three different surgeries. Several times, I thought that this little bun would not survive, but she was a real fighter. The vet said that she actually attacked him when he entered her X-pen, which he said was a first for him. We started calling her "The Scrapper."

Eventually, we named her Star and I have to tell you, I am the world's worst foster parent. After three months of nursing this little bunny, I did not want to give her up and decided to adopt her too, and she has turned out to be one of the most special rabbits I have ever met.

Star is a true lap rabbit who spends every evening sitting on my lap. She likes to go everywhere with me, even if it is just to the corner store. She enjoys car rides with her "dad" and she is the "kissiest" bunny I have ever known. Every day, this girl gives me dozens of bunny kisses. I have taught her to kiss my face when I ask her to, and it always amazes people when she does it for me.

This girl bunny and I communicate perfectly, and she actually tells me when she needs to use her litter box while she is on my lap or in our bed. She likes to hop around on her leash at the beach, and even goes with me to the dentist or on the train in her pet stroller. My accountant has come to expect her being with me when I visit.

I started wondering if there were other families out there who had "bunny buddies" who liked doing things with them as well, so

I launched a monthly group meeting at a local park near the beach that's open to anyone who loves lagomorphs. I wanted a family-oriented, regular event that would include the whole family and their pet rabbits. From this idea, the Beach Bunnies group was born.

It started out with just nine bunnies playing on the sand in their X-pens while their humans had a small picnic, but it has quickly grown into a much bigger gathering: We now regularly have over 20 rabbits and twice as many humans in attendance at our monthly get-togethers! The buns gather on the grass in the park during our cool Southern California falls and winters, and on the sand late in the day during the hot summer months. It's turned into a fun, festive way for everyone to include their buns in an outdoor family event, and each meeting sees more and more attendees of both the rabbit and human varieties.

We have even started marching in one of our local Fourth of July parades to try to raise public awareness about house rabbits. And besides, who doesn't love a bunny?

As you have already surmised, my journey learning about rabbits and how to care for them has been long and often painful. My wife, Denise, and I have gone from doing it all wrong to being passionate educators for people with rabbits. When we work as educators at the annual national veterinary convention in San Diego, we find that we now know more than many of the vets in attendance about proper housing and care for rabbits. How ironic is that?

Whether you're just embarking on or are continuing down your road of house-rabbit education, this book will provide you with a wealth of information. It is the culmination of Denise's and my 20 years of rabbit experiences, as well as what we have learned in education

classes about rabbits from well-respected rabbit veterinarians and from rabbit experts at our local House Rabbit Society. Throughout this book, I'll tell you many stories of our personal experiences with our own family bunnies, as I did in this chapter, so that you can learn directly from my mistakes.

Summary

- **Most people need a book like this before they ever bring their first rabbit home.**

- **Miss Bunners was doomed to have a short life by living outside and being fed nothing but pellets and sweet human food.**

- **Unspayed or un-neutered rabbits are not good pets.**

- **You should only take your bunny to an experienced rabbit vet (also known as an "exotics" vet).**

- **Mr. Bunners is the rabbit who taught me that bunnies should live indoors with their humans.**

- **Most rabbits are not born enjoying being picked up.**

- **Part of the socialization of a bunny is teaching him to be handled by you.**

- **The number-one reason bunnies out there are not living the long lives they deserve is the lack of knowledge of their owners.**

- **Every single bunny is special and has his own unique personality.**

- **I have gone from doing it all wrong to being an educator for people with rabbits.**

- **You can learn directly from my mistakes.**

Chapter 3:
Why Rabbits Need To Live Indoors

Before we get any further into this book, I want to discuss why rabbits should live indoors and never outside. If you read my story, you will know that I have mistakenly kept bunnies outside myself. I now know that this was terribly wrong for so many reasons, many of which I will cover here.

I am not going to pull any punches regarding this subject. If, by the time you read this chapter, you are not planning on having your rabbit live indoors, then you might as well not even bother to finish reading this book. All the information in it is only in regard to house rabbits and does not apply to "backyard" bunnies. If you are stubbornly clinging to some notion that an outdoor rabbit can live as happily, healthily, and safely as one who lives inside, then this book is not for you. The whole purpose of this book is to explain to you how to successfully adopt, live with, and care for a house rabbit—in other words, a rabbit who is kept inside the house (not in the garage, not in the basement, and not in some other building; strictly in your home with you).

One of the things that I feel very strongly about is that pet bunnies are indoor rabbits and livestock rabbits (rabbits raised for meat) live outdoors. If you are going to be companions with your pet rabbit, then he needs to be near you, interacting and enjoying life's day-to-day moments. It is not enough to "go visit" your rabbit outside every day, because rabbits are social creatures. They crave company and social interaction. It is a big part of their natural life; wild rabbits commonly live in warrens of 100-150 bunnies.

A backyard bunny is a terribly lonely bunny, even if he is let out to run loose all day in the yard (which is another no-no). The thing your rabbit needs the most is attention and love. If you have ever watched two bonded rabbits together, they are constantly cuddling and grooming with each other. The natural way rabbits express happiness and love is by being close and giving and receiving attention. This is crucial to having a happy bunny.

Ricky and Lucy flopped out in front of their condo. Ricky is doing the "dead bunny flop" because of how it looks when he lies that way.

When you relegate a rabbit to a lonely, solo existence, you become out of touch with his feelings, needs, and important moments. This is not what having a companion is all about. As a good bunny caregiver, you'll want to be constantly in contact with your bunny in order to ensure your rabbit has everything he needs as well as to immediately be able to see if he is not feeling well or is sick. While healthy, well-cared-for bunnies rarely get sick, it can happen, and it is imperative that you notice this right away to improve your pet's chances of surviving the illness. Rabbits can become extremely sick and even die in as few as 24 hours from some relatively common situations.

By living near and paying close attention to your pet rabbit, you will be quick to notice that he did not want his salad or has not used his litter box that day, which are often the first signs your bun is not feeling well. If a rabbit is living alone outside in a cage, you will not see it when he huddles up in the corner in obvious pain and may discover his discomfort too late to save his life.

A two-story "condo" with a pen attached to the front as a "run space."

The reason people have pets is to interact with and enjoy having them nearby. The best way to interact with a pet rabbit is getting down on the floor on his level. How much crawling around in the dirt in your backyard are you willing to do with your bunny? Learning to communicate with your pet is another big part of enjoying your life together. How are you going to communicate with an animal that you have locked into a cage all by himself? I am pretty sure that the answer to both questions is, "Very little."

Remember also that rabbits are prey animals, and almost every other creature out there in your neighborhood can (and very well may) kill him if he is left unprotected. Dogs, cats, hawks, coyotes, snakes, and raccoons are just some of the predators who pose a threat to your rabbit if he's kept outdoors. And just because you live in the city does not mean there are not predators around.

Many times, the predator does not even have to get inside the cage for your rabbit to die. When rabbits were domesticated 400 years ago, they were bred to have smaller hearts in relation to their body mass than wild bunnies. Farmers did not want hyperactive 20-pound rabbits kicking like crazy every time they went to handle their stock, so they made the rabbits infinitely more docile by breeding them with hearts one-third the size of those of wild bunnies.

While this may make the rabbits easier to handle, the domesticated rabbits' smaller, but less-efficient, hearts lead to many cardiovascular complications. One of these is that they are prone to heart attacks if they become very frightened. Some people think this is so that a rabbit will already be dead if a predator catches him and is going to eat him. The bottom line is that a dog or hawk on top of your rabbit's cage can literally scare him to death. So, even if your backyard hutch is predator proofed, your rabbit can still die from a predator's attempts to get at him. Also, raccoons are very clever and have been known to actually open even complicated latches to a bunny cage in order to get at the bunny inside.

Probably the most important reason that you need to keep your rabbit indoors is that statistics have shown that indoor bunnies live twice as long as outdoor rabbits. The average lifespan of a backyard bunny is about four to six years, while an indoor rabbit typically lives ten to twelve years, depending upon the breed.

There are other compelling reasons for keeping your bunny indoors in addition to his having an improved quality of life, a longer lifespan, and a better relationship with you: A rabbit needs about three hours a day of exercise to run and play. Your backyard is not a safe place for him to do this. Even with close supervision, there is always a certain amount of danger for your pet. A hawk can suddenly swoop down or some other predator can quickly appear. This is why so many rabbit lovers rarely take their bunnies outside.

While in your yard he can jump or dig out, and predators can get in. Just because your rabbit has never tried to dig out of your backyard in the past two or three years does not mean that tomorrow he will not wake up and suddenly decide to do it. This happens all the time. I wish I had a dollar for every time someone told me that their rabbit hopped around in their yard for years until he suddenly disappeared one day.

The safest place for your bunny to play is in a bunny-proofed area inside your home. During this time, you can spend plenty of quality time interacting, petting, and grooming your pet, as well as laughing at the silly antics he's doing specifically to entertain you. Your rabbit will come to crave those moments you spend together, and I hope you do, too. For me, it's the best part of my day, playtime with Ricky, Lucy, and Star.

I have heard every rationalization and excuse there is as to why a person's rabbit cannot live indoors and, as far as I am concerned, none of them hold water. People say things like they do not have any room in their house or that they are allergic to the fur. My answer to those things is, "Maybe you should not have a rabbit in the first place," or "Why didn't you consider those things before bringing the bunny home?"

Another two-story condo with a very tall pen attached, because Star is a "jumper" who can hop out of shorter pens.

Other things I have heard are that "the rabbit has to live in the garage because my husband says he cannot come indoors." Another person told me that one of his bunnies gets to live indoors while his other four have to stay outside because not all of the bunnies get along.

These kinds of excuses are really just more reasons why having a rabbit is not for every family. I had one lady tell me that, when her mom moved back in with her because of old age, her pet bunny had to move into the backyard. I just cannot see how someone could do such a thing, and I think there could have been some other solution that would not have meant exiling a former pet to an inappropriate, dangerous, and lonely existence outside.

Another very compelling reason to keep your rabbit indoors is that outdoor buns are exposed to a lot more diseases and parasites than indoor ones. Wild bunnies are often carriers for rabbit diseases. There are deadly viruses and parasites that your rabbit can get from fleas, ticks, and mosquitoes biting an infected wild bunny and then biting him.

If you have a spacious abode for your rabbit, he will enjoy spending time there.

One of these diseases was intentionally released into the wild to kill domestic rabbits who have become feral. This was done in Australia fifty years ago and in England in the 1980s. Unfortunately, the disease has made its way to America, and we are hearing of more and more cases of this terrible sickness called myxomatosis, or "myxo" for short. There is no cure for myxo and,

if your rabbit contracts it, it is always 100-percent fatal.

The only way to prevent your rabbit from getting myxo if it's in your area is to keep your rabbit indoors entirely and not allow him to be exposed to bites from mosquitoes, fleas, or ticks. Do not believe the fallacy that, if you bring your rabbit in before dusk, he'll be safe from exposure to mosquitoes—this is absolutely not true. Mosquitoes hide during the day in the same places that rabbits like to cool off and take their naps. Your rabbit will most likely want to spend the hottest part of the day underneath something shady to keep cool, which is the exact same place that a mosquito will choose spend it.

As I said, the only way to keep your rabbit from being exposed to myxo is to never allow him outside at all, and there are many people who do keep their bunnies inside at all times. However, I personally take my rabbits for heavily supervised playtime at the park or the beach, and while I understand there is a slight risk involved, I feel the benefits of the fresh air and sunshine outweigh the minor risk of contracting myxo. I also happen to live in an area that is at low risk for myxo, and do not take my rabbits anywhere that has a high concentration of mosquitoes.

Fleas and ticks can be brought indoors by dogs and cats who go out and then bring them back inside. This is usually a minor problem, but you should do your best to avoid allowing them to do so. (Cats also live longer by being indoor kitties.) Should fleas and ticks become an issue in your home, consult your regular veterinarian for the appropriate treatment for your cat or dog. If you find fleas on your rabbit, consult your rabbit vet, and never use Frontline® on your rabbit!

Rabbits who go outdoors are also more prone to a dangerous condition called "flystrike." Some species of common flies, such as the bot fly, will actually lay their eggs on any exposed damp skin, such as a messy bottom or open wound. If not caught early, it can result in crippling damage and even death in extreme cases when the larvae (maggots) hatch and begin to eat tissue. Take steps to ensure that your pet is never exposed to flystrike by keeping him indoors and checking all sores or damp areas on his fur for the fly eggs, which look like tiny yellow spots attached to the end of a hair. This is especially true if he has a case of runny poop that sticks to his butt or he gets a wound of some kind. The flies are attracted to the odor from these things. (Read more in **Chapter 19: Rabbit Health and Wellness**.)

All in all, use common sense and take precautions with your rabbit. Remember that rabbits are not like cats and dogs, and they can get into—and out of—things you might never imagine they would, or that they've never tried to before. Bunnies are prone to overheating (more on this in **Chapter 19**'s section called **"Heat and Your Bunny"**), so keep them inside and out of the sun on hot days, and put ice bottles in their carriers if you have to take them somewhere. Always think of your bunny's safety, especially when you take him with you places. Just being cognizant of your surroundings and always keeping your eyes on your bunny, mixed with a good dose of common sense, can help you keep your rabbit healthy, happy, and safe.

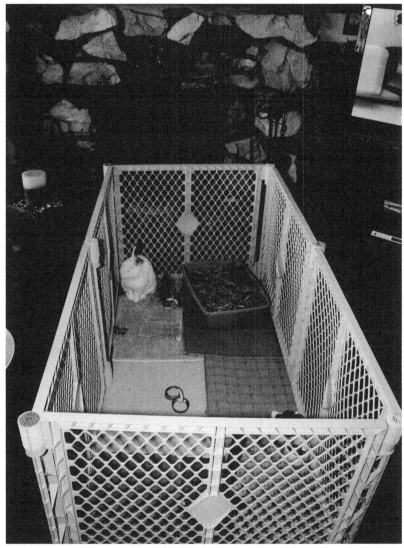

This pen is set up in the living room so that Star can be where the family spends most of the time.

A bunny-proofed area indoors is the only safe place for your rabbit to play.

Summary

- The information in this book only pertains to house rabbits.

- The whole purpose of this book is to explain to you how to successfully adopt, live with, and care for a house rabbit.

- If you are going to be companions with your pet rabbit, then he needs to be near you.

- A backyard bunny is a terribly lonely bunny.

- As a good bunny caregiver, you'll want to be constantly in contact with your bunny.

- By being near to your pet rabbit, you will be quick to notice the first signs your bun is not feeling well.

- Learning to communicate with your pet is another big part of enjoying your life together.

- Dogs, owls, hawks, coyotes, snakes, and raccoons are just some of the predators who pose a threat to your rabbit.

- Many times, the predator does not even have to get inside the cage for your rabbit to die.

- Domesticated rabbits have smaller, less-efficient hearts than wild rabbits.

- Indoor bunnies live about twice as long as outdoor rabbits.

- A rabbit needs about three hours a day of exercise to run and play.

- Your backyard is not a safe place for your rabbit to play.

- The safest place for your bunny to play is in a bunny-proofed area inside your home.

- If you have an excuse as to why your rabbit cannot live indoors, then you should probably not have a rabbit for a pet.

- Outdoor buns are exposed to a lot more diseases and parasites than indoor ones.

- Fleas and ticks can be brought indoors by dogs and cats who go out.

- Never use Frontline® on your rabbit!

- Rabbits who go outdoors are more prone to a dangerous condition called "flystrike."

Chapter 4:
How Much Does Having a Bunny Really Cost?

It is a very common misconception that rabbits are cheap, low-maintenance pets—and nothing could be further from the truth. I believe that this myth stems from bunnies being given to kids as Easter presents. Not only are rabbits not good children's pets because they are too fragile for most young ones to care for and handle, they're not inexpensive—and they're certainly not low maintenance. In fact, rabbits require more daily care than almost any other type of pet I can think of.

Rabbits do not need to get vaccinations, so many people mistakenly believe that rabbits do not ever need to see a vet. The truth is that rabbits need regular veterinary checkups—except they need to see a special type of veterinarian—and emergency vet visits can be necessary, just like with other types of pets.

The time you spend interacting with your rabbit is priceless.

One of the most common questions I hear is, "How much is the rabbit adoption fee?"

My response is always that the adoption fee will likely be the least-expensive bill you will ever pay involving your pet rabbit. By the time you purchase suitable housing, at least one X-pen, a litter box, bedding, hay, food (pellets and fresh vegetables), a water crock or bottle, food bowls, grooming supplies, and toys, your tab can easily reach $250 or more.

Many of these things are one-time expenses, but bedding, hay, and food are ongoing. With the price of food in the stores going up all the time, you can expect to spend at least $10 a week on fresh vegetables for your bun. Bedding and hay are not terribly expensive, but they must be kept in good supply, especially since some buns are very picky and will only eat fresh hay. You can expect to spend about $50 a month for fresh hay, vegetables, and your rabbit's bedding. Once again, you can easily spend a lot more.

One of the most important things you will want to do before you get your rabbit is to find an exotics veterinarian (a veterinarian who specializes in "exotic" pets, such as rabbits, guinea pigs, chinchillas, and other small animals) who will be able to provide regular checkups for and treat your rabbit when the need arises. You do not want to take your rabbit to a "regular" veterinarian who rarely sees rabbits, because experience is very important in treating the common health problems of rabbits. Unfortunately, the likelihood of your rabbit needing to see a vet sometime during his life other than just for his regular checkups is high, and so you must be prepared for it when it happens.

Veterinary medicine for rabbits has changed dramatically in the past decade, and new treatments and medicines are being discovered all the time. Although it's progressed, rabbit medicine is still in its infancy, and if a vet is not keeping up to date, there is a good chance that he or she will be unfamiliar with the latest successful treatments and procedures that your rabbit may need. While exotics veterinarians are typically more expensive than a regular vet, their expertise in caring for your beloved bunny—especially in a life-or-death situation—is invaluable, as I've learned firsthand. I will bring up all the details later in my chapter about veterinarians and medical care (**Chapter 19: Rabbit Health and Wellness**).

The best way to find good, reputable rabbit vets in your area is to seek out your local chapter of the House Rabbit Society. You can locate the closest chapter by visiting the national website at www.rabbits.org.

Once you have selected a rabbit vet and you have adopted a bunny, the first thing you will want to do is have her or him spayed or neutered if she or he hasn't been already. This is much more expensive for a rabbit than a cat or dog, although some counties provide financial assistance for having your rabbit spayed or neutered through their spay/neuter programs for dogs and cats. Some local House Rabbit Society chapters even operate a rebate program; check with your local chapter.

It is always best to try to adopt a rabbit who has already had it done so you do not have to wait four to six weeks for the hormone levels

to recede, meaning that your bunny will be more house friendly the day you bring him home. Otherwise, you will need to schedule your spay/neuter surgery as soon as possible and it will be at least a month before some of the pre-surgery behaviors will start to wane. If you are planning on bonding your new bun with another,

A cozy hidey box is a safe place for your bunny to hang out.

you should also wait at least six weeks for the "settling-down" process after surgery. I cover this subject in depth in **Chapter 8: Spaying and Neutering Your Rabbit**.

I also recommend a wellness check with your new rabbit vet within a week of bringing your new bunny home. Ask for a baseline blood panel to be run at that time. Rabbits vary so widely in their normal test levels that, if your rabbit gets sick, it makes it more difficult for your

As you can see from this chart, except for the adoption fee, everything for a rabbit costs more compared to a dog or cat.

Item	Rabbit Costs	Dog or Cat Costs
Adoption Fee	$30-75	$75-150 or more
Spay/Neuter	$175-400	$90-180
Housing & Supplies	$250+	$100+
Monthly Food & Supplies	$50+	$20+
Annual Vet Checkup	$75+	$50+
Vet Bill if Sick or Injured	$150+	$100+

vet to determine the problem without a baseline to compare to. This is something that you may not need for many years (and hopefully, never), but having it on file can be the difference between your vet being able to diagnose a serious problem with your pet quickly or being panic stricken because none of the tests are allowing him or her to figure our your bunny's issue. Many vets recommend seeing your rabbit at least once a year to have this done, along with a simple, cursory checkup.

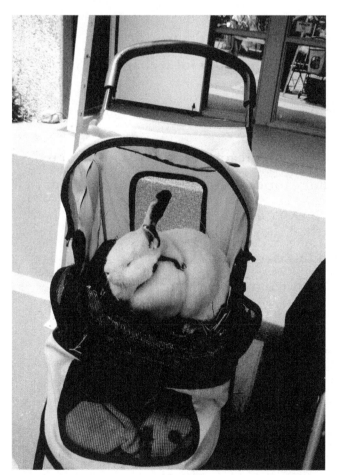

Star likes going places in her bunny stroller.

Again, bear in mind that exotics vets are specialists. This translates into most procedures costing more than they would at a dog/cat vet— sometimes triple what it would be for a dog or cat.

All rabbit owners understand this, and therefore you too need to be aware of this fact before you decide to adopt a rabbit.

You can go for years without visiting your bunny's vet for anything but a checkup, but when you do, the bill is going to be expensive. This is something we all prepare for and expect, having pet bunnies. If an expensive vet bill is something that would really put a big hitch in your budget, then you should consider either a pet insurance policy or a special savings account just for this purpose—or just don't bring a rabbit into your family.

If there is simply no way that you can afford to provide the proper care, then maybe the right thing for you to do is to not have a rabbit at this time. Maybe it will be better for you later, when you have the financial resources to handle an expensive veterinary bill.

The last thing I want to mention about the cost of a pet rabbit is your time. Time is priceless, and taking on any kind of pet is always a big commitment, not just financially, but also with your precious time. It is not fair to adopt a pet rabbit and then neglect to spend the time with him that he needs. This is the biggest sacrifice that you must be prepared to make when considering adopting a bunny.

You should plan on spending at least three hours a day supervising your rabbit's playtime, with some of that time being spent "up close and personal" with your bun. Quality time spent petting and grooming him is critical to forming a trusting relationship and having a happy rabbit in your home. If you cannot afford to give your bunny this much of your time, then it might be better to wait until your life is not so busy and you have proper time for a pet bunny rather than to lock him in a cage or pen to become lonely and unhappy.

Summary

- It is a very common misconception that rabbits are cheap, low-maintenance pets.

- Rabbits are not good children's pets.

- Rabbits need regular veterinary checkups by a rabbit veterinary specialist, also called an "exotics" veterinarian.

- The adoption fee will likely be the least-expensive bill you will ever pay for your rabbit.

- You will want to find an exotics veterinarian before you get your rabbit.

- The likelihood of your rabbit needing to see a vet during his life other than just for his regular checkups is high.

- Veterinary medicine for rabbits has changed dramatically in the past decade.

- To find good, reputable rabbit vets in your area, seek out your local chapter of the House Rabbit Society at www.rabbits.org.

- The first thing you will want to do is have your bunny spayed or neutered if she or he hasn't been already.

- It is sometimes best to try to adopt a rabbit who has already been spayed or neutered.

- A wellness check for your new rabbit with your exotics vet soon after bringing your new bunny home is strongly recommended.

- Most procedures cost more at an exotics vet than they would at a dog/cat vet.

- Everything for a rabbit costs more compared to a dog or cat.

- You should plan on spending at least three hours a day supervising your rabbit's playtime.

Amy getting some "run time" at the shelter.

Chapter 5:
Dispelling Some Common Myths About Rabbits

There are so many myths, misconceptions, and misunderstandings about rabbits that I've decided to devote an entire chapter to try to dispel some of these untruths. At the beginning of this book, I said that bunnies are one of the least understood pets by their owners, and many of these "lagomorph lies" have contributed to the problem, even for those people who've had rabbits for many years.

Myth #1:
Rabbits are good pets for children because they are cuddly and soft.

The Easter Bunny may be the reason for this popular myth. Believe it or not, some families still give young children rabbits, baby chicks, and ducklings for Easter. I feel it is a barbaric practice, because a very large percentage of those animals do not survive a month after being presented as nothing more than "play toys" for those youngsters. Kids under age seven rarely understand their size in comparison to a rabbit (much less a baby chick or duckling), and that simply stumbling and falling on these little animals can result in serious injury or death. Picking them up and/or squeezing and hugging roughly is also something young children seem to like to do with bunnies, and they do not realize they are causing great harm to the animal.

Since the bunny does not make many sounds and he naturally hides his injuries, you may not even know that he is hurt. This is an important reason why rabbits are not suitable pets for young kids under the age of about ten. Even then, all children should be closely supervised with rabbits until they are taught the proper way to interact and handle them. When younger family members have contact with your rabbit, consideration must be given so that both parties are completely supervised and protected from harm. If you have babies, toddlers, or quite young children (under age ten), a rabbit is really not a good choice of a pet for your family unless you have considered how you will be able to safely have both. Most families realize it is a smarter choice to wait until their children are older before bringing a bunny into the house.

Myth #2:
Since rabbits do not need shots, they never need to see a veterinarian.

It is hard to explain to people how a bunny that only cost them $30 or so at the feed store or pet shop can possibly cost $200 or more to have spayed or neutered by a qualified, experienced exotics veterinarian. When deciding to bring a rabbit home, most people do not understand that, like all pets, rabbits need to be spayed/neutered and also need to visit the vet for checkups as well as when they are sick. As stated in the previous chapter, since rabbits are considered "exotic" pets, their doctors are specialists and therefore are more expensive than your regular dog or cat vet.

Myth #3:
Rabbits only live about four or five years.

I think this myth started because rabbits who are kept in backyard hutches and eat pellet-only diets typically do live only about five years, give or take a year. However, rabbits who are kept indoors can live literally twice as long as outdoor rabbits if they're fed a correctly balanced diet of hay, pellets, and a few veggies every day. Some of the larger breeds will only live eight to ten years, but most of the small- and medium-size bunnies live an average of ten to twelve years. I have even heard of some bunnies making it to 13 and 14 years old with good, loving care indoors. The fact that indoor rabbits commonly live twice as long as ones housed outside is the most compelling reason to have your bunny inside.

Myth #4:
Rabbits should eat lots of carrots.

No, I have never met a bunny who does not like carrots, but carrots are very high in sugar, and since bunnies have a sweet tooth, they adore munching on them. Just like you would not feed your child a diet of mostly ice cream and candy, you should also limit the amount of carrots your rabbit gets on a regular basis. These calories quickly add up and so it is best to give carrots to your rabbit in very small amounts. My rabbits only get a piece no bigger than half the size of my pinkie finger, daily. The smaller the rabbit, the smaller the pieces of carrot he should have. A tiny dwarf or mini rabbit may only need to get a tiny piece—perhaps half a baby carrot per day—and it is always better to give him less than more, especially if other treats are being given during the day.

I cover the topic of how to feed your rabbit properly in **Chapter 9**.

Myth #5:
Rabbits do not need to be spayed or neutered.

You **must** have your rabbit spayed or neutered in order for your bunny to be a good indoor companion. There are too many behaviors that rabbits who have not been spayed or neutered display. Males mark their territory like cats by spraying urine, and females can become grumpy and dig everywhere, even on your carpet. These and many other aggressive behaviors are eliminated by having your rabbit spayed or neutered. I would never consider having a pet bunny who has not been "fixed."

Another consideration to think about is that pet rabbits who have escaped their homes have formed extremely large feral populations in some areas. This causes many municipalities to use very inhumane methods in order to deal with this problem. To avoid accidentally contributing to this situation, you should never have an unaltered pet.

For complete information on this topic, see **Chapter 8**.

Patrick enjoying some beach time with his mom, Kacie.

Myth #6:
Everything a rabbit needs to be healthy is in rabbit pellets.

Pellets were designed for farmers to quickly fatten up their rabbits in order to quickly bring them to market. Longevity was not why pellets were fed to these rabbits in the first place. If you want your bunny to live a long and healthy life, he needs to mainly eat grass hays and does not need pellets at all, once he is past six months of age. Rabbits need a very high-fiber diet, and when hay is pulverized to form the pellets, its fibrous properties are removed.

Without sufficient fiber, many digestive issues—along with a number of other chronic conditions—can develop. However, most of these can be avoided when 85-90 percent of your

Star likes exploring and playing in the sand at the beach.

rabbit's diet is comprised of fresh timothy hay and orchard grass, with a smattering of oat hay mixed in. Bermuda grass is an inferior grass hay for rabbits and should not be fed exclusively to buns. If you decide to give your rabbit pellets, be sure that they are timothy hay pellets and not alfalfa pellets. Alfalfa pellets should only be given on the advice of your vet, which is usually when your rabbit needs to put on weight. I recommend 1/8-1/4 cup of pellets for your bunny when they are given. Some of the larger breeds can tolerate a little bit more, but in the long term, the fewer calories your rabbit gets daily from pellets, the better. A daily salad made up of several different leafy greens (I like to give them at least five different kinds daily) equal to twice the size of

your rabbit's head makes up the last part of a healthy rabbit diet.

See **Chapter 9** for everything you need to know about feeding your bunny correctly and which greens are safe for your bunny.

Myth #7:
It is OK for a pet rabbit to live outside in a cage.

Rabbits are very social animals and living outside in a cage all alone will make them miserable. After a while, just like in other species, rabbits get a kind of kennel neurosis that causes them to eventually become anti-social.

As I've already discussed in depth, outdoor rabbits live only half as long as indoor ones, and so companion bunnies must always live indoors to protect them from predators and to monitor their health. A rabbit's health can quickly take a turn for the worse, and if you are not there to notice the slight change in behavior, he may die before you ever know he is sick.

Myth #8:
Any veterinarian can treat a sick or injured rabbit.

Again, taking your sick rabbit to a vet who does not treat many rabbits is the recipe for disaster.

I cannot stress enough how important it is to seek out a rabbit veterinarian before you ever bring a rabbit home. I know in some parts of the country it can be a several-hour drive to reach a vet like this, but it's much better to know where you have to go during a crisis than to be searching for an exotics vet *after* you already need one. Often, every hour—and sometimes every minute—counts when your bunny is sick.

Myth #9:
All rabbits enjoy being picked up and cuddled, or sitting on your lap.

The truth is, rabbits are born with an instinct to dislike being picked up or held off the ground. In the wild, when a rabbit leaves the ground, he is about to die because some predator has just snatched him. This is hardwired into all rabbits, and it is only through socialization that a rabbit learns to not become panicked when you pick him up. Some rabbits never get used to it and will avoid it at all costs. Others can become somewhat accustomed to it and at least they will not run and hide when they realize that you want to pick them up. It is a rare exception for a bunny to become a lap rabbit who enjoys being held and who will sit quietly in your lap while you pet or groom him. You're truly lucky if you ever come across a lagomorph like this—many folks have rabbits all their lives and never meet a bunny who loves being held.

Myth #10:
If you only have one rabbit, you do not need to worry about spaying or neutering.

Rabbits who are not spayed or neutered can have many bad habits that result from their hormones, as I've explained, and I believe having your house rabbit "fixed" is one of the key components to making your relationship with him a success.

Spaying or neutering your rabbit is also very important in order for your rabbit to become easily litter box trained, since once a rabbit has been spayed/neutered, she or he will usually pee and poop in one location. Simply put a litter box there and you have a litter box-trained rabbit.

Another issue to consider in regard to having your bunny fixed, which I have also addressed, is to not contribute to huge feral domestic-rabbit populations already in existence in some areas should your house rabbit ever accidentally get loose or lost.

I'll cover this subject completely in **Chapter 8**.

Myth #11:
Small rabbits do not need very much space to live.

Actually, the opposite is true. Dwarf and mini breeds of rabbits tend to be very high-energy pets; some of them border on hyperactive and, at times, they seem to be literally bouncing off the walls. It is these tiny rabbit breeds who actually need rabbit-experienced humans and are not recommended for first-time rabbit owners. I tell people who are getting their first bunny to get the biggest one they can find because the larger breeds were bred more for their mellow temperaments and less for their looks, and thus tend to be the most docile and friendly. Dwarf breeds are famous (or should I say, infamous!) for their "dwarf-itude": I tell people that they are the chihuahuas of the bunny world, since these bunnies jump, bounce, and hop around almost non-stop. So, do not make the mistake of thinking that because you are going to get a very small bunny that you can get by with a very small cage. If anything, you will need a larger cage and play area for a smaller bun.

Myth #12:
If you set your domestic rabbit free, he will be happy running wild with his "buddies."

Rabbits are *prey animals* and they absolutely do not have any "buddies" outdoors. Even wild rabbits will have nothing to do with a stray house rabbit. Domestic rabbits have no self-preservation skills whatsoever, nor do they possess the camouflage of the natural coloring wild rabbits have to avoid being eaten. Coyotes, wolves, raccoons, owls, hawks, and many other common wild creatures will easily catch and eat a stray domestic rabbit, as will both domesticated and feral dogs and cats.

If you find yourself with a rabbit that you cannot keep, you should do the responsible thing and take him to your local shelter. If your local Humane Society is not accepting rabbits, then contact your closest House Rabbit Society chapter and ask them where you should take the rabbit. *Do not* just set him free, because you are issuing him a *de facto* death sentence, and that is a very cruel thing to do to any animal.

Myth #13:
Rabbits make great classroom pets.

This is the misconception that I have seen in practice many times over the years. For some indescribable reason, teachers feel that they are teaching something to their children by keeping a pet rabbit in a small cage in their classrooms. To me, this is absolutely wrong.

If we were to teach anything to the children, it should be to always properly care for an animal. Often I hear it rationalized that keeping live animals in classrooms are good learning experiences, but I contend that, instead, we are teaching the kids that all of these common myths are true.

Some classroom teachers even have different students taking the class bunnies home each night or on weekends. How can a little kid who has no idea how to properly handle or feed a rabbit be left responsible for a bunny? How can the child's home possibly be bunny-proofed and safe for a rabbit to hop around in? Since none of these things have been considered, that poor bunny is probably going to spend all of his time in a cage too small for him in the first place. What about his daily exercise and playtime?

Even if the rabbit is housed in an X-pen, which is much preferred over a too-small cage, the temporary "parents" for the bunny (aka the student's parents) will most likely have no bunny experience or knowledge whatsoever. This means bad food and treats will probably be given to the poor rabbit as well.

There is just nothing right about this scenario that I can think of. It is so sad for the poor rabbits who are forced to endure the rough handling of the usually rather young children (elementary and middle school seem to be the most-popular grade levels in which this animal-in-the-classroom story occurs) who have not been shown how to properly pick up and carry a rabbit. If the rabbit were to get sick or injured over the weekend, would the babysitting family get him to the correct vet in time? Would they even know the signs of pain or sickness in a bunny? Would they even bother to take him to the vet at all?

This is terribly wrong on so many levels, and I wish that this was not a common practice, but it is. I run into this all the time, and when I tell the teachers all the different reasons why I do not condone this, they always make excuses and go away thinking I am the bad guy. If they could only see the awful lesson that they are teaching the kids. It would be one thing if they got a book like this and studied rabbits together, but this does not ever happen, to my knowledge. So I feel that the lesson the children *do* come away with is that rabbits are disposable pets who do not need special care, feeding, or handling, while the exact opposite is true.

It will probably take a law to stop this from occurring in our schools, but until then, I am afraid that it will continue. Almost every elementary and middle school out there has at least one bunny locked up in a cage in some classroom. If you run across this, you would be right to tell the teacher that the bunny does not belong in a classroom.

Summary

- Rabbits are not good pets for children.

- Rabbits do need regular veterinary care.

- Properly housed and cared-for rabbits ideally live eight to twelve years.

- Rabbits should not eat lots of carrots.

- Rabbits need to be spayed or neutered.

- Rabbits do not need rabbit pellets to be healthy.

- Rabbits should never live outside in a cage.

- Rabbits need to see only rabbit veterinary specialists (exotics vets).

- Rabbits do not always enjoy being picked up and cuddled, or sitting on your lap.

- Rabbits always need to be spayed/neutered, even if you have only one, to improve litter-box training.

- Rabbits need plenty space to live, especially the smaller varieties.

- Rabbits should never be set free.

- Rabbits do not make good classroom pets.

Sometimes when you look into a rabbit's eyes, you can really see their gentle soul.

Chapter 6:
Is a Rabbit Really for You?

I am going to be brutally honest with you in this book. Some families are just not a good match for rabbits as pets, and I want to help you logically answer the question as to whether your household would be a good fit for a pet rabbit. Too many people do not ask themselves these critical questions before taking home a rabbit. This is big reason why we have so many rabbits in shelters right now. I would ask that you please be honest in assessing whether having a rabbit is really a good choice for you.

You will notice that many times I say that "maybe a rabbit is not for you." If you fit into any of those categories after which I make that statement, then you must seriously consider that a rabbit might not be the right kind of pet for you. You should not be a rabbit when you really should be adopting a dog, cat, goldfish, or some other critter that better suits your family's lifestyle.

It is critical to ask yourself some very important questions before you decide to adopt a companion rabbit. Some of these things are important no matter what kind of animal you want to bring into your family, but others are very specific as to whether your family is the right place for a pet bunny to live. There is a big difference between just wanting a house bunny and actually committing to the responsibility of being a good bunny parent.

Your first consideration is whether you are truly going to be able to care for your new rabbit for eight to twelve years. This is a long-term commitment that is not to be taken lightly. If your life is unstable at the moment, do you really want to take on a very high-maintenance pet in addition to the other stresses that you have? This is common sense but, believe it or not, I see a lot of people trying to adopt when they're in between apartments or just before they go off to college. It is selfish to take on a pet rabbit with the attitude that you can just give him away or find some other way to get rid of him if he becomes too much of a burden.

Will you be able to afford not only the spay or neuter surgery, but any other medical needs that should arise? It is not right to let a companion pet suffer or have him euthanized because you do not have the money to pay to get him help. (This is part of owning any pet.) A truthful analysis of whether you now have—and will have in the future—the space and resources to keep and care for a bunny is an important part of the decision to adopt one.

Rabbits have especially dense, fine fur and so you must consider if anyone in your household is going to be allergic. Rabbits' super-fine fur can, and likely will, get into and onto everything unless you vacuum and dust almost daily. Everyone in your household will be exposed to it. You do not want to discover that your spouse or child is terribly allergic to rabbits a month after you get a new bunny. I cannot tell you how many times I have heard this story from people: "Oh, I had to get rid of our new bunny; turns out my [husband, daughter, son] is allergic."

If you are allergic to cat dander, then there is a very good chance you will also be allergic to rabbit fur. I suggest that, if you are in doubt, visit a shelter or someone who has rabbits and pet their bunnies for several minutes. After 20 minutes or so, go home and monitor for symptoms. I have found this experiment to be enough to show most people whether or not they are going to have an allergic reaction. I highly recommend that you not bring a rabbit home if someone in the household is allergic.

Is everyone in your home happy about adopting a pet rabbit? You are going to need to bunny-proof your house, and special considerations are going to have to be made. This will affect everyone in the house, and so it is very important that everyone is in agreement about bringing a bunny home. It is never a good idea to try to surprise someone with a new pet, particularly one as unique and high maintenance as a rabbit. Everyone in your household should talk about it, especially if you have never had a bunny live indoors with you before. There are many things that you must learn about how to house and care for your rabbit before you bring one home. Everyone in the family should be aware of these things.

Are you willing to take the time and energy to learn how to properly house and care for a companion rabbit? I cannot tell you how many times I have been contacted by folks who want me to tell them how to care for their rabbit after they've already had him six months or more. Doing your homework and learning at least the basics before bringing a bunny home is important.

You cannot learn it all in one day, and so you should make an ongoing commitment to continually educate yourself about your bunny. The more you know, the better you can properly care for him. You can learn how to better communicate and interact with your rabbit. You can also find ways to enrich his life and to promote his better long-term health. This does not mean that you should attend a rabbit university (there's not one anyway—I checked; that's why I'm writing this book). Reading and learning about rabbits regularly

can accelerate your knowledge base, rather than waiting for a problem to arise and then suddenly having to educate yourself.

Do you travel for work or frequently go away for days at a time? Rabbits cannot be left for days inside a cage or X-pen. They need fresh water, greens, and hay every single day, in addition to several hours of exercise time. What kind of arrangements are you planning on making for your rabbit when your family goes away on vacation?

Star likes watching TV with me.

Are you thinking of getting a bunny for a child? Regardless of age, a child is not capable of being the one primarily responsible for a pet bunny. Ultimately, that responsibility falls upon the adult. Please do not try to delude yourself that an eight- or nine-year-old kid is going to maintain the responsibility of a complicated, high-maintenance pet like a bunny for the next 10 years. It may actually happen for a year or two, although that's extremely unlikely, but the children always grow up and move on to other interests, and the parents end up stuck with caring for the rabbit—or worse, the rabbit gets no care at all.

Dwarf rabbits are often adopted on an impulse because of the "cuteness factor."

More often than not, within months, the adult finds him- or herself with a burden that he or she was not expecting. Therefore, this is why you never get a rabbit for a child unless you're the one who truly wants the bunny for yourself, and you accept that you will be the one taking care of the bunny for the long term. Every time I hear parents say that their child(ren) will not lose interest in a bunny, I silently laugh, because I know it is inevitable. Girls discover boys, guys discover wheels, and suddenly childhood rabbits are not a big part of their lives. Do not fall into the trap, and do not adopt a pet that you, the adult, do not want.

Are you going to have several hours every day to supervise a rabbit while he gets out for exercise? It is an important part of a happy

rabbit's life to get at least three hours a day of run time. It is best if at least part of that time is spent interacting with you, but you must have a safe containment or bunny-proofed area if you are not completely supervising your rabbit at all times. This is when you can socialize your rabbit, and you both learn about each other. Without this time together, it is hard to really appreciate and understand your pet.

If you are not planning on spending some significant time daily with your bun, I feel you must ask yourself why you really want to get a bunny in the first place. If you are going to shut him in a hallway, back bedroom, or bathroom every day and expect playtime to be equal to being near you all the time, I must tell you it is not the same. Your rabbit learns to be friendly by interacting with you. Trust comes the same way.

I recommend at least one hour of hands-on socializing with your bunny each day. Sometimes you may spend more and some days a bit less, but if you are not planning on including your rabbit in your everyday life due to lack of time, then you may not be a good candidate for adopting a rabbit.

If you love animals, why would you want to sentence a rabbit to a miserable and lonely existence exiled from the family because he and his special requirements do not fit into your lifestyle or household? Wouldn't it be better not to get that bunny in the first place?

Are you patient enough to handle and understand that a rabbit has special needs and requirements? They do not always do what we expect them to do, especially when we are just learning about them. Rabbits can be even less inclined to cooperate or "obey the rules" as cats, and they do not react well to any kind of punishment or scolding. If you are lacking patience and prone to yelling or getting upset easily, then are you mature enough and endowed with the qualities that will make for a good bond with a bunny? Rabbits require patience, gentleness, and understanding and are not a good pet for everyone for these reasons.

Are you expecting a pet who will jump up in your lap right away and be your friend? This is not a very normal scenario for a new pet rabbit. Some bunnies are very confident and trusting right away: They may display affection and allow contact right away, but this is quite rare. Most rabbits want to first know that you are a true ally before trusting you and allowing you to approach them at any time. Every human-rabbit bond occurs differently, and so you must let it happen in its own time and not force it, or you will risk causing your rabbit to avoid you.

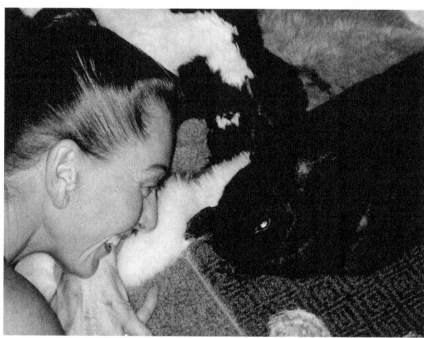

The way to interact with your rabbit is down on the floor at his level.

It usually takes some time for a new rabbit to become completely accustomed to a new home and to accept you as part of his family. It can take as little as a few days, but I have seen abused rabbits take a couple of years to become comfortable. It is hard to predict the length of time the settling-in process will take, so you must

be prepared for this. Part of love is acceptance, and so accept your rabbit's new trust in the small stages in which it's given.

Impulse-acquired rabbits are encountered every day at the local shelters: People who, 15 minutes prior to meeting some cute little fluff-ball and had no intention or idea of adopting one, suddenly decide to become rabbit parents. They often do not know beans about how to house or care for a rabbit and are totally unprepared. The right time to learn and prepare for these things is not after you have already brought one home. This is not a formula for success.

You must prepare for bringing home a bunny by getting all of his food and supplies such as X-pens, abode, litter box and bedding, and water crocks or bottles beforehand. Locating a rabbit-savvy vet is also very important. Only after all of these things have been obtained and set up should you be walking through the front door with your new rabbit.

Good, successful rabbit adoptions involve learning about proper feeding and care and what to look out for in case your bunny gets sick or injured. Reading a book like this will go a long way toward helping you prepare for a new rabbit in the family. I am sad to say that many people do not do these things, and so their success rate with their new pet is not very good. I contend that you should want to have an extremely high chance of things working out by considering all of these important questions.

Rabbits are very high-maintenance pets. They require daily litter-box cleaning, daily interaction, daily exercise, and weekly grooming.

They also can be quite destructive. A good bunny parent will monitor food and water intake and observe poops in the litter box daily. This is one of the most important ways to be aware of your rabbit's state of health. This daily commitment of time and high level of observance is especially important to rabbits, so I cannot overstate the potential negative impact if you do not provide it.

Over and over again, I have heard that the reason people do not interact with their rabbits is because their rabbits are "mean." Rabbits only become "mean" (and I feel that's a subjective term in many cases) because they have not been treated correctly, and often it is because of a lack of close contact. Like a dog who is locked in a cage too long, rabbits eventually develop a neurosis of sorts where they shun humans. I feel it is a coping mechanism that arises from wanting emotional contact so badly that eventually they decide it is better not to want it at all, rather than go crazy from wanting it and not ever getting it. This is especially common with backyard hutch bunnies who rarely get attention. I have seen some of these rabbits become quite vicious.

No one wants a "mean" bunny, so if you are not prepared to spend the time to bond and develop trust with yours, then you are risking a poor relationship that may end with you wishing you had never met this little critter. I cannot stress enough the time commitment involved with having a pet rabbit. Don't be one of those people who leaves him locked in a cage all day, occasionally leaving him some food and water. This is why I am posing all of these crucial questions to you. Now, I hope you can be honest enough with yourself to make the right decision for you and your future rabbit—if, that is, a rabbit is in your future.

Rabbits with Other Pets

I get asked all the time whether rabbits will get along with other household pets already in the home. I think the better question is whether your other pets will get along with a rabbit. I know many rabbit families who have dogs and cats running around the house with their rabbits, but some real care must be taken when entering into one of these types of living situations.

You must be completely honest with yourself about the kind of cat or dog you are trying to get to live with a house rabbit. If there is any kind of prey drive at all in your dog, or if your cat is the supremely jealous type who is going to end up attacking a bunny because you give the rabbit any kind of attention, then a rabbit is likely not a good idea for your household.

Dogs

If you are considering bringing a bunny into your home with a dog, then you must ask yourself these questions—and answer them with complete honesty—about your dog:

- Does your dog chase cats, squirrels, or other small animals when he is out for his walk?
- Does your dog like to play chase and fetch games?
- Is your dog super-active and/or does he tend to be overly playful, excitable, and/or jump up on people?

These are all signs that your dog is probably not a suitable candidate to live with a rabbit.

Often, a dog is not trying to kill or hurt a bunny when he injures one. When your rabbit takes off on a fast run and the dog chases and grabs him, there will likely be an unintentional injury to the bunny such as puncture wounds or broken vertebrae. This happens a lot more than I would care to say.

Other dogs will outright attack a defenseless rabbit and so, even though you believe that you have the gentlest, most easygoing dog around, there must be 100-percent, constant supervision during the first six months the bunny and the dog are together so that you can watch for any sort of dangerous play or aggressive interactions that could result in injury.

I do know some families who have a big-enough house that the rabbits and other pets are never together. Of course, this is impractical for many families and still requires vigilance to see that the animals never get together unsupervised. It only takes a few seconds for a rabbit to become seriously hurt from being snatched up in even a small dog's mouth.

Good candidates for dog-rabbit relationships are older, relaxed dogs who are not hyperactive. Puppies tend to be too playful and do not understand that it only takes one playful bite to terribly injure a bunny friend. Dogs who are friends with cats are usually friendly with rabbits, too. Any dog who chases cats and/or other small animals when he's outside will most likely do the same with a rabbit indoors.

Cats

Cats are a lot like rabbits in that they are always taking baths and are very clean. Both use litter boxes and usually require grooming. I have known several close cat-and-rabbit relationships; my one-eyed girl, Star, was totally bonded with a very old male cat, and would sleep with him. She became very lonely after he passed away.

In all of the relationships that my rabbits have had with other species, the rabbit was always the dominant critter. While our dog was so gentle, he never challenged the rabbit for dominance from day one. Our cat did become aggressive a couple times, but the rabbit would charge and send him flying, even though the kitty was much larger than the bunny.

After doing this twice, the cat decided that the rabbit could be the boss. Your biggest fear when rabbits and cats are having a little tiff is that a scratch from the cat can cause terrible eye damage on a rabbit's exposed and vulnerable eyes. Ear bites can also be very dangerous, because bunnies have so many large blood vessels there. They can bleed to death in minutes from a severe bite to their long ears.

This is why you need to be honest with yourself about whether your existing pets are suitable bunny companions. It is not fair to the defenseless rabbit to be made to endure punishment and possible injury from other pets.

There are often dogs at our educational events, so we must be very vigilant.

Jealousy is also a big problem when bringing any kind of new pet into the home. I have seen this happen a lot. Usually it does not happen when your pet thinks you are watching. I have turned my back or left the room, only to see a jealous cat or dog take out after another critter to try and make it go away. Jealous pets do this so that they can have all of your attention for themselves.

It is very important that you do not dote on a new pet and suddenly give your existing pet less attention, as this will certainly cause jealousy. Better to focus on and give even more attention to your existing pet, so that he does not associate less time with you with the arrival of your new pet bunny.

Even with careful consideration and lots of extra attention for your existing pets, there will sometimes be a jealousy issue. This is a red flag that these animals can never be left alone together until these issues are completely worked out. I have seen new rabbit owners lulled into a false sense of security, even though there is a huge jealousy issue seething just below the surface. All of a sudden, months later, a big fight or argument breaks out between the two animals, typically when you are not right there to intervene.

If your animals are fighting, you must break it up and stop all aggression immediately. I recommend that you do not completely separate the animals; otherwise, they will learn that by fighting, the other will be made to go away. Instead, you must put both animals together and make them lie quietly together for at least five minutes. This way your pets learn that, by getting into a tiff, you are not going to separate them; otherwise they will fight more often to make this happen. Similar procedures are used when bonding two rabbits.

There are few diseases that you should worry about that can be transferred from dogs or cats to bunnies except ringworm. Most diseases are species specific and so you should not be concerned about this. Fleas can be brought indoors to your rabbits by cats and dogs that go outside. If a flea bites a wild rabbit who has myxomatosis and then bites your bunny, it could give your bunny the disease. All rabbit owners should be aware of this danger and act appropriately. The ASPCA now recommends that all cats and dogs be indoor pets.

Summary

- Some families are not a good match for rabbits as pets.

- It is critical to ask yourself some very important questions before you decide to adopt a companion rabbit.

- Your first consideration is whether you are truly going to be able to care for your new rabbit for eight to twelve years.

- A truthful analysis of whether you now have—and will have in the future—the space and resources to keep and care for a bunny is important.

- You must consider if anyone in your household is going to be allergic to a bunny.

- Is everyone in your home happy about adopting a pet rabbit?

- Are you willing to take the time and energy to learn how to properly house and care for a companion rabbit?

- Do you travel for work or frequently go away for days at a time?

- Regardless of age, a child is not capable of being the person primarily responsible for a pet bunny.

- Are you going to have several hours every day to supervise your rabbit while he gets out for exercise?

- Your rabbit needs at least one hour of hands-on socializing each day.

- Rabbits do not always do what we expect them to do, especially when we are just learning about them.

- Rabbits require patience, gentleness, and understanding, and are not good pets for everyone for these reasons.

- It usually takes some time for a new rabbit to become completely accustomed to a new home and to accept you as part of his family.

- Impulse-acquired rabbits are almost always a bad idea.

- You must prepare in advance for bringing home a bunny.

- Rabbits are high-maintenance pets.

- Rabbits only become "mean" because they have not been treated correctly.

- Are your other pets going to get along with a rabbit?

- If your dog likes to chase cats, squirrels, or other small animals; likes to play fetch or chase games; or is overly playful, excitable, and/or jumps on people, he may not be suitable to live with a pet rabbit.

- Often, a dog is not trying to kill or hurt a pet bunny when he injures one.

- There must be 100-percent, constant supervision during the first six months the bunny and the dog are together.

- Good candidates for dog-rabbit relationships are older, relaxed dogs who are not hyperactive and who already get along well with cats.

- Cats are a lot like rabbits in that they are always taking baths and are very clean.

- When rabbits and cats are having a little tiff, a scratch from the cat can cause terrible eye damage to your bunny.

- It is not fair to the defenseless rabbit to be made to endure punishment and possible injury from other pets.

- Jealousy is a big problem when bringing any kind of new pet into the home.

- If your animals are fighting, you must break it up and stop all aggression immediately.

- There are no diseases that can be transferred from dogs or cats to bunnies except ringworm.

Star bonded with an older male cat who also had only one eye.

Chapter 7:
Selecting Your New Rabbit

I teach a lot of children about rabbits, and the first thing I always teach them is to never *buy* a rabbit. There are thousands of rabbits languishing in shelters and rescues around the country, and until every one of them has a home, no one should ever buy a bunny. Every time you buy a rabbit, there is one at a rescue or shelter who does not get a home. Even worse, when you purchase a bunny, you are supporting breeders who make their livings off of overpopulating the public with unneeded rabbits. There are plenty of bunnies of every breed, size, and color available at the local shelters.

The reason I will not spend a lot of time talking about the different purebred rabbits that are available is that I do not want to encourage people to obtain their pet rabbits from breeders. Often, when a person gets his or her mind set on owning a certain breed of rabbit, it might not be readily available at the local shelter or rescue.

If the exact rabbit you desire is not currently at your local shelter, just wait a little while, because he will undoubtedly appear there. You should also check with any local rabbit rescues or sanctuaries to see if they have a bunny that you might like to adopt. Tell your local shelter that you are looking for a certain kind of rabbit—they will call you when he appears on their doorstep.

It is really most important to adopt a rabbit with whom you are going to make a connection, not because of his looks or appearance. Many times, when an adoption is decided because of the looks or breed of a bunny rather than how he fits into the family, it is bound to cause many disappointments. Since you will not be adopting a rabbit to show or breed him, you do not need a purebred. A trusting relationship is more important than a pretty purebred bunny.

For this reason, I will show you pictures of some rabbits who look typical of some breeds, but I will not go into all the differences or specifications about them other than to mention some very general behavior traits that are commonly found in some of them. I usually advise people that the larger breeds tend to be more relaxed and friendly, while the smaller breeds will usually be much more energetic and often have "attitude."

A Himalayan girl shows off the colored points of her matching nose and ears.

Unfortunately, inexperienced people often gravitate towards the "cute" mini and dwarf breeds, but those are really breeds that are best left for experienced rabbit owners. I always tell adopters to bring home the biggest bunny they can find, because those breeds will be easier for first-time owners to bond and socialize with.

Lop-eared rabbits are very popular for their easygoing personalities as well. Some people will only have "loppies" for this very reason. I think that many of the other kinds of larger rabbits are just as lovable and friendly. When the smaller breeds were created, the breeders were looking for a certain appearance, not a personality. The larger breeds are usually more sociable than the tiny ones, because they were bred for temperament and ease of handling. Also, please note that there is no breed that is known for being more bright or intelligent—it depends more on the individual animal, because I have met clever rabbits in all breeds (purebred and mixed), sizes, and colors.

The reason you have a pet living indoors with you is so that you can form a relationship and a bond. It must be a mutual one where both sides benefit, resulting in everyone experiencing happiness. If you focus more on the personality and communicating with a bunny during the

Groucho and Pink are brothers, yet you can see that they look completely different. This is quite normal within a litter.

adoption process and less on the looks, you will end up bringing home a rabbit who is a better fit for your family.

Inexperienced rabbit adopters also tend to glorify and seek out certain looks or breeds without a truly valid reason. Since you're not bringing home a show rabbit, don't become too focused on this while selecting one. Having an idea about the size of rabbit you want and are able to house is more important, because you should have prepared an abode for your new bunny in advance.

In addition, part of preparing to adopt should be deciding what kind of rabbit would be the best match for your family. Are you seeking a rabbit who will provide many hours of entertainment each day with his high-energy antics, or are you looking for a rabbit who is more of a friendly love lump who is going to let you cuddle up close to him on the floor?

These are two totally different kinds of rabbits, and I would recommend knowing in advance which of these types of bunnies is what you are looking for. When you go to the shelter or rescue to adopt, you should tell them the kind of temperament you are seeking in your new pet. Then they can let you meet the bunnies who will best fit into the lifestyle that you have in your home. Everyone in the family needs to participate in the adoption interaction. Most shelters and rescues will not allow an adoption to take place until all the members of the family have visited with the bunny.

The reason for this is that it is important for all family members to understand how fragile rabbits are and to know something about their handling and care. Both spouses need to be on the same page when making a 10- or 12-year commitment. Families with young children may not be suitable adopters unless the parents realize that the small kids and the rabbit will need to be kept separate. Small children can easily severely injure pet bunnies, and no one wants that. Many shelters will also try to provide as much information as possible in order to help educate first-time rabbit parents. Still, it's up to you to make sure that you follow up and continue learning about your new pet after your adoption. Just because the adoption process is over does not mean that you should stop learning about your new bunny.

Rabbits with short, flat noses—such as lops and dwarfs—tend to have the most dental issues. A rabbit has 28 teeth inside his tiny mouth that are constantly growing and, in order to not have dental issues, these teeth must mesh perfectly. Just like humans can have crooked teeth, some rabbits are genetically predisposed to this problem. Where the real issue arises is that in rabbits, if those teeth are not wearing down when they chew, they can literally grow right out of their mouths.

Getting one of these breeds dramatically increases your chance of adopting a rabbit with dental issues. If a rabbit does not show signs of this problem (malocclusion) within the first six months of his life, then it does not usually appear again until he reaches senior status (over eight years old). When it appears during adolescence, then it is almost always a genetic problem. These rabbits will need regular vet visits their whole lives, unless tooth-extraction surgeries are performed.

Baby or young rabbits are a lot more work and cost more than older buns. You must spay or neuter them, you must train them, and they are more active and therefore more destructive. It takes a while for them to learn about living in your home. Older rabbits usually already know all these things, and have been spayed or neutered previously if you are adopting from a shelter or rabbit rescue.

Long-haired (Angora) rabbits are also not for beginners. They are a huge commitment because most need daily combings or their fur

becomes terribly matted and uncomfortable. This is the main reason that many people will not opt for one of these kinds of rabbits.

If you are looking for a lot of attention from your rabbit, then you should only have one. Bonded pairs spend more time with each other than they do with their people. If you are

Ruby is a playful bun who sports a mane, denoting that she is a Lionhead mix.

someone who works a lot and will have less time at home with your rabbit, bonded pairs can keep each other company when you are not around. Remember that you will still need to spend at least one hour a day in hands-on interaction, so getting another rabbit does not absolve you of the responsibility to give your rabbit(s) daily attention.

Contrary to popular belief, two or more rabbits are not as easy as caring for one. Two rabbits are twice as much work, and don't let anyone tell you any differently. Maybe there is only one litter box and water bowl to clean and fill, but two bunnies make the litter box twice as dirty, and two bunnies will eat twice as much hay. Two bunnies can really mess up their abode and play area, and so it will require more cleaning, as well. Still, for many people, this is a great option if they know that their rabbits will be spending most of the day at home alone.

Following are some of the most-common rabbit breeds you're likely to come across at shelters and rescues. Please note this list is simply for reference, and again, it's not to encourage you to choose a specific breed of rabbit when you go out to adopt, but rather to help you potentially identify what type of rabbit you have adopted so that you can learn more about that specific breed.

Niblet is a male Dutch.

Jennell is a French Lop mix.

Gertrude & Heidi are Mini-Hotots.

Lionheads come in all colors & sizes.

Lucy is my New Zealand girl.

Squirt is a Mini-Lop boy.

Lily is a full-size Hotot.

Ruby is a white Lionhead.

Madea is a Silver Martin.

Ricky is my black Havana boy.

A young Rex.

Lonnie is a Netherland Dwarf.

Saul is a Palomino boy.

Netherland Dwarf.

Netherland Dwarf.

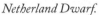

Peter is a black Mini-Lop.

Probably the most important thing in selecting a rabbit is if, when you meet and interact with the rabbit, there is a connection. Often, one particular rabbit just catches our fancy and we immediately feel like we can bond with him. This is usually how experienced rabbit lovers adopt a rabbit.

Now, you should also be aware that a rabbit can be quite clever: If he is in a shelter, he instinctively knows that a person he's meeting is the key to his getting out of that shelter. I have personally seen a rabbit "kiss up" to a potential adopter because he just wanted to go home with anybody.

After you get him home and he starts to feel comfortable, you may find that your bunny does not act quite as friendly as he did at the shelter. This is very normal. Many people do not give rabbits credit for comprehending many situations, but I think that they do. Once the bunny knows that he does not have to perform gratuitous acts of friendliness, he may suddenly become a bit aloof. This also is quite typical. Now it is time to begin your personal bonding and development of trust.

Respect is the key to all long-term relationships, and it is no different with bunnies.

A pet should be a companion, not a conversation piece or status symbol. Therefore, I believe that, other than relating to temperament, a rabbit's breed is pretty much irrelevant. I feel that many of the most popular rabbit breeds are the least well-suited for many inexperienced

and first-time owners. This is why you should be completely honest with the staff members who are introducing you to rabbits at a shelter or rescue: They can be invaluable in helping guide you to just the right rabbit, if you tell them the personality that you would like.

Your priority should be finding a rabbit who will bond with and fit into your family. Your lifestyle should match the personality of the rabbit you are adopting. In the long run, this will make for a much happier match for both the rabbit and everyone in your family.

If you are the nurturing, caring type of person who wants to save an unhappy rabbit, then you might take on a special-needs rabbit who will need extra care and love. If you are the kind of person who is looking for a lot of attention from your pet, then make sure you adopt one who is very friendly and who wants to have your attention as well. If you want a bunny pal who will appreciate a lot of closeness, then you will not want to select a bunny who is shy and reserved.

I cannot stress enough that cuteness and looks should not play a big part in the selection process. As with humans, looks only go so far and, if a true long-term relationship is to develop between you and your rabbit companion, there has to be a more mutually beneficial bond to cultivate. If you are not the kind of person to spend a year or two developing a trusting bond with a painfully shy rabbit, then by all means do not bring one with that type of personality home just because he is the lop-eared bunny you always wanted as a child. This is not the correct way to select a bunny.

One thing you can be sure of, though, is that when you save a rescue or shelter bunny, he will be eternally grateful in a bunny sort of way. Just be sure that once you make the commitment, you are willing to accept and enjoy the rabbit you've brought home for whatever kind of bunny he is.

I have found that rabbits I adopted have turned out to be nothing like I expected. Part of being a bunny lover is learning to accept each rabbit for his or her own uniqueness and personality. I think it is because of my willingness to accept—and love—each bunny just the way he or she is that I am (and will always be) a lifelong "bunny slave."

Determining the Sex of Your Rabbit

I cannot tell you how many people I have talked to who do not even know if their bunny is a boy or a girl. Of course, this means that they have not been spayed or neutered; otherwise, they would know. I have also seen many rabbits named Joe turn out to be Josephine, so I am giving you this easy guide to help you determine whether your bunny is a boy or a girl.

It is different sexing rabbits when they are young and immature (under four months old) than when they are older. Older rabbits are somewhat easier, because un-neutered males have pronounced testicles and, when you "pop out" their sex organs, they are easy to see. Unspayed mature females also have more pronounced genitalia, so it is very easy to distinguish between the two.

A dewlap is a large roll of skin that develops under the chin of mature females. Both male and female rabbits of some breeds can have dewlaps, but females have much larger ones than males do. (A dewlap is a handy place used to pull out fur to make a nest for their young when they give birth.)

To turn your rabbit over, first hug him to your chest.

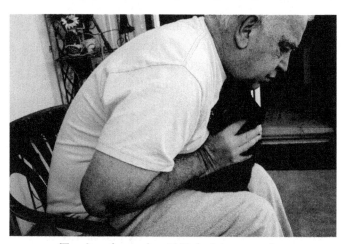

Then lean forward until his back is on your legs.

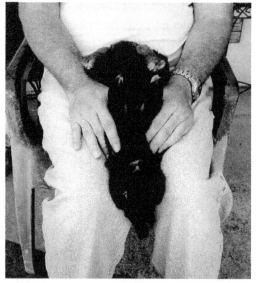

When you sit up, your rabbit should be laying on his back in your lap.

Neutered adult males are missing their testicles, so you must "pop out" their penises to see that they are boys. When you do this for a mature female, you will see a more cone-shaped protrusion that slants back towards her tail, with a slit running the length. Do not confuse this with a male penis, which, when it protrudes, has a more tubular shape without the slit running down the whole side. The opening is at the top and forms a full circle for the males.

It is a little harder to tell the difference in younger buns, because the distinguishing features are so much smaller and the differences more slight. Still, on an immature female you will notice the slit running the length of her protrusion towards the back. Usually, you will also easily see two red stripes running the length of the cone-shaped genitalia, which will pop out when pressed on either side.

There are two techniques for turning the rabbit over to check the sex organs. The one-handed cradle can be done more easily with smaller bunnies than with larger ones. However, it takes a bit more practice, so I recommend laying the bunny over on his back in your lap for novices.

Hold the bunny to your chest while sitting down with a towel across your lap. Bend over at the waist until the bunny's back is on your lap. Make sure to hold the bunny tightly so that, when bending over, he does not feel like he will fall. Once the bunny is on your lap, sit back up while holding the rabbit firmly. If you spread your legs slightly, it will form a trough in the towel and you can let the bunny slip into that furrow. If you keep a hand on his chest or stomach, he should stay still for you.

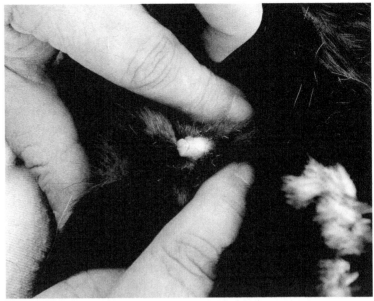

A male rabbit's sex organ.

Wait until you have control of the bunny and he is calm before manipulating his sex organs. Right in front of his anus you will see where his genitalia are located. By pressing softly on both sides of it, you will see that it pops out or protrudes. By closely discerning the shape, you can then tell whether you have a boy or a girl.

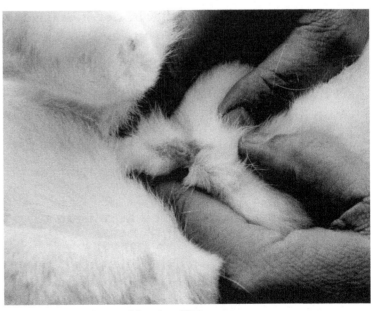

A female rabbit's sex organ.

Summary

- Never *buy* a rabbit; always adopts from a shelter or rescue.

- If the exact rabbit you desire is not currently at your local shelter, just wait a little while, because he will undoubtedly appear there.

- It is really most important to adopt a rabbit with whom you are going to make a connection, not because of his looks or appearance.

- Inexperienced people often gravitate towards the "cute" mini and dwarf breeds, but those are really breeds that are best left for experienced rabbit owners.

- The larger breeds are usually more sociable than the tiny ones, because they were bred for temperament and ease of handling.

- Rabbits with short, flat noses—such as lops and dwarfs—tend to have the most dental issues.

- Baby or young rabbits are a lot more work and cost more than older buns.

- Long-haired (Angora) rabbits are also not for beginners.

- If you are looking for a lot of attention from your rabbit, then you should only have one.

- Contrary to popular belief, two or more rabbits are not as easy as caring for one.

- Probably the most important thing in selecting a rabbit is making a connection with him.

- Once the bunny knows that he does not have to perform gratuitous acts of friendliness, he may suddenly become a bit aloof.

- Respect is the key to all long-term relationships, and it is no different with bunnies.

- A pet should be a companion, not a conversation piece or status symbol.

- Your lifestyle should match the personality of the rabbit you are adopting.

- Cuteness and looks should not really play a part in the selection process.

- Be willing to accept and enjoy the rabbit you bring home for whatever kind of bunny he is.

- Part of being a bunny lover is learning to accept each rabbit for his or her own uniqueness and personality.

- It is a little harder to tell the difference between males and females in younger buns, because the distinguishing features are so much smaller and the differences more slight.

Chapter 8:
Spaying and Neutering Your Rabbit

There is a lot of misinformation on this subject. Just last week I was coaching a new bunny owner who had unfortunately bought a rabbit from a very uneducated breeder who told him that he should not get his female rabbit spayed because it would cause cancer.

Actually, the exact opposite is true: Unspayed female rabbits have an 85-percent chance of developing breast or uterine growths by the time they are four years old. These kinds of cancers and tumors do not have a very high survival rate, even with surgery.

There are also behavior issues associated with unaltered bunnies. Intact males are known for marking their territory with their urine, just like male cats do, and unspayed female rabbits will be more prone to cage protectiveness, chewing, and digging. All rabbits are territorial, and chewing, scratching, and digging are normal marking behaviors performed by both sexes, but it's very hard to keep a boy bunny indoors with you if he is spraying urine all around to mark his territory. These kinds of behaviors are usually minimized by spaying or neutering your rabbit. I am not saying that they will never do these things again, but if you are trying to modify your rabbit's behavior, you cannot even begin until after you have had her or him spayed or neutered.

You'll also find that your bunny will usually be more friendly and docile after the procedure, especially if he or she was prone to aggressive behavior before. My own experience with a very aggressive unaltered male was such

that we could not wait for him to be neutered after we brought him home. He literally mounted any female, including human ones (those hormones are *strong*) who came within reach, which was quite obnoxious. It was hard to explain to our guests, "Don't mind our rabbit; he is just going through a phase." Of course, this stopped after we had him "fixed."

Another very good reason to do the surgery is that spayed and neutered buns are a lot easier to litter-box train. In fact, a rabbit will tend to teach her- or himself to use the litter box after being spayed or neutered. This is a very desirable thing!

Two sibling rabbits can usually remain bonded if they are both spayed or neutered.

Why doesn't everyone spay or neuter their bunny? Because many rabbits are impulse buys. People who, fifteen minutes before they saw a little baby bunny in a store, had no thought of bringing a rabbit home that day. Whether it is because he is so cute or suddenly connects with the person, quickly and on a whim that person decides that he or she is now going to be a rabbit owner. Usually this is done by someone who has never had a bunny as a pet and does not know the first thing about rabbits.

Once this cute baby bunny gets to his new home and settles in, the new owners are shocked to find out that this $29.95 cute little bunny that they just got from the feed store or pet shop is going to cost upwards of $175 to get neutered or $300 to be spayed!

Now that they have already spent a couple hundred dollars on top of what they paid for the bunny for an X-pen, litter box, and other supplies, they were just not planning on it costing so much for the bunny to get fixed. This unexpected cost is why a majority of "pet-shop bunnies" never get spayed or neutered and often go on to become unwelcome house "pests" because of behavioral issues.

Many others are never spayed or neutered because their owners simply do not know how important the procedure is. While most cat or dog owners would never consider having an unspayed or un-neutered pet, they do not realize that all pet rabbits should be fixed, too. They mistakenly think that the only reason it should be done is so that their pet does not have babies. If they only have one bunny, they feel that it is impossible for their rabbit to mate, and so it is not necessary. Most people do not realize how dangerous it is for their female bunny to not be spayed and how different her behavior would be if it was done.

Another big problem within many American communities is that unspayed females are being released by their owners who no longer want them. You read articles in many local newspapers about feral domestic-rabbit populations developing from bunnies who have either escaped or been released and then are reproducing in our local communities.

This has created a huge moral and ethical problem for many local governments that are trying to find a way to reduce these massive populations of feral domestic rabbits. I have followed several of these cases, and it is not a pretty story. I will say no more than that, if these rabbits had been spayed or neutered when they were adopted, there would not be this problem in the first place.

The best way to not have to pay this substantial expense is to adopt a bunny who was previously spayed or neutered. You can go to your local humane society or shelter to adopt, since most shelters will spay or neuter all animals before they are adopted. When you adopt from a shelter, the adoption fee is rarely more than a fraction of the cost of taking your bunny to be spayed or neutered by a rabbit vet (*do not* allow a cat or dog veterinarian to spay or neuter your rabbit—rabbits are very difficult to anesthetize properly, and only an experienced exotics vet who has performed many rabbit spay/neuter surgeries knows how to do this safely).

Furthermore, if you are planning on bonding two rabbits, they both must be spayed and/or neutered (regardless of what sexes the bunnies are that you intend to bond, even if they are the same sex), and you must wait four to six weeks after the procedure is done before the hormones have left their both of their systems. Sometimes it takes a while for the benefits of the surgery to be fully apparent, but virtually everyone reports big changes in their rabbits from it.

It is best to use an exotics veterinarian with a lot of experience treating rabbits when obtaining a spay or neuter, because that vet's experience translates into a much lower mortality rate for your bunny. As with all surgeries, there is risk involved, but the risk is minimized when using a veterinarian who has performed many rabbit surgeries. I have seen hundreds of spay and neuter surgeries during my time working at a shelter. The work done by inexperienced vets or vets who don't regularly work on rabbits had more complications than the procedures performed by the more-experienced rabbit specialists. Several rabbits did not survive their surgeries, due to what I feel was lack of experience. You do not want your rabbit to be the first or the fifth spay or neuter that a veterinarian has ever done on a bunny. I strongly recommend that you seek out an exotics vet who does five or six of these a week, not a year. I think it dramatically increases the chances of your rabbit surviving the surgery without any complications.

Of course, there is never a guarantee that there will not be any complications. Stitching up a rabbit's skin is much more difficult than a dog's or a cat's (rabbits have surprisingly thin, delicate skin), and doing sutures on a rabbit properly is as much an art as a skill that takes practice. And you don't want a vet who will be "practicing" on your rabbit when you take him in for his surgery. I have seen stitches completely pull through a rabbit's spay incision because the vet was not experienced. For this reason, many of the rabbit-savvy vets now use glue and staples for rabbit surgeries. It reduces tearing and stress because a rabbit's skin is so fragile. Bear in mind as well that exotics veterinary medicine is a *specialty*, like neurology is a specialty in human medicine, and it requires additional education in order for a DVM to call him- or herself an "exotics veterinarian." This is why their services cost more, but also why you can feel more confident that the care your beloved bunny is receiving is better.

If, however, you are unable to use a rabbit specialist because they are more expensive than a dog or cat vet, then a rabbit is probably not the right pet for you. The bottom line is that you will need a vet for your rabbit again, sooner or later. Part of being a good rabbit owner is providing good medical care to your fluffy charge, and this means seeking out and always using an exotics veterinarian. When a budget doesn't allow for this type of additional expense, it's a prime signal that a rabbit isn't a good choice for that person or family.

Caring for Your Bunny After Surgery

Once you have returned home with your rabbit after the surgery, he may still be a little groggy from the anesthesia. Often the bunny will have been given a mild painkiller, which may also make him woozy. Do not allow your rabbit to sit on anything up off the ground without holding him, because he may misjudge his own condition,

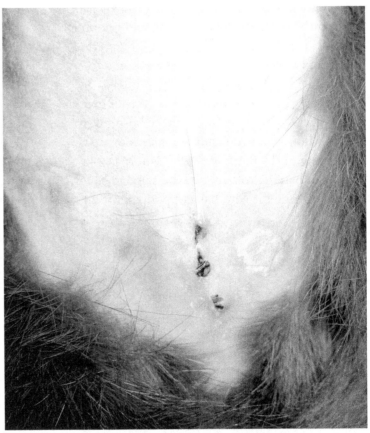

A normal spay incision a few days after surgery.

fall, and injure himself. Also, it is very easy to pull stitches on spays apart from any rough handling or your rabbit kicking while you are holding her.

Your rabbit's sutures may ooze some clear fluid and even a little blood, but any continued bleeding of more than a few drops of blood after the first day after surgery means your rabbit needs to revisit the vet immediately. If blood can come out, then bacteria can get into the wound and cause an infection.

The safest, cleanest place for your rabbit to spend the first couple days after surgery is inside his X-pen or condo. Do not let him hop around outside for at least a few days to allow his wounds to heal up and not allow dirt inside. Most rabbits will not want to be very active the first day after surgery, but usually by the second or third day, they will be mostly back to normal.

The most important thing is to pay attention to is whether he is eating and pooping properly. It is important that your rabbit start eating and pooping as soon after surgery as possible. If he's not, that qualifies as an emergency: Take your bunny back to your exotics vet or nearest emergency veterinary hospital (if it's after hours and you cannot reach your vet). Not eating or drinking water for as few as 24 hours can be fatal to a rabbit. The same goes for pooping—a rabbit who has not pooped for 24

hours should also be rushed back to his vet. Never withhold food from your rabbit like you would a human, cat, or dog before or after surgery. This can start a gastrointestinal (GI) stasis condition that will be very difficult to remedy after the stress of surgery. Rabbits should be allowed to eat and drink right up until their anesthesia.

If your vet is telling you to not feed or water your rabbit before surgery, do not let him or her do the surgery. An exotics veterinarian who regularly sees rabbits should not advise you to do this unless there is some highly unusual circumstance also in play.

Watch your rabbit's surgical incision for a couple of weeks post-op for redness and signs of infection such as pus or crusty areas. A little crustiness is normal, but continued oozing of anything but clear fluid indicates a recheck by the vet is needed.

I will end this chapter by again asking you to always spay or neuter your companion rabbits. Please do not even consider having a house rabbit as a pet unless you are planning on having it done. It will make both of your lives better and happier together.

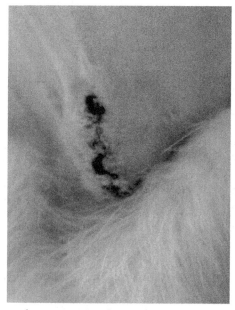

A crusty incision that needs vet attention.

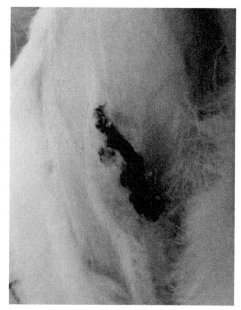

This incisicion is oozing blood and is not OK.

Summary

- Unspayed female rabbits have an 85 percent chance of developing breast or uterine growths by the time they are four years old.

- Intact males are known for marking their territory with their urine, just like male cats do.

- Unspayed female rabbits will be more prone to cage protectiveness, chewing, and digging.

- You'll find that your bunny will usually be more friendly and docile after being spayed/neutered.

- Spayed and neutered buns are a lot easier to litter-box train.

- Many rabbits are impulse buys and people do not plan for the need to spay/neuter.

- It can cost between $175 to over $300 for a rabbit-experienced vet to do a spay/neuter surgery.

- Many rabbits are never spayed or neutered because their owners do not know how important the procedure is.

- A big problem within many American communities is that unspayed females are being released by their owners who no longer wanted them, creating huge feral populations.

- The best way to avoid the expense of a spay/neuter is to adopt a bunny who is already done.

- If you are planning on bonding two rabbits, they both must be spayed and/or neutered.

- It is best to use an exotics veterinarian with a lot of experience treating rabbits when obtaining a spay or neuter.

- There is never a guarantee that there will not be any complications during or after surgery.

- If you are unable to use a rabbit specialist because they are more expensive than a dog or cat vet, then a rabbit is probably not the right pet for you.

- Part of being a good rabbit owner is providing good medical care whenever he needs it.

- Once you have returned home with your rabbit after the surgery, he may still be a little groggy from the anesthesia.

- Any continued bleeding of more than a few drops of blood means your rabbit needs to revisit the vet immediately.

- The safest, cleanest place for your rabbit to spend the first couple days after surgery is inside his X-pen or condo.

- It's important to pay attention to whether he is eating and pooping properly in the days after surgery.

- You should feed your rabbit hay and water right up until the surgery.

- Watch your rabbit's surgical incision closely for a couple of weeks post-op for redness and signs of infection such as pus or crusty areas.

This girl is part of a group of five bonded bunnies.

Ricky and Lucy having their daily salad.

Patrick and Tilly pose for their portrait.

Chapter 9:
Your Rabbit's Diet

It is very important that you feed your pet house rabbit properly if you want him to live a long and healthy life. Years ago, people were told to feed their bunnies unlimited amounts of rabbit pellets, and that was that. My first rabbits had a hopper that continually fed them pellets in their cages. I was even told by a vet that this was the correct way to feed my pets.

Little did I know that this was one of the unhealthiest things I could do for my bunnies. Rabbits who live solely on pellets tend to live only half as long as rabbits who are fed properly balanced diets of grass hays and a variety of fresh greens daily. Rabbits typically do not need pellets at all in order to be healthy. It was once thought that pellets were needed for their vitamin content, but bunnies can get all the nutrients they need from their daily green salads. Many bunny lovers do not ever give their buns pellets, and those bunnies are happy and healthy.

I like to call pellets "bunny crack" because they are more or less addictive and, given a choice between hay and a bowl of pellets, most rabbits will shun the hay and eat only the pellets. People tell me all the time that their rabbits will not eat hay; my advice is for them to remove the pellets from their rabbits' diets and stop feeding fruit or treats. Once your bunny is eating mostly hay, then you can reintroduce a few very small treats once in a while. Grass hay should be at least 80 percent of your rabbit's diet because, for optimal health, rabbits need a high-fiber and low-carbohydrate diet without too much protein or fat.

Pellets are extremely dense nutrition and were designed for farmers to be able to fatten up a baby rabbit for market quickly. Of course, a farm rabbit rarely lives over a year and so there is no thought about longevity or long-term health; it's all about reaching market weight. Pellets are good for a rabbit when he is under six months old and after he becomes a senior citizen (age eight and older) if he has trouble maintaining his optimal weight.

A proper diet will extend the life of your rabbit and, conversely, a poor one will shorten it.

Otherwise, pellets should be fed judiciously, around a quarter-cup per day or less. This amount can be adjusted up or down, depending on the size and breed of the rabbit. A tiny, two- to three-pound dwarf should get no more than about an eighth of a cup (two tablespoons) daily, while a big eight- or nine-pound New Zealand may be need a quarter-cup or more daily, depending upon his weight and appetite.

Remember, rabbits do not need pellets at all, and they will easily ignore a lot other healthier options when given too many pellets. Rex rabbits, who were bred to quickly gain weight in a farming scenario, should probably never have pellets at all once they are adults (one year old), especially the mini-Rexes. Most of them seem to gain a lot of weight from eating them, and it is a good idea not to feed Rex bunnies pellet food at all after they are adults.

The proper amount of green salad is twice the size of his head daily.

Plus, you must watch your rabbit for signs of weight gain and adjust your bunny's diet accordingly. When your bunny is standing in a side profile, you should be able to see air underneath his belly. If your bunny's tummy is touching the ground or you cannot see a big space there, he needs to lose weight. Another good test is to rub your rabbit along his upper back to determine if you can feel his ribs. If you cannot, then your rabbit is probably overweight. And, it's much easier to keep your rabbit at a healthy weight than it is to get excess weight off your rabbit, which is another reason why it's critical to monitor your bunny's diet so carefully.

An important thing to know about a rabbit's physiology is that rabbits do not store most of their excess fat under their skin like humans. They store their extra fat in their livers, which reduces liver function. For example, if your rabbit has 25 percent fat in his liver, then his liver function is reduced by 25 percent. Eventually, the liver ceases to function entirely and death is inevitable. The best vet in the world is not going to able to save a bunny whose organs have shut down due to liver failure. This condition is called "fatty liver disease."

The most frightening thing about fatty liver disease is that, usually by the time you can see that your rabbit has a weight problem, he is very sick inside. It is imperative that an overweight bunny be put on a healthy diet immediately, before it is too late. Rabbits can repair their fatty livers if the excess nutrition is gradually removed from their diets, but this must be done as soon as possible. Your exotics vet can help you do this. The first things that should be removed from an overweight rabbit's diet are fruit, treats, and pellets. These high-calorie foods are frequently the culprits for excess weight on your bun.

Many rabbits who fail to live to be at least eight years old are victims of being overfed. As I've previously mentioned, all rabbits have a terrible fondness for sweet stuff, and will eat all the wrong things if allowed. Thus, it's your job as a good bunny parent to be in total control of your rabbit's nutrition for his own good by limiting treats and carbohydrates, and encouraging him to eat lots of grass hay.

Rabbits require a very high-fiber diet that is low in protein, fat, and carbohydrates. Rabbits do not ever need to eat sugars or fats. They should never be allowed to eat starchy or sugary foods such as beans, peas, corn, popcorn, and people cereals, crackers, and cookies. Nuts are also too high in protein and fat for rabbits. I am not saying that they will not eat these things and love them— they will, but it can cause your bunny to get very sick for several reasons, and not just with fatty liver disease.

Because bunnies are constantly shedding and are natural self-groomers like cats, they will bathe all day long to stay nice and clean. When they get their fine fur down their throats, rabbits cannot throw up furballs like a cat—rabbits are unable to vomit. There is only one way for the fur to get out, and that is to go all the way through their digestive systems. For this reason, their intestines must always be moving. When a rabbit has too much nutrition, it causes the speed, or motility, of their intestines to be reduced, which in turn makes them much more susceptible to an intestinal blockage from ingesting their fur. This is actually a very common problem and can be fatal.

For a truly happy, healthy rabbit, you should feed him unlimited amounts of grass hays, such as timothy hay, orchard grass, oat hay, and bromme (or Bermuda) grass. The best of these nutrition wise is timothy, followed by orchard grass. Oat hay can have too much protein and carbohydrates for it to be fed exclusively, but some people like to mix a bit of it into their rabbits' hay; in limited amounts, it's fine for some variety in the diet. Oat hay is my rabbits' favorite hay, but remember that bunnies like a lot of stuff that is not good for them.

When rabbits are young and growing (less than six months old) they can tolerate some alfalfa and higher-protein hays such as oat hay to help them grow. After they are no longer juveniles, most rabbits should not have very much of these foods. Some breeds such as Angora rabbits will need these higher-protein diets in order to produce the wool that they are known for. Also, when rabbits become older and are having trouble keeping weight on, they will be given this type of diet to try to put some on them. I would recommend seeing a vet before putting your rabbit on a special diet like this because, as a rule, high-protein diets consisting of lots of alfalfa or oat hay should not be given to most adult rabbits.

A daily green salad of several different leafy greens provides all the vitamins and other nutrients that your rabbit will need to be healthy. A rabbit needs roughly one cup of greens per day, once again adjusted up or down according to your rabbit's size. This would be the amount of greens that you could pack down into a measuring cup. It will fluff up and look a bit larger when spread out, but a good rule of thumb to remember is that your bunny should have enough greens to be equal to two times the size of his head. If you follow this simple rule, you will not overfeed your rabbit.

I have said before that caring for a rabbit is not always intuitive, and here is one good example. In humans, we believe that the more fresh greens and salad that you eat, the healthier you are. With rabbits, this is not necessarily true, because you can overfeed your rabbit by giving him too many greens. Too much nutrition can be very unhealthy for a rabbit in the long term—you can actually make your rabbit sick by giving him too much green salad every day.

These are examples of healthy bunny treats, including an herbal mixture, two kinds of bunny crackers, and a timothy hay cube.

Make a mix of about five different kinds of greens so that your bunny has access to all the different vitamins that he needs. I will include a complete list of these greens later in this chapter, but a short list would be: parsley (all kinds), kale (all kinds), romaine lettuce (never iceberg), leaf lettuces (green and red), spinach, dandelions, celery, watercress, and herbs such as basil (all kinds), fennel tops, and dill.

Some rabbits can tolerate Brussels sprouts, cauliflower, and broccoli, but these cabbage-family veggies can be gassy for your rabbit, which is painful and can cause bloating. Bloating can even become fatal for a bunny, so caution should be used when feeding these to a bunny. They should be introduced carefully and in very small amounts until you know that your rabbit can tolerate them.

The amount of timothy pellets I feed my rabbits is 1/8 cup each per day.

Many rabbits are very reluctant to try new veggies and will often shun them the first time that they encounter them. This is normal, and you will find upon reintroducing them again at another time your bunny usually will try them. Like people, rabbits have preferences and their likes and dislikes often change. What your rabbit's favorite veggie is this month may not be his favorite next.

One of my rabbits' current favorites is the silk from an ear of corn. When it is summer, I get fresh corn at the local farmer's market.

They should not get the brown part of the tassel on top of ear, but the fresh yellow silk inside is yummy for a rabbit. Rabbits should never eat any vegetable that is wilted or has gone bad. Bacteria can get transferred to your rabbit this way, and so you should carefully remove all spoiled or wilted portions of your rabbit's veggies. Also, your rabbit should never be given the actual corn kernels since they are too starchy for your bunny.

When introducing any new food into your rabbit's diet, always proceed cautiously. Carefully look for signs of discomfort after feeding your rabbit new foods. He might get a tummyache from that piece of cauliflower or dill that you tried with him. It is hard to tell when this happens, since bunnies are masters at hiding their pain because they are prey animals.

A sign that a rabbit has a problem or is in pain is that he will be sitting hunched over and not moving much. They will sometimes click their teeth loudly and will refuse to eat their favorite things (even treats) or their hay. When your bunny feels good and is happy, he will relax by stretching out his legs and lounging or he will simply flop over on his side. If, instead of relaxing after dinner, your rabbit goes into a corner and stays there, tensely hunched over, you will want to take note.

Usually, this discomfort will go away in a few hours; still, you should always keep a very close eye on a rabbit who is showing signs of pain or discomfort. A rabbit who does not eat or poop for just 24 hours can die. Watch his litter box for fresh bunny poops. (This is something all good bunny owners do every day anyway.) If you ever go a day without seeing any poops in your rabbit's litter box, take your rabbit to his vet immediately: This is a life-threatening condition.

The same thing goes for eating hay and drinking water. If your bunny does not feel well and stops eating his hay or drinking his water, you will need to pay very close attention and not let it slide, as this indicates a very dire situation that must be dealt with quickly to improve your bunny's chances of survival.

The condition of not eating and pooping in rabbits is called gastrointestinal (GI) stasis, and it is a very common and deadly problem for rabbits. This is why you should be constantly monitoring your rabbit's litter box and food and water intake every day. It is also another important reason why rabbits need to live indoors near their owners. You must be aware on a daily basis how your bunny is eating and pooping so that if your rabbit ever does get sick, you can save his life by taking him to the vet.

As I've expressed before, all rabbits love treats. However, the subject of treats is very controversial amongst bunny lovers, because many people feel that it is wrong to deny your rabbit the pleasure of eating special treats, especially since they all love them so much. The problem arises when the human owners are not able to properly judge how much is too much.

Some people give their rabbits a small piece of fruit daily as a treat, but fruit has a lot of natural sugar as well as carbohydrates, which can quickly add up to extra weight on your rabbit, especially when given on a daily basis. Bunnies are very small critters and only a few extra calories over a long period of time will add up.

Many people give their bunnies raisins or Craisins® as treats. Others give them dried fruit, such as dried apricots, dates, and pineapple. I highly discourage this, because dried fruit has a higher sugar content than fresh fruit. Some folks will rationalize that they are only giving their bunnies one or two raisins a day, but think of it in terms of body size: Think how big a raisin is in relation to a bunny's body size. It would be like you eating a small bag of

chocolate chip cookies—or two—by yourself (one raisin = one bag of cookies). It may not be bad for you to do this once in a while, but if you did this every day, the calories would catch up with you.

Rabbits love roses, leaves, thorns, stems and all.
Just be sure that no pesticides have been sprayed on them.

Be aware that most of the treats for bunnies sold in pet stores are very bad for rabbits. Rabbits should never eat dairy products, so those yogurt-drop treats they sell should never be given. If you look at the ingredients for many of the other bunny treats and cookies in the stores, you will see that they have lots of flour and fruit in them, which makes them very high in carbohydrates and/or sugar, and therefore they should be given very sparingly if at all.

Rabbits also do not need the salt licks found in pet stores with a picture of a rabbit on the package. Neither should they ever get something with seeds or nuts in or on them. For years, we bought these treats for our bunny because they had an image of a bunny on the label. Looking back, that treat had peanuts and all kinds of seeds including sunflower seeds—all bad stuff for rabbits.

The most common sign that you are giving your rabbit too much nutrition is finding his cecotropes lying around. Cecotropes are soft, mushy poops that look like a small bunch of grapes. They do not resemble the hard, round poops that you normally find in your rabbit's litter-box, and cecotropes usually have a much stronger odor.

Rabbits love to forage and dig in their fresh hay all day long.

Normally, a healthy rabbit will always eat these cecotropes (sounds gross, but it's a natural thing for rabbits to do, and part of how they get their vitamins from food) and you will never see them, but if you start finding these several times a week, it should be a red flag for you. When rabbits don't feel the need to eat these, it is often because they are being overfed.

It is up to you if you choose to give your bunny treats or fruit, but let me tell you this short story that has convinced me not to give unhealthy treats to my bunnies anymore: After my last bunny passed away and I found out it was due to fatty liver disease, I went to my bunny's vet and asked what the proper diet for my next bunny should be. He described the regimen I have been explaining to you, but I distinctly remember him telling me not to give fruit, and that you are "dancing with the devil" if you do.

Anyone who's ever given fruit or a treat to a rabbit knows how excited the bunny gets. We all like to see our little furry kids happy, and I have never met a bunny who does not get very happy when given a treat. Mine literally dance in circles and binky all over the place for their favorite goodies.

Most rabbits will do anything for a treat, especially sweet stuff, and it is very easy to train rabbits as a result of this. My bunnies will come and sit up, jump in my lap, and all kinds of other tricks for their treats. Of course, this delights me to no end, but it is just too easy to get caught up in the cycle in which your bunny does his tricks that get him a treat, so he does even more tricks to get even more treats, and the next thing you know, you have fallen into the "treat trap."

I used to give my Ricky, Lucy, and Star a little piece of fruit every day, in spite of what my vet had told me, even after losing our beloved Pamela to fatty liver disease. I saw my vet again at an event about a year later, and he reminded me about what he had said about not giving my buns fruit. I thought about it, and realized I was back to my old habits of giving fruit daily to my three rabbits, so I stopped.

For over a month, my bunnies did not get any fruit, and they quickly forgot about it. Several weeks later, I had some leftover watermelon in the refrigerator and I remembered that it happened to be my bunnies' favorite fruit. I gave them each a small piece—and by morning, they were all sick.

None of them wanted to eat their salad the next day, so I got out their favorite bunny crackers and tried to give each of them a piece of that as a test. None of them were takers. By the following day they were all back to normal, but this episode told me everything I needed to know.

I did not give any of them fruit again for about three months, and the same thing happened again. There was some cantaloupe in the refrigerator, and for some reason I decided to give them all a small treat. The next day, it was the same thing: Not one rabbit would eat, and it was a sign that they all had tummyaches.

How could they have been eating fruit like that every day and not get sick, but when I gave it to them just one time, they did?

The answer is that sugars have no part in a bunny's natural diet. When they are present, they literally change the whole flora of the bacteria inside the gut. It is very similar to a human getting Montezuma's Revenge from drinking strange water, which comes from ingesting bacteria that our gastrointestinal systems are not used to. Rabbits get the same kind of thing, and this was a very graphic and easy-to-understand example that really hit home with me.

A rabbit who never gets sugar, from sweets or fruits, has a totally different set of bacteria inside his gut, and the sudden introduction of a food like that can immediately throw his GI tract out of whack.

When I removed all fruit from my bunnies' diets, they eventually became all excited about the other, more nutritious and healthy foods that they got such as their salads or rose petals from the garden. Yes, bunnies love roses . . . leaves, stems, thorns, and all. Just make sure that they have not been sprayed with pesticides, or your bunny could get sick.

With all of these warnings and things to watch out for, it makes it sound as if rabbits are very fragile pets—and they are. That is why rabbits are used so often to test different products before they are given to humans. Rabbits' ultra-sensitivity to so many things is the reason that they are frequently used for lab animals.

This is another reason I tell people that rabbits are not low-maintenance pets. There is some knowledge and effort required in order for your bunny to live a long and healthy life. Even making well-meaning mistakes in feeding can cause illness, and as you've already read, the vet bills can be very expensive, and that is only if you catch it in time.

Simply put, what I have learned is that rabbits love treats, but it is we humans who associate treats with sugar and sweets. Your rabbit will be just as happy to get a big sprig of his favorite green or herb for a snack or treat as he would be to get some fruit. Teach your rabbit that his treats will be healthy ones and believe me, in a few weeks he will forget about those bits of dried fruit—or better yet, never get him started on them in the first place.

I like to give my rabbits at least five different kinds of greens each day.

I have read some books on the market that say it is OK to occasionally give your rabbit human cereal and fruit treats. Some even go so far as to describe how big the pieces of fruit should be and how often you can give them cereal. I disagree completely with these writers. Too many people will misjudge the amounts and slip right into the "treat trap," not to mention that people cereal is high-carb and has lots of added sugar. It is better to never get involved with giving your rabbits any of these kinds of foods.

Not only are bits of fresh greens good, healthy treats, but I know some rabbit lovers who make special treats for their buns with a food dehydrator. They put stems from things like parsley and cilantro and pieces of hearty greens like kale and spinach in them until they are crispy. Those crunchy bits that look so insignificant to us are a grand treat for your rabbit.

I have found a bunny lover in my area who makes what I call "guilt-free" bunny crackers. She does not load them up with fruit and wheat flours, but bases them on some oats and ground pellets. These things are still not good in large amounts, but my bunnies wait all day for their one-inch square of these crackers. Still, I see to it that they never get more than one of these per day.

It may take some work on your part to find the best treats for your bun, but you can if you always look at the ingredients that are in them. Avoid those whose main ingredients are flours (carbohydrates), and watch out for added sugar or sweeteners such as honey. If there is fruit in it, it should be one of the last ingredients. Choose ones that have the lowest calorie counts.

And remember portion control: The single cookie that each of my bunnies is allowed every day is usually broken into four even-smaller pieces. Bunnies don't know the difference between a whole cookie and a part of one. All they know is that I am bestowing treats on them.

Crockery bowls are useful rabbit equipment because they resist being tipped over.

Healthy Bunny Food List

Unlimited Grass Hays – not Alfalfa unless prescribed by your vet or your bunny is a juvenile

Timothy hay
Orchard grass
Oat hay
Bromme/Bermuda grass

Fresh Vegetables and Herbs – Daily mixture twice the size of your bunny's head

Romaine lettuce	Mint (all types)
Leaf lettuces (red and green)	Thyme
	Oregano
Parsley (all types)	Chervil
Cilantro	Carrot tops
Watercress	Bok choy
Cucumber	Snow pea pods
Celery	Beet tops
Kale (all types)	Collard greens
Bell pepper (red, orange, and yellow)	Mustard greens
	Chard (all types)
Green beans	Fennel
Spinach (all types)	Dill
Basil (all types)	Dandelion leaves

Unlimited access to water

Very limited treats

Very limited rabbit pellets, if at all (around ¼ cup or less, depending on size)

These Items Are Absolute No-No's

Iceberg lettuce	Dairy of Any Kind
Any beans	Seeds or Nuts
Corn kernels	Human cookies
Peas or Legumes	Sugary cereal
Avocado (too fatty)	Chips or Popcorn
Chocolate (toxic)	Most Houseplants

Summary

- It is very important that you feed your pet rabbit properly if you want him to live a long and healthy life.

- Rabbits who live solely on pellets tend to live only half as long as rabbits who are fed properly balanced diets of grass hays and a variety of fresh greens daily.

- Given a choice between hay and a bowl of pellets, most rabbits will shun the hay and eat only the pellets.

- Pellets are extremely dense nutrition and were designed for farmers to be able to fatten up a baby rabbit for market quickly.

- You must watch your rabbit for signs of weight gain and adjust your bunny's diet accordingly.

- Rabbits store most of their extra fat in their livers, which reduces liver function and can cause a fatal condition called "fatty liver disease."

- Many rabbits who fail to live to be at least eight years old are victims of being overfed.

- Rabbits require a very high-fiber diet that is low in protein, fat, and carbohydrates.

- When a rabbit has too much nutrition, it causes the speed, or motility, of their intestines to be reduced, which in turn makes them much more susceptible to an intestinal blockage from ingesting their fur when they groom themselves.

- For a truly happy, healthy rabbit, you must feed him unlimited amounts of grass hays every day.

- A daily green salad of several different leafy greens provides all the vitamins and other nutrients that your rabbit will need to be healthy.

- A good rule of thumb to remember is to feed your bunny a fresh green salad equal to two times the size of his head daily.

- You can actually make your rabbit sick by giving him too much green salad every day.

- A mix of about five different kinds of greens daily should provide all the different vitamins that your bunny needs.

- Cabbage-family veggies can be gassy for your rabbit, which is painful and can cause bloating.

- Many rabbits are very reluctant to try new veggies at first.

- When introducing any new food into your rabbit's diet, always proceed cautiously.

- You should always take notice of a rabbit who is showing signs of pain or discomfort, and take him to the vet promptly if needed.

- Not eating and pooping in rabbits is a very common and deadly problem, and he needs to see a vet immediately.

- Be aware that most of the treats for bunnies sold in pet stores are very bad for rabbits.

- The most common sign that you are giving your rabbit too much nutrition is finding his cecotropes lying around.

- Most rabbits will do anything for a treat.

- Don't fall into the "treat trap."

- Sugars have no part in a bunny's natural diet.

- There is some knowledge and effort required in order for your bunny to live a long and healthy life.

- Your rabbit will be just as happy to get a big sprig of his favorite green or herb for a snack or treat as he would be to get some fruit or other sweets.

- Some rabbit lovers make special treats for their buns with a food dehydrator.

- It may take some work on your part to find the best treats for your bun.

- Remember portion control when feeding your rabbit except when it comes to hay.

Angelo has a funny way to lounge.

Lucy cooling her heels.

Lucy sprawled out on the floor.

Chapter 10:
How To House Your Rabbit

There are three different ways to have your rabbit live indoors with you, and I am going to explain each method along with their pros and cons.

X-Pens

Many house rabbits live in an X-pen environment. These are multi-panel, metal (or heavy plastic) pens that can be folded up for storage or transport. X-pens are very versatile because you can adjust their shapes, making them one of the simplest ways to provide a safe and secure place for your bunny to spend most of his time, especially when you are not able to supervise him. We also use them to take our bunnies to the park or beach, as well as set them up in the yard to make it easier to keep an eye on the buns when they are outside playing. You can connect a couple of X-pens together to make very large run spaces. We use the clips like the ones on the ends of dog leashes to connect multiple X-pens together, although many other kinds of clips work too.

X-pens come in a variety of heights and you will need to make sure you get one that your rabbit cannot hop out of. Most rabbits are fine with a 36-inch-high pen, but one of my bunnies, Star, is a jumper and she easily clears pens that high so hers is a 48-inch-high pen. I have met bunnies who are fine in 24-inch-high pens and others who are OK with 30-inch-high pens. When you purchase your X-pen, be sure to check the store's exchange policy so you can exchange it if you find that it is not tall enough.

I recommend that you start with a 36-inch-high pen if you have a new bunny and you don't know whether he is a jumper or not. Younger rabbits tend to hop and jump more, as do dwarfs. Older rabbits, just like older cats and dogs, are not as active and generally will not be as inclined to jump over tall fences. I have kept older rabbits in a 24-inch-high pen and they never once hopped out.

The good part of using an X-pen for your rabbit's abode is the large space it offers; the drawbacks are that many rabbits learn how to jump or climb out of them. If you are going to be away from your rabbit for long periods, you will not want to arrive home after a long day to discover that your rabbit has gotten out and chewed through every cord he could get his teeth on. For these clever buns, consider purchasing covers for their pens or keeping them inside large cages (indoors of course) when you are not at

Two English Spot boys playing in an X-pen.

home. The covers are not that expensive and work very well for containing rambunctious rabbits. With X-pen living, you'll need to give your rabbit an enclosed place to hide and sleep. A "hidey" box inside your rabbit's X-pen will provide some privacy and a cozy place for him when he wants it or when it's naptime. There are many of these on the market, or you can simply make your own by cutting some doors in a good-sized cardboard box.

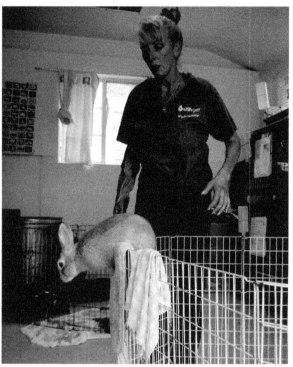

Kevin is an escape artist and illustrates why you need to make sure that your rabbit's X-pen is tall enough that he cannot jump out.

X-pens are not inexpensive (around $100, plus or minus $20, depending on size), but they are an excellent piece of equipment to invest in when you have a pet bunny.

A 3' x 6' or 4' x 8' space is ideal for your bunny to have inside an X-pen, as long as he gets about three hours' run time out of it each day.

Rabbits are crepuscular, not nocturnal as many people believe. This means that they are the most active in the early morning and early evening hours. They sleep most of the night and will usually nap for several hours during the day—in fact, rabbits get their deepest sleep about midday, between the hours of 10 a.m. and 3 p.m.

Cages/Condos

Another, but more expensive, way to house your rabbit is in a large cage or bunny condo.

Kevin shows another way to escape an X-pen.

Many people do not like to have cages in their homes because most cages are made of wire and look like they belong in the backyard, not your living room. We found one made partly of wood and partly of metal that we really like because it looks more like furniture. It is a two-story affair with textured plastic floors that are easy to clean.

You should avoid wire-bottomed cages at all costs. Rabbits tend to get their toenails caught in the wires and can pull them completely out. I have actually met a bun who lost his leg from an infection that set in after pulling out a toenail in a wire-bottomed cage. If you must use a wire-bottomed cage, make certain that you cover the entire bottom with carpet squares and keep your rabbit's toenails trimmed at all times.

If you elect to go with a cage, the exact size of it (we like to call it the bunny's "condo") should depend on the size and activity level of your bunny. Very small rabbits, such as dwarfs, can be happy in a 2' x 3', one-story condo, as long as they get plenty of time each day outside of the cage for exercise and running. A larger bunny will obviously require something bigger, such as a two-story setup or larger square footage.

If you do not give your bunny enough space in his condo, then he will not be happy spending long periods inside when you are away. My rabbits all have two-story condos that are 2' x 4'. They absolutely love them and, when I come home and let them out, they will often continue to sit inside for a half-hour or more before coming out to play. This tells me that they really like their abodes and do not mind being inside them.

You need to ensure that your rabbit's condo is large enough to hold his litter box, water crock or bottle, hay manger (if you choose to use one), and toys, and still have enough room for him to move around and stretch out. You will be surprised how big even a medium-size rabbit will stretch out to when flopping over. My large New Zealand girl, Lucy, can easily measure well over two feet long when she's only slightly stretched out. Remember, your bunny will be spending many hours inside this structure, and it is always better to have a condo that is too large than too small. If you get a durable model, it will last through several bunnies. Expect to pay between $200-400 for a high-quality, well-constructed, good-sized cage.

My bunny's two-story condo looks like it belongs indoors.

Ricky and Lucy relax in front of their two-story abode (condo).

You'll find a lot of small, plastic-and-wire cages sold in pet stores, but most of them are not large enough for a rabbit; they are better suited for rats and guinea pigs. Your rabbit's X-pens and condo will be some of your biggest expenses in bringing home your new rabbit, and so if you cannot afford large-enough housing—either due to cost or to space in your home—then perhaps you cannot afford a rabbit at all. If you give your bunny plenty of room, he will be a happier, more relaxed rabbit. If you keep him in too small an area, it creates tension and makes him nervous because he's always wanting to get out of his "jail cell."

Custom Built

If you are a do-it-yourselfer, then you might consider making your own bunny condo. I have seen lots of unique and clever abodes made with materials that you can purchase at your local housewares or hardware store. Avoid using press-wood or particle board, since your rabbit will most likely chew on it at some point, and you do not want him ingesting the resins that are used to manufacture these materials.

Rough-textured plastic flooring works best for the bottom level, and is easy to clean. Do not use something that is extremely smooth because your bunny will have trouble keeping his footing on the slick floor. If you must use something smooth, then cover it with carpeting that is easily replaceable in case your bunny chews it, too.

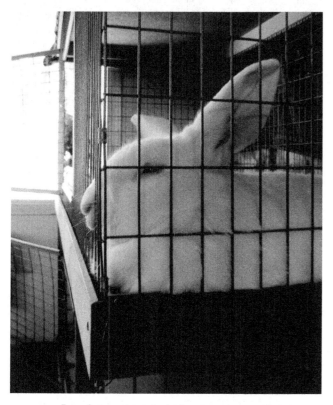

Lucy lounges upstairs in her two-story condo with her nose sticking out.

There are components that are for building stacking cubes in stores that sell housewares that make nice condos. You can even find instructions and designs for using them online. Just make sure to build it large enough for your bunny. I suggest no smaller than 2' x 3' with room above for your bunny to be able to stand up and stretch.

However, I have found that, by the time you buy all of the parts and construct your bunny's home, you are only saving about $100 from the cost of buying a similar, pre-built abode new. If you enjoy making things, then maybe it will be worth it for you. If you are not that handy and do not have all the tools, it is probably easier to buy one already made.

Whatever type of housing you select for your bunny, there are a few features to keep in mind when you're buying or building. First is that the entrance/exit is down low enough to the floor so that your rabbit can hop in and out easily. For this reason, I think the better designs have doors that open sideways and not up or down. Ones that open upward can fall down and close accidentally, and they get in your way when you try to reach inside. Those that fold down will need to be covered so that your bunny's toes do not get caught in the wire, and this is not very convenient.

The second important feature is ease of cleaning. Hay, poops, and occasionally urine are going to get on it. Having a big, wide door or lid on the top that lifts will dramatically improve your ease in cleaning. Try vacuuming or sweeping out stuff from a condo with a one-foot-square door that is four inches off the ground and you will see what I mean.

Be sure not place to your rabbit's abode in front of any sunny window, radiator, heater, vent, or drafty spot for his comfort. (You know how warm you can get in the sunshine coming through a window.) Rabbits do not tolerate heat well, and actually prefer cooler temperatures than most humans. Do not put his condo over the top of the heater vent thinking it will make him nice and cozy—he's already wearing a fur coat, so he's plenty warm.

You may find that you need some urine guards for around your rabbit's condo if he is spraying. This behavior usually goes away after spaying/neutering, but sometimes rabbits will mark their abodes if they sense another rabbit or animal near their territory. They may even do it to express displeasure with some perceived slight. If you have a bun who does this, you may want to consider external urine guards on his cage.

The main benefit of housing your bunny in a condo is that, when you are not there, you know your rabbit is controlled inside a safe place and he cannot get into trouble. The drawback to a condo is that if you do not get one roomy enough, your rabbit will become frustrated if he spends a lot of time in there. Rabbits who are locked inside bunny cages while you are at school or at work will need to have more run time than those who stay in X-pens, since they're not able to hop and run at all while inside.

My rabbits are let out of their condos the minute we get up in the morning or get home from being away. They are only put in there when we go to bed at night or leave the house for any period of time.

The "Rabbit Room"/"Free-Run Bunnies"

Another method of housing a rabbit is to completely bunny-proof a room and to shut your bunny inside that room when you are away. This is far more difficult than it sounds, because bunnies can hop up on almost anything and I have met several rabbits who were expert climbers. They can get up on top of many things and so nothing can be left on a chair or table-top that you do not want turned into confetti. Any food other than hay—rabbit or human—is another thing that you do not want to have accessible in a "rabbit room," because rabbits will eat many foodstuffs that are not good for them. Some human foods can make your bunny sick.

I have seen rabbits open cabinet doors and tear out everything inside. They can easily hop up on a bed and, if they have a mind to, shred your very expensive comforter. There are many places you may not think a rabbit can get to, but

do not underestimate their abilities. This is why I am saying that it is a lot harder than it sounds to completely bunny-proof a whole room (or house).

For many devoted rabbit lovers, they opt to give their rabbits the run of the house. These lucky house rabbits are never in a cage or pen. They are allowed to run freely inside the whole house, but it takes a real rabbit expert to completely bunny-proof an entire home, and note that some of these free-run bunnies are limited to certain areas by natural barriers such as steps or slick flooring that they refuse to cross.

The benefit of this kind of living arrangement is that your rabbit never has to be locked in a cage or pen, but as I pointed out, to bunny-proof a complete room or house is difficult

Ricky and Lucy are a bonded pair, and they are free-run buns who have the run of the house.

if not impossible for many families. Your rabbit will find every single thing that you missed over time—and trust me, they will find every last one of them. I recommend that people get down on the floor and look at a room from a rabbit's point of view; even tiny spaces and cracks as small as a couple inches can provide an opening for a rabbit to crawl in between or under furniture and appliances, or to start chewing and creating a hole in your wall or floor. This means that the wires for a refrigerator or TV become fair game if not suitably protected, and it's why most people will not give a rabbit full run of the house until they have truly bunny-proofed every single part of the home.

I once had a rabbit who would not cross the slippery tile floor in my kitchen or go back to the bedrooms because of a slick slate floor. For over two years, this rabbit minded her natural boundaries, but then one day she learned how to hop on those surfaces and I found her in my computer room, exploring everything.

Ricky surveys the living room from the top floor of his Cottontail Cottage.

That led to us having to bunny-proof the rest of the house to prevent any problems. It took months before the whole family learned to always close the door to the computer room because that room was not able to be bunny-proofed. Never assume that, just because your rabbit has never

explored a part of the house, someday he will not suddenly decide to do so. Rabbits learn every day and get smarter as they get older. You may suddenly find your rabbit hopping up and down a set of stairs that for years he would not go near. That is just how rabbits are.

As you can see, each of these three housing methods has its benefits and disadvantages. If you choose one method and then decide to opt for another down the road, do not worry: Rabbits are quite adaptable and will usually get used to a change in their abode very quickly.

I have seen some rabbits who were allowed to run free and were never in cages get a little angry about suddenly being locked in a cage or X-pen. These rabbits will need extra time out so that they do not come to resent their new living conditions. Your rabbit will communicate his feelings about his home to you, if you pay attention to his signals. I have found that if a rabbit is upset about being in a cage after having had the full run of the house, you may need to go for the X-pen option instead of a cage; this usually solves the problem.

Just be certain not to tuck your bunny away in a part of the house that no one in the family frequents. He could end up being just as lonely there as he would be out in the backyard. Most people want their pets in the part of the house where they spend the most time, like the den or family room. The main reason you should want this is so that you can enjoy spending time and communicating with your little furry friend.

More About Bunny-Proofing

The areas where your bunny stays, plays, and runs will need to be bunny-proofed. This means that all things that you do not want him to chew on or dig at need to be protected or removed. There are only three ways to protect something from your rabbit. You can make a barrier to prevent him from getting near it, you can cover it with something that is chew-proof, or you can completely remove the item from the area that your rabbit is in. You will also need to visually (and actively) supervise your bunny very closely during his time out to play. I guarantee your rabbit will show you every weakness in the barriers and covers you put up to prevent him from going where you don't want him to go. And, the minute you tell your bunny that he is not allowed to go in a certain area, he is going to spend the rest of his life trying to get there to see what it is that he is not supposed to see. It is amazing the single-mindedness a bunny can have when he decides he wants to go somewhere.

Think of rabbits as two- or three-year-old children: Everything they come in contact with goes into their mouths. If you already have your bunny, you've likely found out by now that bunny teeth are super sharp, and can chew through things in a flash. Some rabbits chew more than others, but all bunnies chew at one time or another—it's a natural rabbit behavior. Make sure that your rabbit does not get into trouble or hurt himself by chewing on the wrong things. And just because a bunny does not normally chew does not mean that one day he will not just suddenly decide to chew everything in his path, including the legs on Grandma's antique table you inherited. You can't train your rabbit not to chew, so don't even try; again, chewing is natural, normal rabbit behavior and you can't change it. Just give him other, safe things to chew on, like toilet paper tubes stuffed with fresh hay or an old telephone book. It sometimes helps to put lots of his personal toys in his play area to divert his attention from chewing or digging on your stuff. You can also use an X-pen to limit the area in which your rabbit spends his time.

Do not make the mistake of thinking that you can watch your bunny closely enough to keep him from chewing your television cord or computer cables. One of my bunnies is famous for her "drive-by chompings" and will literally hop by a cord of any kind and nip it without ever breaking her stride. I have spent hundreds of dollars and countless hours replacing cords due to a bunny getting away into an un-bunny-proofed area in the house. Your rabbit can also electrocute himself by chewing on cords.

The best way to protect cords is to purchase some cord protectors, which are available at most hardware stores. Cord protectors are hollow plastic tubes that slip right over your cords and computer cables to discourage rabbits from chewing. Warning: Cord protectors aren't chew-proof, and some rabbits will chew through the cord protectors. They're still a good investment, because they can buy you enough time to save the cord in most cases.

Also be sure to cover the flooring in your bunny's X-pen area, even if it's carpeted. Some rabbits like to dig (another natural behavior) or chew on carpet, and you can prevent the destruction of your good carpeting by covering it with something that doesn't matter if it gets dirty or chewed on. We like to use carpet-sample squares discarded by carpet stores. You can also use inexpensive carpets from discount stores— they can often be machine washed—but don't buy rugs with fringe or unfinished edges; your bunny can swallow and choke on the fibers. Some people like to use carpet remnants in a size slightly bigger than the X-pen to reduce the rate at which their bunnies chew through the carpet remnants, if their rabbits are big chewers. I have also seen people use office-style plastic chair mats as floor protectors or a remnant of linoleum if their bunny likes to constantly chew on carpet squares.

Summary

- There are three different ways to have your rabbit live indoors with you—and all pet rabbits should live indoors.

- Many house rabbits live in an X-pen environment.

- X-pens come in a variety of heights and you will need to make sure you get one that your rabbit cannot hop out of.

- Rabbits are crepuscular, not nocturnal as many people believe.

- Another, but more expensive, way to house your rabbit is in a large cage or "bunny condo."

- Avoid wire-bottomed cages because rabbits tend to get their toenails caught in them.

- The size of a cage/condo should depend on the size and activity level of your bunny.

- Your rabbit's condo needs to be large enough to hold his litter box, water crock or bottle, and toys, and still have enough room for him to move around and stretch out.

- Small, plastic-and-wire cages sold in pet stores are not large enough for a rabbit.

- If you are a do-it-yourselfer, you might consider making your own bunny condo.

- The cage/condo entrance should be down low enough to the floor so that your rabbit can hop in and out easily.

- A big, wide door or lid on the top that lifts will dramatically improve your ease in cleaning.

- Do not place your rabbit's abode in front of any sunny window, radiator, heater, vent, or drafty spot for his comfort.

- The main benefit of a condo is that, when you are not there, you know that your rabbit is controlled inside a safe place.

- Another method of housing a rabbit is to completely bunny-proof a room and to shut your bunny inside that room when you are away.

- Many rabbit lovers opt to give their rabbit the run of the house, but it takes a real rabbit expert to completely bunny-proof an entire home.

- Never assume that, just because your rabbit has never explored a part of the house, someday he will not suddenly decide to do so.

- Do not tuck your bunny away in a part of the house that no one in the family frequents.

- The areas where your bunny stays, plays, and runs will need to be fully and carefully bunny-proofed.

- You will need to visually and actively supervise your bunny very closely during his time out to play.

- Think of rabbits as two- or three-year-old children and always supervise them that way.

- Do not make the mistake of thinking that you can watch your bunny closely enough to keep him from chewing your television cord, computer cables, or other items when he is out for playtime.

- The best way to protect cords is to purchase cord protectors; while not chew-proof, they can usually give you enough time to save the cord if your bunny gets hold of it.

- Your rabbit can be electrocuted by chewing on electrical cords.

- Cover the flooring in your bunny's X-pen area, even if it's carpeted, to protect your good carpets and rugs from digging and chewing.

Chapter 11:
Handling and Socializing Your Rabbit

Learning how to safely handle your rabbit in order to avoid either you or him getting injured or him possibly escaping is very important. Many people panic when their rabbits start kicking and squirming, which can result in bunnies being dropped or, even worse, their backs being injured.

Since bunnies are fragile creatures, you will want to always handle yours with care. I will illustrate the proper way to pick up and handle your rabbit, as there are several safe methods to use as well as some that are completely off-limits.

Never, ever pick up your bunny by his ears or the scruff of his neck. I have seen even vets do this (typically dog-and-cat vets who are inexperienced with handling rabbits), and I cringe every time I see it happen. A rabbit's ears are one of the most sensitive parts of his body, and his very thin skin is subject to bruising if you pick him up by the scruff of his neck. It physically hurts a bunny to be held this way, and it is a very poor way to build trust with your pet. You do not want your bunny running and hiding from you every time you want to pick him up. Picking up your rabbit by the ears or his neck is a sure way to have this happen.

Like I've said in previous chapters, the main reason rabbits do not like to be picked up is because, in the wild, when a rabbit leaves the ground, he is about to die. So, you're asking your bunny to go against a basic instinct when you pick him up and carry him around. This is why most unsocialized rabbits will put up a fuss when you try picking them up.

To pick up your rabbit, form a "V" with your hand.

Find the balance point behind his front legs.

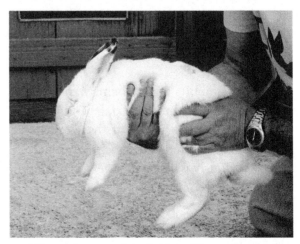

Lift your bunny and steady him with your free hand.

Rabbits will learn to tolerate handling the more you do it. Some bunnies trust their owners so much that they will not fight being turned over on their backs and carried like a baby, but this is something that has developed from thoroughly trusting that they will not be dropped.

Hold your rabbit behind his front legs with your hand and pinch his behind between your elbow and your side to firmly hold him.

When approaching a bunny who is skittish, it helps to get down low on his level. When you come at him from above, it resembles being attacked by a predator. With time and patience, you can get your rabbit used to being approached to the point where he will not try to escape when you go to pick him up, but this takes working with your bun.

Some rabbits take to being handled more readily than others, often depending upon the rabbit's past history. Rabbits have excellent memories and will remember being dropped or hurt previously when someone was trying to handle them, even if it wasn't you.

If a rabbit is being aggressive when you approach him by grunting, growling, charging, or boxing at you, then it is best to gain control over the bunny first by placing your hand gently but firmly on top of his head. All but the feistiest rabbits will flatten out and settle down once your hand is on their heads.

If your bunny is socialized and used to being handled, you will be able to skip putting your hand on top of his head. If your rabbit shows any resistance, do not hesitate to use the hand-on-top-of-the-head method to make him relax a bit.

If the bunny continues to try to resist or fight with you even with your hand on his head, then gently apply a little more pressure to control his head so that he cannot nip or bite you. Most rabbits will resign themselves to being handled with your hand merely resting lightly on their heads with virtually no pressure at all. This technique seems to work with virtually all rabbits.

Be very careful if a struggle ensues to not use so much pressure that an injury can occur. If your rabbit is that aggressive, then you may want to consider putting on some gloves in order to avoid getting bitten. This is a very rare occurrence; I have handled hundreds of bunnies in my time working at the animal shelter and have never had to resort to this extreme tactic. I have heard stories about super-aggressive bunnies who did need this, though. I just have not run into one myself yet.

For 99 percent of bunnies, simply placing your hand on their heads will calm them right down. Once you have the rabbit calm, you should then use your other hand to scoop underneath his belly between his front and hind legs. I like to make a "V" with my thumb and forefinger and use that as a cradle under the bunny's chest right behind his front legs.

When you start to lift the bunny with your hand under his chest, you will want to seek the balance point so that you can lift the bunny up. You should use your free hand to control the bunny's legs if he kicks or his head if he tries to nip you.

Once I have picked up the rabbit, I like to gently pin his hind legs and rump between my elbow and my abdomen. This generally will keep most bunnies from kicking and flailing around while you are holding them. If he does break away from between your elbow and your side, then you can use your free hand to regain control of him.

You want to avoid a bunny flailing and kicking while he is being held if you can, because that can result in the rabbit being dropped and escaping, or even a skeletal injury. Rabbits have hollow bones like birds, which makes them more delicate than most pets, especially when being handled.

An important thing to remember is, if a bunny feels in peril of being dropped, he usually will react by kicking and flailing around. The ironic thing is that, when they do this, it usually results in their being dropped. The solution is to always hold a bunny firmly so that he never feels like he can fall. This will go a long way to prevent him from doing any kicking when you are holding him.

Once your rabbit develops trust in you and gets used to being picked up, he may allow you to hold him for long periods of time—some rabbits will permit this, and some won't. I feel it is important to work with your bunny by picking him up often, even if he does not like it at first, because the more you do it, the more used to it he will become.

You will need to handle your rabbit for his weekly grooming sessions. This is a good time to practice picking up and holding your rabbit.

Use your free hand to hold his legs if he kicks.

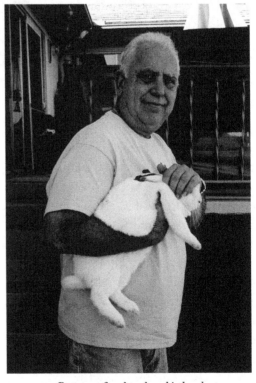

Put your free hand on his head if he tries to nip at you.

Many rabbits will learn to enjoy their time being groomed and, to a bunny, being groomed by you means that he "owns" you. It is good for his self-esteem and well-being to have regular grooming sessions. Most rabbits need combing at least once a week and sometimes every day during molting season. Rabbits also need their toenails trimmed about every six to eight weeks. Be sure to check your bunny's toenails to see if they are in need of trimming every time you groom.

Be sure and hold your rabbit snugly when carrying him. Otherwise he will flail around if thinks he might fall.

Some highly socialized rabbits will actually allow themselves to be easily turned over and cradled like a baby. Not many bunnies will tolerate this kind of handling, and it usually comes from years of building trust. You must be careful that your rabbit, in trying to twist out of the upside-down position, does not strain, injure, or fracture his back. If your rabbit is resisting being held this way, then don't do it until he becomes more trusting of being handled and carried by you. You do not want him to injure his spine and end up a paraplegic, which can easily happen if he is struggling to get free or flip himself over.

Many rabbits never learn to tolerate being carried that way and that is normal, so do not try and force it if he is resistant. You would be surprised how many bunny owners never learn how to pick up and carry their rabbits. Just having a bunny who tolerates being picked up and carried is sometimes a big win, depending on your rabbit's age and past.

Often it is easier to train your rabbit to do things on his own so that you do not need to pick him up, such as when you want him to go back in his pen or condo. Using a treat or a toy that he likes can often have your bunny running to his pen when it is time to go in, instead of precipitating a big chase and then struggling to pick him up and carry him back.

Still, I feel it is important to master the skill of picking up and carrying your bun. I once had a bunny who did not like to be picked up. I never handled her for years until she got sick and had to go to the vet. Then it became the most traumatic experience imaginable. I realize now that, if she had been socialized to being picked up, the whole car ride and trip to the vet would not have been so terrible for her.

Rabbits are so smart that, sometimes, as soon as they see their pet carrier, they know they are about to go on a car ride. If your bunny hates car rides, he may bolt and hide the second he sees the carrier. Then all the socializing and training in the world will not get your bunny to willfully enter the carrier.

I have found that putting my buns into their pet carriers on a regular basis eventually gets them used to the whole thing. They still may not like it, but they no longer act like it is the end of the world. I still may hear a thump or two from them inside the carrier as they tell me that they disapprove, but at least it is not an all-out battle to catch them and get them inside.

I recommend getting your rabbit in a position where you do not have to chase him to pick him up. I like to corral my buns in their condos before picking them up to be put inside their carriers. This way, they cannot escape because they do not want to be put in there. However, I would not advise using this method for a cage-protective rabbit (one who becomes aggressive when you enter his cage).

You can do the same thing with your rabbit's X-pen: Simply corral your bunny inside his pen and then keep reducing its size until he can no longer run from you. If he is resisting, remember the hand-on-the-head trick. This will usually stop all attempts to escape.

Remember to gain a firm grip on your bun as you approach the pet carrier because he will often freak out and try to get away when he sees it coming. It is best to use your free hand to control his hind legs so he does not kick himself free.

You can use this advice for anything that requires handling your rabbit, especially for things that some rabbits do not like doing, such as being combed or having a nail trim. Firm-but-gentle handling goes a long way to calming your bunny down when carrying him someplace that he really doesn't want to go.

A little trick I learned from a very experienced rabbit lover is to put the bunny into the pet carrier or condo rump-end first. This way, he won't see it coming and therefore does not squirm to avoid it. The trick is learning to securely switch him from being held facing forward to facing the opposite direction. It does take some practice, because if your rabbit feels you fumbling when you do the switch, he will start to squirm anyway.

Carrying your rabbit loosely is an invitation for him to kick his legs and end up being dropped. If your rabbit is relaxed and not fighting being held, you still must not relax your hold on him. If he feels insecure and in danger of being dropped, this will usually cause him to suddenly start flailing around.

After you become very used to handling your rabbit and he becomes used to you doing it, then you might be able to become more relaxed in how you pick him up and carry him. This takes time for some bunnies, and others never do reach that stage. You will begin to get the feeling from your rabbit whether or not he is stressed from you handling him.

I can feel the tension in my bunny's body when I am holding him, and I can usually sense when he is preparing to try to jump from my arms or if he is just going to relax and allow himself to be held. Handling rabbits becomes easier and easier with experience, and confidence is important when you go to pick up your bunny, because he can also sense when you are not sure about it.

Most rabbits will not let you hold them like this.

If, for some reason, your rabbit is kicking and flailing around and you start to lose control of him, it is best to quickly kneel down and get your bunny as close to the floor as possible. This will avoid him becoming injured if he kicks his way out of your arms. Better to have him only falling a foot or so and escaping than to break a bone or get a severe back strain. You should always be prepared to put your bunny's feet on the ground quickly to stop yourself from losing control of him while he is being carried.

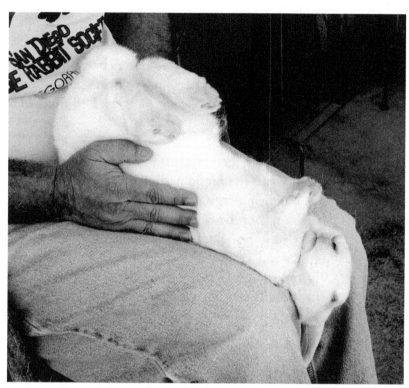

Regularly handing your rabbit for grooming builds trust and allows him to get used to being picked up, touched, and examined.

Many rabbits get injured each year from improper handling or being dropped. In order to build trust, it is your job to make sure that your rabbit is never one of these buns. Practice makes it easier every time you pick up and handle your rabbit, so do it often and you both will learn how to do it.

Some rabbits have some serious baggage from their previous owners or situations. They may have been dropped so many times that they never learn to stop fearing being picked up. For a hard-to-handle rabbit, a method that can often be employed is to use a towel when picking him up. When we have particularly fierce rabbits at the shelter who are very aggressive, we put a towel over them to keep them from being able to nip or kick while they are being picked up.

I would only do this as a last resort, because you should learn how to handle your rabbit without a lot of drama, and I feel that the towel method keeps him from ever learning to tolerate being picked up. In other words, it will prolong the time that your rabbit refuses to let you handle him. I think it is better to struggle with it for a short while in hopes that eventually the fighting will end through trust.

Still, there are some very tough cases where you may find that you need to use the towel method. With some extremely unsocialized rabbits, this is the only way that you can handle them. I hope that the rabbit you choose to adopt does not have these issues—they are tough to get past and sometimes they never do quite get over it. When you run across a bunny like this, just remember that it was a human who made him this way, so don't be too hard on him. Only with love and understanding will you ever be able to help him overcome his fears.

Special care should be taken when allowing children or strange pets to approach your rabbit. I recommend holding your rabbit and then kneeling or sitting down to present your bunny for petting or an introduction. Watch for any rough handling, and describe to children how to rub your bunny's head and ears while avoiding his eyes. Rabbits' eyes are very exposed, and a kid's dirty hands should not be allowed touch your rabbit's sensitive eye area.

It is always better for you to hold your rabbit safely than to allow him to be approached by a toddler on the ground. Toddlers may lose their balance and fall over when they bend down to pet a small critter. You do not want them to fall on top of your rabbit, because severe injuries occur this way. It is never a good idea to let small children hold your rabbit unless they are sitting down and they have been shown the correct way to do it. Even adults who do not understand the proper way to hold a bunny can lose control and drop your rabbit suddenly if he squirms or kicks. This is why I rarely let others hold my rabbits unless I know for sure that they have enough experience to do it correctly.

Socializing Your Rabbit

Socializing your rabbit is a bit different from training him, because when you are training a rabbit you are using treats to get him to do a specific behavior. Socializing is more about getting him used to interactions and events that he is not used to. Once he becomes accustomed to them, it makes day-to-day activities easier and less complicated.

What at first was a terrifying experience for your bunny can, in most cases, become a normal activity over time by using gentle repetition. One example of socialization in action in our house is the vacuum cleaner: When we first brought our rabbits home, they used to run and hide whenever they saw Denise dragging out the vacuum. Now, through repetition, they no longer care and the noisy, whirring machine can come right up to their feet and you almost have to nudge them with it to get them to move.

However, some rabbits dislike or fear some things so much that they never get used to them—or they are so stubborn that they never come to accept their occurrence. This is not uncommon. It really depends on your rabbit's personality and his trust in you. Usually, when bunnies learn that a thing they fear will not hurt them, they can get used to it. They may never like it, but it will no longer cause all-out panic.

You also need to be realistic in your expectations when socializing. If you put a harness on your bunny and he freaks out, screaming and flailing around, it may be too much to expect that he is going to someday become a leash rabbit if you just keep putting a harness on him often enough. Maybe it is possible, but is it really worth freaking out your rabbit over and over again until he becomes used to it? And what if he never does?

Rabbits are not terribly forgiving, and they have good memories. Always consider how your rabbit is dealing with your socialization efforts: Is he mildly annoyed, or is he having full-blown panic attacks over what you're doing? Most likely, it is somewhere in between, so use your common

Some rabbits can be socialized to enjoy walks on a leash.

sense to decide whether what you are trying to accomplish is something that is worth it to both you and your bunny.

To me, the most important thing in socialization is the relationship and trust building with the bunny. If you are losing your rabbit's trust and he is starting to avoid you because you are trying to force him into doing things that he does not want to do, it's not worth completely destroying your relationship with him over it.

This is why daily interactions involving petting and just being near your rabbit are the basis for moving on to the socialization stage, not the other way around. If you just come barreling into your rabbit's area every day, demanding that he perform for you without ever getting his trust and friendship, then he is not going to respond well. This kind of approach may work with a dog, but not with rabbits.

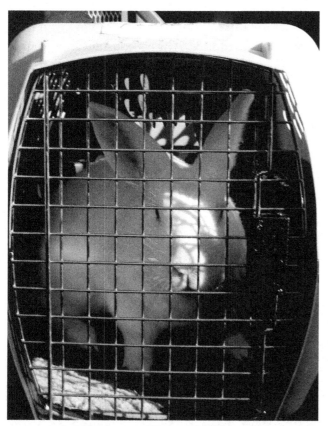

Socializing your rabbit to tolerate a car ride in a pet carrier is very important.

I have one rabbit who likes to walk on a leash in a harness and another who absolutely goes crazy when she feels "caught" by the leash—to the point where she screams and cries. I know that I could probably work with her and perhaps eventually get her to accept it without screaming and flailing around, but do I really need a rabbit who hops on a leash?

If we were talking about riding in a car in a pet carrier, then my response to that question

would probably be yes—I need my bunny to be able to visit the vet and handle a car ride occasionally. Mind you, no rabbit I have ever had liked car rides at first. I could tell that they were quite scared and unhappy about it each time, but over time they learned it was not the end of the world and so, gradually, it became less traumatic. But I do not really need to have a leash-trained rabbit.

My one-eyed bunny girl, Star, actually likes going places with me and hops into her little carrier as soon as she sees it. That is extremely rare, and Star is one in a million. I am reluctant to even tell you this, because I don't want people out there to start looking for a bunny like her who loves to ride around and go everywhere. Rabbits like her are exceptionally uncommon; in fact, I've never met another bunny like Star.

And so, this is where acceptance by you becomes the key. We need to play the hand that we are dealt and we never know what the next ten years with our bunnies is going to be like when we adopt them. Sometimes it is more about learning how we are going to fit into our bunny's life and personality, rather than trying to mold the rabbit into our "vision" of what a pet bunny should be like. Just like human children, you never know what you're going to get with a house rabbit, and you simply love, enjoy, and accept them for

Secure the pet carrier in the back seat of the car.

precisely who they are. It can be the quirks that make your bunny even more lovable, just like with people.

It can take years of constant, loving, gentle interaction before some rabbits come around. Often, we never know the "backstory" that a rabbit carries with him. His life before you saved him could have been just horrific; he may have been abused and lived in such terror of humans or feared for his life so often that it can take a very long time to help him get over that.

Never give up trying to work on your relationship with your pet bunny. We adopt our pets for their companionship and love, and our ultimate goal should always be to enjoy as much time and to spend as many quality moments with them as possible. If this is not your goal, then having a pet of any type—particularly one requiring as much attention and time as a rabbit—may not be right for you at this time.

I personally find it easier to calm an aggressive rabbit and get him to look forward to quality petting time than it is to make a timid, fearful rabbit learn to like me. Aggressive rabbits who will charge at and box with you when you come near them have a lot of self-confidence, which is very hard to cultivate in bunnies if they lack that quality.

Still, shy, fearful, or aloof bunnies are good candidates for socializing as much as more self-confident ones are. Teaching your shy bunny that you coming into the room or getting down on the floor is not a reason to run and hide is an important part of building a bond with your pet. You cannot give up or just forget about him if he does not want to have anything to do with you at first. Part of adopting a rabbit is the commitment to never give up on him.

All my rabbits over time, no matter how feisty or aloof, have come to look forward to

a little head rub or scratch between the ears. Some bunnies will let you do this from day one and others will force you to "earn" the privilege. Whether you are considered "worthy enough" can vary from day to day and even hour to hour, and this is where socialization comes in: The more your bun gets used to you approaching and petting him, the more he will actually come to expect it.

Ricky and Lucy rode on the train in their stroller to a street fair.

Here are some other things that you can socialize some—and truly just some—rabbits to enjoy:

- playing bunny games with you
- stroller rides to the corner store or around the block

- hopping on a leash with a harness
- grooming and nail trims
- car rides in a carrier with the family
- sitting on the couch with you
- accepting and giving kisses
- being picked up or held
- coming when called for a treat
- going into his condo or X-pen upon your request
- going outdoors with you to a park for a picnic
- digging in the sand at the beach (my rabbits love this)
- taking stroller rides on the train (another favorite of my bunnies)

If you are in tune with your bunny, he may tell you about the things he likes to do. Go with the flow and explore those things with your rabbit. You may find that he likes to crawl under the blanket with you when you lie on the floor to watch TV, or he may decide that he likes to jump up on you and then quickly hop away when you

Star relishes going places in her pet carrier.

get down on the floor to hang out with him—this could be his way of playing a game with you. It's easy to make games out of lots of things like this that your bunny initiates.

I have had a bunny who liked to jump up on the couch and toss all my stuff off onto the floor. When I scolded her for that, she would hop away quickly, doing lots of binkies. I finally realized that she was just trying to play with me. I had another bunny who enjoyed ripping up my newspaper as I was trying to read it. Rather than become upset, I started taking a section that I was finished reading and tossing it on the floor. It only took a couple times before she knew that it was "playtime" and would proceed to shred the paper. Of course, it created a bit of a mess, but cleaning it up was a small price to pay for my rabbit having fun playing with me. In her mind, it was "recess time" when she heard me opening up the morning paper.

My rabbits get out a lot to do educational events, which has led to them also going with me to many other places. They go with me so many places that my dentist and accountant will ask where they are if I show up for an appointment without one of them. They also regularly go to the park or beach to spend a few hours in their X-pens. We actually have a group of rabbit lovers who meet monthly to give our buns some time out in the fresh air.

Keep in mind that bunnies cannot tolerate heat. For this reason, most of the time I wait until the late afternoon or early evening to take my rabbits on most outings. When in their X-pens outside, I always shade them from direct sun with a sheet clipped to the pen. Pink-eyed rabbits do not like bright, direct sunlight and will tend to avoid it.

Just as with all good relationships, living with a house rabbit is a two-way street. As you socialize and teach your rabbit to live with you,

you and your family must also learn how to make your household an accommodating and happy place for your bunny. It is not realistic to expect that all the learning be done by your rabbit; you, too, will need to learn and make compromises in order for a good relationship to develop.

A big part of bringing a rabbit into your home is building your rabbit's trust of all the family members and bolstering your bunny's self-esteem. Some rabbits already have a lot of confidence and, as soon as they feel that their new home is a good, safe place for them to be, they hop right into their role within the family. Other rabbits are more shy and need much more time and work to develop that trust. It could be because they have had bad experiences prior to coming to you, or it could simply be due to their personalities. Sometimes we never know the true reason.

Paramount in helping your rabbit settle into his new environment is constant reassurance from you that he is now in a safe and friendly place. Think how it must feel to suddenly find yourself in a strange place with new, scary sounds and smells that you do not understand. Then imagine strange creatures who are much bigger than you moving all around you. You would probably be wondering the same things that your rabbit is wondering like, "Am I safe here?" or "Are these big, noisy creatures going to hurt me or even eat me?"

This is why a concerted effort must be made to help your bunny become secure and happy in his new home. Give him a "hidey" box in his area so he can go inside and feel cozy and safe there. You should not barge into your bunny's hiding box with your hands right away. That is his safe place and it is scary for a big hand to be thrust into his face. Rabbits do not see very well up close, so it is best to try to coax your bunny out to see you.

Quiet talking and encouragement, along with you being down on the floor and not looming over him, will help a lot to soothe your nervous bun. It is probably better to visit him down on the floor just outside his hiding spot several times a day, but resist the temptation to keep invading his safe space by constantly putting your hands on him at first.

China has been socialized to be a therapy bunny. She visits hospitals and retirement homes as part of her job.

If your bunny approaches you or shows interest by having his ears facing toward you, then approach his head from above with one hand and place it on top before stroking and petting him there. Do not try to pat or rub his rump, as this is insulting to most rabbits. Your rabbit may be too scared to nip you for it, but a more aggressive bunny is likely give you a bite for touching him there before you are very good friends. It is very rare for a rabbit to allow you to pet or touch any of his undersides when he is standing on all fours, since that is his most vulnerable area and, instinctively, rabbits do not like a lot of human touch there.

You should be studying your rabbit's body language when you are near him, especially when he is new in your home. Is he happy to see you or quite afraid? (See **Chapter 15: Bunny Communication** for a complete description of rabbit body language, signals, and sounds.) Does he get angry if you get too close, or does he easily allow you to pet him? It is critical to see how your interactions are affecting your rabbit's mood by closely watching his signals.

The reason you want to do this is so that you can adapt and adjust your demeanor to suit the way your bunny is feeling about you being there with him. If your rabbit panics or gets angry when you come into his space, then you know you will need to tone things down and proceed more slowly so that you can gradually build his trust.

If a rabbit has had months—or even years—of bad relationships with humans, it may take just as long to undo all that psychological damage. You have to show your bunny that you are a "good human" and not one of those "bad people" who forced him to do all kinds of things

Lucy is an educational bunny and goes to many events to teach the public about house rabbits.

he did not like, abused him, or ignored him. This can be an agonizingly slow process for some bunnies, but your patience and persistence will pay off.

If you are lucky and your bunny does not come with a lot of past baggage, then you may find that you and your rabbit take only a few weeks to hammer out a friendly, amicable relationship. The more "in tune" you are with your bunny's body language and signals, the more you will be able to interact in a way that makes your bunny feel comfortable and safe.

Being prey animals, rabbits by nature are shy and timid until you get to know them. There are always exceptions to this: Some rabbits are very outgoing and gregarious and accept almost anyone as a friend, but they are not the majority. More often than not, your bunny will require you to earn his respect and affection.

Ignoring your bunny's requests to be left alone every time he tells you will cause you to be seen as a threatening pest who cannot be communicated with. I have found that, when you get a positive response from your rabbit regarding something you do, take that opportunity to build on that positive interaction. Then other positive interactions can grow from it.

If, when you bring your bunny fresh hay, he is suddenly friendly and approaches you when he is normally standoffish, then that is the time you should take advantage of his friendliness and give your bunny some touches. If, when you lie on the floor, your rabbit likes to come closer to you, then you should be getting down onto the floor more often to start your interactions with your bun.

When I pick up a bunny and hold him on my lap, I am not restraining him to make him stay there against his will. Most rabbits are never going to want to sit in your lap for hours, but many will tolerate being there for five minutes or so. If your rabbit is panicking or squirming a lot, then let him jump down and hop away. If you try to force him to stay, he will resent it and start trying to avoid you.

Some bunnies never stay long and you are lucky if they sit calmly for a full minute. Others may stay four or five minutes before telling you that they are ready to go. Watch for your bunny's signals and act accordingly. If he thinks he can come and go as he pleases, then you may find him actually jumping up to be on your lap, especially if you happen to have a yummy bunny treat for him.

I used holding a rabbit on your lap as an example because most rabbits never really come to enjoy spending long periods on their owners' laps. It is pretty universal amongst rabbits that they will not enjoy it very much. So you, being the intelligent, loving owner, need to strike a balance between socializing your rabbit to not freak out if he needs to be in your lap (think combing and nail trims) and being a "lap rabbit." Almost all rabbits will fall somewhere in between these two extremes.

If you have any children in your family, you must be extremely vigilant to never allow your bunny to be tormented or played with roughly. Many little girls insist on playing with a rabbit as if he were a Barbie doll or tea-time partner. If your rabbit is not interested in these kinds of interactions with your daughter, then all efforts to build trust can be erased. This is one reason why rabbits are often not good pets for families with children under the age of ten. It is very important that every member of your family understand what fragile creatures rabbits are and what building trust is all about.

It is up to you as the parent to ensure that your bunny's trust is not betrayed. I believe that if you do have younger children in your family, all interactions between the children and the

rabbit must be closely supervised. You do not want your six-year-old undoing a year's worth of work building trust with your pet because he inadvertently scared or manhandled your bunny while you were not looking. I feel that, for most families with young children, a dog is a usually a much better choice than a small, delicate bunny.

Something else that you should always bear in mind is that aggressive rabbits are simply afraid, and they should never be disciplined. That will only make them mistrust people more. You must show your rabbit that you are not going to hurt him, no matter what. This is a difficult thing to do with a fierce bunny, but any aggression returned by you just reinforces to the rabbit that you are to be feared; therefore, he should stay away.

If you or anyone in your family does not have the self-control or patience to never hit or intentionally hurt a rabbit, then you absolutely must consider another kind of pet. Rabbits need patient handling and understanding parents. Never punish a rabbit, even if it is something as benign to you as a swat with a rolled-up newspaper. Rabbits do not respond well to this kind of training, and you will be undoing any respect or trust that you may have spent time developing. Rabbits can be a challenge to understand and to socialize to your household. Even experienced bunny lovers find bringing a new rabbit into the family a lot of work.

Some rabbits like hopping on a leash.

Summary

- It is very important to learn to safely handle your rabbit.

- Since bunnies are fragile creatures, you will want to always handle yours with care.

- Never, ever pick up your bunny by his ears or the scruff of his neck.

- The main reason rabbits do not like to be picked up is because, in the wild, when a rabbit leaves the ground, he is about to die.

- Rabbits will learn to tolerate handling the more you do it.

- When approaching a bunny who is skittish, it helps to get down low on his level.

- If a rabbit is being aggressive, gain control over the bunny first by placing your hand gently but firmly on top of his head.

- Be very careful if a struggle ensues to not use so much pressure that an injury can occur.

- Use your free hand to control the bunny's legs if he kicks or his head if he tries to nip you.

- I like to gently pin his hind legs and rump between my elbow and my abdomen.

- If a bunny feels in peril of being dropped, he usually will react by kicking and flailing around.

- You will need to handle your rabbit for his weekly grooming sessions.

- Many bunny owners never learn how to pick up and carry their rabbits.

- It is very important to practice picking up and holding your rabbit.

- Sometimes it is easier to train your rabbit to do things on his own so that you do not need to pick him up.

- If your rabbit is kicking and flailing around and you start to lose control of him, it is best to quickly kneel down and get your bunny as close to the floor as possible.

- Putting your buns into their pet carriers on a regular basis eventually gets them used to it.

- Firm-but-gentle handling goes a long way to calming your bunny when carrying him.

- Carrying your rabbit loosely is an invitation for him to kick his legs and end up being dropped.

- Many rabbits get injured each year from improper handling or being dropped.

- There are some very tough cases where you may need to use the "towel method."

- Special care should be taken when allowing children or strange pets to approach your rabbit.

- It is better to hold your rabbit safely than to allow him to be approached by a toddler on the ground.

- Do not let others hold your rabbit unless you know for sure that they have enough experience to do it correctly.

- Socializing is about getting your rabbit used to interactions and events that he is not used to.

- What at first was a terrifying experience can become a normal activity over time by using gentle repetition, in most cases.

- You need to be realistic in your expectations when socializing your rabbit.

- The most important thing in socialization is the relationship and trust building.

- Always consider how your rabbit is dealing with your socialization efforts.

- Sometimes it is more about learning how we are going to fit into our bunny's life and personality.

- Never give up trying to work on your relationship with your companion bunny.

- Whether you are considered "worthy enough" by your rabbit can vary from day to day.

- If you are "in tune" with your bunny, he may tell you about the things he likes to do.

- Keep in mind that bunnies cannot tolerate heat when taking them out of the house.

- A big part of bringing a rabbit into your home is building your rabbit's trust of all the family members.

- A concerted effort must be made to help your bunny become secure and happy in his new home.

- If a rabbit has had months or years of bad relationships with humans, it may take just as long to undo all that.

- Ignoring your bunny's requests to be left alone when he tells you will cause you to be seen as a threatening pest.

- You must be extremely vigilant to never allow your bunny to be tormented or played with roughly by your children.

- Rabbits should NEVER be disciplined; that will only make them mistrust people more.

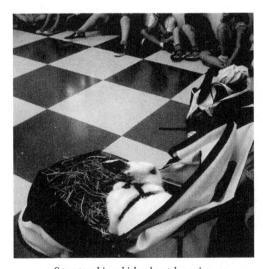

Star teaching kids about bunnies.

Star posing for her Christmas card picture.

Rabbits can be socialized to have fun with the family at the park or beach.

Chapter 12:
Making Your Home Safe for Your Bunny, aka Bunny-Proofing

What Is Bunny-Proofing?

"Bunny-proofing" is the act of making your home safe for your rabbit by removing or protecting every single thing within your rabbit's reach so that he cannot chew on or dig at it. Rabbits are very inquisitive and are experts at persisting long enough to figure out how to get into places you never thought possible. Thoroughly bunny-proofing includes removing/protecting anything you want to keep that's made of paper or cardboard, since these are favorite things for rabbits to chew. My rabbits happen to have an affinity for television remotes, and the buttons on them will quickly disappear once in the jaws of a bunny.

Why Bunny-Proof?

As I have said before, rabbits explore the world with their mouths, and so something that is actually unappetizing to your bunny may end up with teeth marks on it during your rabbit's examination of it. He may not actually be trying to eat it, but instead just exercising his jaws or simply trying to figure out what the thing is.

Rabbits are prolific chewers by nature and necessity: Their teeth grow several inches a year, and so your bunny has a need to chew all the time to help keep his teeth worn down and in healthy condition. It also means that your bunny is going to chew no matter what, so you need to protect or remove everything in his path that you do not want in his mouth.

Chewing habits also change with the seasons. I find that my rabbits chew a lot more while they are shedding or molting. They will chew and swallow extra fiber from paper, cardboard, and wooden objects. It helps to move the excess fur through their guts. This is why I always make sure my rabbits have lots of cardboard and wooden toys around. I also give them paper to shred like newspaper or old phone book pages. Most of the time, when my bunnies want to chew on something, they will use these items since they are readily available. Better those things than the furniture or baseboards.

A bigger concern is that your bunny can actually hurt himself if he chews on something that is not good for him. Toxic substances and items such as houseplants should not be left within reach of your bun. Remember that rabbits can jump and climb well, so even if these things are up on a chair or table, they are still within your bunny's reach. Sometimes the smell of something sweet or new can entice your rabbit to suddenly hop up to a place where he would not normally venture to go exploring.

Some buns learn how to open cabinets, so you must not allow your bun to run in an area with poisonous household cleaners and supplies in low cabinets. Some day, your bun could discover how to open one or you may accidentally leave it slightly ajar and then you could have a serious pet emergency on your hands.

Houseplants are another big danger for rabbits. Many of the most-common houseplants are extremely toxic, so it's best to not keep them anywhere near where your rabbit plays. Leaves can fall off onto the floor and your bun will eat them. Rabbits have an amazing ability to climb and hop up onto counters and tables, too. I have seen them use objects and chairs as stepping stones to get up where you would never think they would get, and then plants that were seemingly out of reach are suddenly gotten hold of. To your rabbit, any houseplant is just a big green treat. Over the years, domesticated rabbits have lost the ability to know good plants from bad ones, like wild bunnies do.

You can go on the Internet and see all the fantastic homemade bunny videos of rabbits scaling heights and getting into all kinds of trouble with their cat-like climbing abilities. You would never leave a three-year-old child alone in a room unsupervised for any amount of time, and the same goes for your bunny.

Cord with a homemade cord protector. You can buy ready-made versions at office supply and hardward stores.

Lagomorphs can, and will, find all kinds of things to get into, so it's imperative to plan and bunny-proof the area(s) where you're going to let your bunny stay and play in order to prevent mishaps—and disasters. It only takes seconds (literally) for a bunny to leave tooth-induced gouges in a piano leg, rip a hole the size of a baseball in an antique Persian rug, or chomp every computer or lamp cord in the room in two. Electrical cords are particularly dangerous, because not only can your rabbit get electrocuted by chewing on them, I have actually seen cords chewed by a rabbit spark and start a fire.

Cords are the biggest thing you will need to protect in your home, because anyone who has ever had a rabbit will quickly tell you that rabbits seem to have a pathological need to munch on every cord they can find. I have had some people say it is because cords remind them of roots inside their burrows that need to be chewed to remove them. I know when my buns go outside on their leashes they chew on every single twig and leaf that crosses their paths, so maybe there is some truth to that.

Regardless of why they do it, rabbits have destroyed more telephone, computer, and electrical cords in my house than you would believe. Just when you think you have made a barrier or protected every cord that your bunny can reach, he'll find another one that you missed. He will find the only weakness in every barrier or the only unprotected spot on the cord, guaranteed.

My second rabbit, Mr. Bunners, never chewed cords during the several years he hopped around my house, but every two years he made the rounds and chewed every single cord in the house in one day. Then for two years he would not do it again until one day he would suddenly wake up and do it all over again. It only happened two times, and back then I thought it was due to my "superior rabbit-training abilities."

It was not until I got my next rabbit, Pammy, that I knew this was a delusion. Just like some rabbits chew more than others, some go after cords more often, but the truth is that they all will chomp a cord at any time. You cannot train your rabbit to not chew your cords.

The only way to protect your cords is to either remove them or put cord protectors over them. There are all kinds of them made, and you can find them at your local hardware store, pet shop, or computer store. Most cord protectors can still eventually be chewed through if your bunny works at it long enough, which is another reason why your rabbit should still be supervised when he is running free in an area with cords, even protected ones.

I recommend that you never have cords of any kind—even protected ones—in your rabbit's abode or play area. Out of boredom, your bunny can work on a cord long enough to remove the protector and get to the wires inside. It only takes the slightest chomp by your rabbit's ultra-sharp front teeth to shear a cord in two.

Star and her now-infamous "drive-by chompings" are testament to how a rabbit can chew two or three cords in just one second. She has escaped from my lap several times only to race to the computer room to gnaw on as many cords as she can before I can recapture her. It's her obsession.

This is where your supervision comes in. You will always want to be near your rabbit when he is out running around a bunny-proofed area of your house until you know what his behaviors are going to be. This can take several months, because as a rabbit becomes more comfortable and familiar with his new home or area, he will explore more and more.

Where and How To Bunny-Proof

Some of the simplest places to bunny-proof are bathrooms, kitchens, and hallways.

Usually, there are not many cords present in these rooms that will need to be protected and very little furniture to worry about. Most rabbits will chew on carpet at times, and while they do not usually ingest the actual carpet, they do like to pull on the fibers and can gnaw holes completely through down to the floor. Some rabbits do this more than others.

Sometimes, rabbits are too nervous or unsure of their surroundings when they first come into a new territory, but once they gain confidence, they will end up in places that they

Blueberry knew there was food up there somewhere, so she hopped out of her X-pen.

Then she launched herself over to where the food was. You cannot turn your back on a rabbit for even a minute.

never strayed into before. This can be on top of any piece of furniture and certainly underneath any as well. Rabbits can flatten down to a pancake when they want to go under something: My nine-pound New Zealand girl, Lucy, can squeeze under a two-inch gap to get underneath my chair, which is pretty amazing.

The safest way to protect anything from your rabbit is to simply remove it from his area. If your rabbit is attacking your carpet or baseboards, either cover them or give your bunny replacement items to chew on instead. Things like phone books, empty toilet paper tubes, cardboard boxes, and wooden chew blocks and sticks can often distract a rabbit from chewing things you do not want gnawed on, but this does not work for all bunnies.

Here is an example of why you may need to cover or protect your carpet. This carpet square has been heavily damaged by a bunny chewing.

If your bunny is tearing up your carpet, I suggest that you cover the areas that they can chew with some carpet-sample squares or remnants that you can regularly replace. If your rabbit is chewing the baseboards, you can either create a barrier to keep him away from them such as an X-pen, or move his abode area so that he cannot be near them. I have heard of some people

crafting baseboard protectors out of clear plastic strips that they screw into the wall. The strips are just high enough to protect the baseboards from being chewed and, because they are clear, they do not stand out as much. Wallpaper is another favorite target of some buns, so any loose corners or edges at bunny height should be glued back down before your rabbit is allowed in that area.

A good story about the trials and tribulations of bunny-proofing has to do with Lucy. She had a terrible habit of digging my carpeting in the corners of the living room, especially underneath a big curio that she liked to lie under a lot.

I tried putting carpet squares over the area to prevent her from destroying my wall-to-wall carpet. We were having to replace the carpet squares almost every week and, if she got really busy, Lucy would tear right through them and still cause damage to my good carpet.

It was not until I placed 12-inch tile squares over the area that I solved the problem. At first she would hop under there and then thump when she found there was no carpet to chew on. She refused to sit on top of the tile, which is great for keeping rabbits cool during the summer.

After a couple weeks, though, Lucy discovered that the cool tiles felt great on her tummy and she started sleeping on top of them. She no longer chews the carpet in that area and we no longer have to worry about protecting the carpet under there. This is a great example of the process that you may have to go through with your rabbit, making his area secure and suitable.

While thorough bunny-proofing takes time, it is well worth it (and necessary), and it can often be an ongoing process of trial and error, with your bunny finding all the "chinks in the armor" that you missed. But be persistent, be patient, and know that you're being a good bunny parent in the process.

Discouraging Chewing Even After Bunny-Proofing

Should your bunny start going after something you don't want him to, gently move him away from the area he is chewing. Never hit or punish your rabbit—it will destroy all trust that the bunny has in you and he will become afraid of interacting or coming near you. If he refuses to keep his teeth off something, it is usually better to simply remove it from his area than to have an ongoing battle of wills.

Another tactic I have found useful is a spray bottle full of water set to shoot a stream. A squirt or two will make even the most determined chewer stop what he is doing. My rabbits have actually become trained to the sound of me picking up the water bottle and will immediately abandon any illicit chewing activities now when I just shake the bottle. The sound alone alerts them that they are about to receive a squirt and most of the time, they will stop chewing.

This is not to say that, in 30 seconds, they do not return and start chewing again. Rabbits definitely have minds of their own and can be quite stubborn. (Again, think three-year-old.) This is why you cannot discipline your rabbit into not being destructive. You might make them stop temporarily, but they will go back to doing whatever they were doing as soon as you look the other way.

Here is my last and most important point: Never discipline your rabbit. If he chews something dear to you, it is not his fault. It is your fault for allowing him to be in the position to do it.

Do not get carried away with the squirt water bottle method, either. Even though it can be an effective method of training, it can also have negative results if you use it too often. It's much better to thoroughly bunny-proof and closely supervise.

Part of having a rabbit is understanding—and accepting—that rabbits are very destructive at times. If you have a bunny in your home long enough, things are going to get chewed. If you cannot deal with this and cannot control your temper when it happens (because it will), then a bunny is not the right pet for you.

Eating Other Pets' Food

I have had people express concern that their rabbits will occasionally eat their dog's or their cat's food from the other pet's bowls, and have asked me if this is really bad for their rabbit.

Rabbits share food with other rabbits as a sign of love and bonding, so sharing food with your dog or cat could represent that your rabbit considers the other animal a good friend. That being said, most cat and dog food has meat or meat by-products that are not digestible by a rabbit, and while a bite or two is unlikely to make your bunny sick, you should always keep your rabbit away from any other pet's food. The easy solution is to simply take up your other pet's food bowl before your bunny gets out to play.

The clear tubing is a cheap alternativeto the store-bought black tubing for protecting cords.

Summary

- "Bunny-proofing" is the act of making your home safe for your rabbit.

- Rabbits explore the world with their mouths.

- Rabbits are prolific chewers by nature and necessity.

- Chewing habits also change with the seasons.

- Toxic substances and items should not be left within reach of your bun.

- Do not allow your bun to run in an area with poisonous household cleaners and supplies in low cabinets.

- Most common houseplants are extremely toxic.

- Lagomorphs can, and will, find all kinds of things to get into.

- There are only three ways to prevent chewing: remove it, cover it, or create a barrier.

- Cords are the biggest thing you will need to protect in your home.

- The only way to protect your cords is to either remove them or put cord protectors over them.

- You should never have cords of any kind—even protected ones—in your rabbit's abode area.

- You will always want to be near your rabbit when he is out running around a bunny-proofed area of your house.

- The simplest places to bunny-proof are bathrooms, kitchens, and hallways.

- The safest way to protect anything from your rabbit is to simply remove it from his area.

- If your bunny is tearing up carpet, cover the areas with some carpet-sample squares or remnants.

- Bunny-proofing takes time, and it can often be an ongoing process of trial and error.

- If your rabbit refuses to keep his teeth off something, simply remove it from his area rather than have an ongoing battle of wills.

- Never discipline your rabbit; it will only make him mistrust you.

- If your bunny chews something dear to you, it is not his fault; it is your fault for failing to properly bunny-proof.

- Do not get carried away with the "squirt water bottle method."

- Part of having a rabbit is understanding—and accepting—that rabbits can be very destructive at times.

Chapter 13:
Hay in Your Bunny's Litter Box and Litter-Box Training

Once your rabbit is spayed or neutered, in 99 percent of cases, he or she will almost always litter-box train him- or herself.

Rabbits are grazers, like cows and horses, and like to eat their grass hays throughout the day. While they are eating, it stimulates their need to pee and poop, and so it is natural for a bunny to use the litter box and eat at the same time.

The first thing you need in order to litter-box train your rabbit is, of course, a litter box. A large, plastic cat litter box obtained from a pet store works just fine for most rabbits. Do not use a litter box that has previously been used for cats—you must buy a new litter box just for your bunny! Get the largest, deepest box that is practical for the area in which it will be placed. The only time you might have to use a special litter box is if your rabbit is old or handicapped and cannot hop up into a taller box. For these bunnies, they make boxes with one low side; these are typically easy to find in most pet stores as well as online.

You will also need fresh grass hay of the types I discussed in **Chapter 9**, and an absorbent bedding made from unscented paper pulp (such as Care-Fresh®) for the bottom of the litter box. Do not use pine or cedar shavings in the litter box, because the aromatic oils in them are toxic to your rabbit and can cause sudden liver failure. Aspen shavings do not have these oils and are safe to use. Likewise, never use cat litter in your rabbit's litter box because the dust from it can damage your rabbit's respiratory system. Cat litters are made from clay and the dust forms clumps in your bunny's lungs. An economical product that many people use in their rabbits' litter boxes that is safe to use is hardwood-stove

pellets, which can be found in many feed stores. Some people use a combination of both stove pellets and paper-pulp bedding and find that very economical.

Hay should be as fresh as possible; many bunnies will not eat hay that's not extremely fresh. The prepackaged hay usually found at pet stores is often many months old; try to find a local hay supplier or feed store, or contact your nearest House Rabbit Society chapter to locate the freshest hay source you can. If you live in an area where you have trouble getting fresh hay, you can also use the Internet as a resource. There are all kinds of websites that will ship big blocks of fresh hay anywhere in sizes from a couple pounds to fifty-pound bales.

I store my hay in clean plastic trash cans so it cannot get wet. Wet hay will mold quickly, and moldy hay is toxic for your rabbit.

A rabbit will eat where he poops and pees, and this is not unhealthy or unnatural for him in any way. Rabbits eat all their food twice and you will often see your bunny hunched over looking like he is cleaning his private area. If you look closely when he sits up it will appear that he is chewing on something. This is your rabbit eating his cecotropes, which is his food after it passes through his body the first time. While it sounds disgusting, it is actually a necessary function of your rabbit's digestive process, and part of how he obtains his vitamins and nutrients from his food.

First rinse the litter box with fresh water.

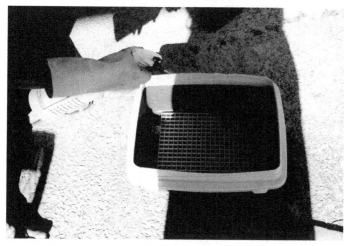

Then spray with a 50-50 vinegar and water solution.

If your rabbit is healthy and eating properly, you will very rarely, if ever, see his cecotropes in his litter box because he should always be eating them. Regularly seeing these sticky, smelly, dark poop clusters that look like small bunches of grapes almost always means that

your rabbit is getting too much nutrition. See **Chapter 9** for information on how to properly feed your bunny and how to adjust his diet if you are noticing cecotropes in his litter box. Also, if you find sticky poop or cecotropes stuck to your rabbit's rear end, that indicates he is eating too much nutrition and a diet adjustment is called for—this is frequently a sign that your bunny is overweight and on the path to a shortened lifespan. However—and this is important—if amending your bunny's diet does not resolve the issue within two days, contact your exotics veterinarian. While uncommon, there are medical conditions and parasites that can cause this problem.

The nice, hard, round bunny poops that do not smell much (if at all) have been through your bunny's system twice, and these are the only kind of poops you want to find in your rabbit's litter box.

Change the bedding in your rabbit's litter box every day if he is a larger bunny (over seven pounds). With a smaller bun, you can probably get away with changing his litter box every other day; it all depends on the size of the litter box in relation to the size of the bunny. The absorbent bedding at the bottom of the litter box needs to only be between a quarter-inch to a half-inch deep. You can adjust this according to whether you are changing it every day or every two days and the size of your rabbit.

Fresh hay should be given every day in the litter box, whether the bedding is changed or not. You should always inspect your bunny's hay and keep it dry and out of all moisture. Mold on your rabbit's hay creates toxins that can be deadly for your bunny. If you see some white or black coating on the hay, it should be thrown out and not fed to your bunny. When in doubt, smell it. If it smells moldy, then it is. Better to throw it away and be certain than to take the chance of your rabbit getting any bad hay. Rabbits are very sensitive to toxic materials, which is why they are so often used as lab animals. You do not ever want to accidentally poison your pet by giving him hay with any kind of mold on it.

Always store your rabbit's hay in a cool, dry container. I like to use clean trash cans with lids that I bought just for this purpose. Do not use one that has ever been used for trash. There are also specially made, plastic hay-storage bins available if you are buying your hay by the bale. The important thing is to keep the hay dry so that it does not mold. I'm always on the lookout for mold on my rabbits' hay because it is toxic.

Your rabbit will eat lots of hay if you get the kind he likes. My bunnies each eat around one pound of hay per week, so I have to keep a lot of fresh hay on hand in order to satisfy their appetites. A rabbit can simply never eat too much grass hay—the more that they eat the better.

Completely empty your rabbit's litter box of hay when you clean it. Rabbit urine is extremely caustic and contains a lot of calcium salts that form into a hard, white layer that will build up over time. In order to prevent this buildup and to remove calcium that is present, use white vinegar diluted 1:1 with water. We will sometimes save part of the absorbent bedding material to reuse if it does not have any urine on it, but we take it out of the box to clean it thoroughly before putting it back in. If conserving the material is not important to you, it is definitely easier to just dump the whole box in the trash or your compost bin. I find that, even with a strong vinegar solution used daily, the calcium can still build up, requiring using a large spoon or spatula to scrape the deposits from inside our bunnies' litter boxes. If you don't remove the deposits, the stuff will continue to build up and become more difficult to get off later.

Never use household cleaners in your rabbit's litter box or living area. They contain chemicals that can make your rabbit very sick and even cause liver failure and death. Diluted vinegar is the only cleaner you should ever use around your rabbit to be safe, and it has the added benefit of neutralizing the caustic properties of your bunny's urine.

Put a nice layer of safe absorbent material on the bottom.

Cover with the grate and then fill to overflowing with hay.

After cleaning your bunny's litter box, place a layer of bedding all across the bottom. You will need to use enough to last at least one full day. The larger your rabbit, the thicker the bedding layer should be. Then add several large handfuls of hay—enough to allow your bunny to graze on all day and some extra to dig in and throw out of the litter box, too.

I like to put a little grate in between the layer of bedding and the hay. Since you are always using an absorbent material that is safe for your rabbit to ingest, it is not to stop them from eating it. The reason we put a grate there is that it actually makes the box easier to clean and allows us to save the part of the bedding that does not have any urine in it.

If you do not have a grate, when your rabbit digs down in their hay, they disturb the bedding layer. Rabbits were born to dig and they adore spending lots of time digging way down into their hay to get the last good bite. It is fun to watch them eating in a litter box full of very fresh hay. They will feverishly dig for the very best pieces, sometimes with only their ears sticking out

The only safe cleaner for your rabbit's health is a weak vinegar and water solution. Most household cleaners are toxic for your bun and should never be used.

from underneath. My bunnies often come up with pieces of hay all over the tops of their heads. It often makes me laugh.

There are some litter boxes made just for rabbits that come with a stainless steel or plastic grate inside. You can make one yourself very easily by purchasing some plastic grating at a hardware store and cutting it to fit inside your litter box. The honeycomb plastic inserts for overhead florescent lighting fixtures also work very well and are very inexpensive.

Another good reason for having a grate is that it separates your rabbit's feet from the wet bedding. If you notice that your rabbit has yellow fur on his feet from standing in his well-used litter box, then you may want to consider putting a grate in there. If you have a grate and your rabbit's feet are still getting stained yellow, then you should consider changing the box more often or putting more absorbent material and hay into the box.

Yellow feet are a sign of contact with urine, and the caustic urine can cause severe damage to your rabbit's fur and skin if contact is prolonged and/or regular. At first the fur will literally melt and form big mats. Then the skin will become inflamed, similar to a child's diaper rash, and this can eventually lead to baldness and serious infection if left unchecked. Unlike dogs and cats, rabbits do not have protective paw pads on their feet—they just have their tender skin directly under the fur.

It is a good idea to check your rabbit's underside and feet regularly for evidence of this phenomenon called "urine scald." If you catch it early, it is easy to correct, but once it gets bad it can take up to three or four months for your bunny's skin and fur to heal.

Really severe cases can send your bunny to the vet's office, so a bit of prevention and observation can go a long way. The best way to prevent this is to give your rabbit a clean litter box full of fresh hay every day and to never let it get so dirty that his body ever comes in contact with his own pee.

Never use a wire-bottomed cage to solve your litter-box issues, because rabbits who live in wire-bottomed cages regularly pull their toenails out by getting them caught in the wires, which is extremely painful. Living in a wire-bottomed cage also wears the fur off the bottoms of their feet, which is a permanent thing and can lead to a lifetime of sore foot conditions. I have seen rabbits lose their whole legs from neglecting the kind of sores that develop from wire-bottomed cage environments.

If your rabbit ever makes a mistake and pees somewhere outside of his litter box, the lye-like qualities of his urine can quickly stain or discolor many things, especially your carpet. To neutralize this effect, use a 1:1 white vinegar/water solution on the area to remove the stain and the odor.

If your rabbit is peeing in a specific corner or area and not using his litter box, then either move his box there or place a second box there. When litter-box training a rabbit, I have seen folks set out two or thee litter boxes in areas that the bunny is using. Most of the time, the bunny will get the idea and use the box instead of the floor.

Of course, I need to stress yet again that litter-box training is only effective on spayed and neutered rabbits. If your bunny is not, then all bets are off. Training unaltered males is incredibly difficult: They have an instinct like un-neutered male cats to mark everything in their territory by spraying urine on it. Intact male rabbits also have unprecedented spraying capabilities: I have seen them spray over 15 feet while wiggling their backsides back and forth to get maximum

dispersal. All of these behaviors go away within four to six weeks after being neutered, so you will need to be patient during this period of time.

Sometimes, not using a litter box is just a bad habit. The longer your rabbit has gone without being litter-box trained, the longer it can take to train him to use the litter box. I recommend to novice bunny parents that the easiest way to deal with the litter-box issue is to adopt a rabbit from a rescue who is already spayed or neutered and litter-box trained. You are not only making it easy on yourself so that you do not need to do the training, but you are also saving a rabbit at a rescue who needs a forever home.

If it has been over two months and your rabbit has still not gotten the hang of using his box, then you may need to give him some remedial training. This is rare, and will not be necessary most of the time. If your bunny has been fixed and has a fresh clean litter box daily, he will almost always take to it on his own.

These are cecotropes and you should not see them.

More cecotropes. See Chapters 9 & 19 if you find them.

Summary

- Once your rabbit is spayed/neutered, he or she will almost always litter-box train him- or herself.
- Rabbits are grazers and like to eat their grass hays throughout the day.
- A large, plastic cat litter box obtained from a pet store works just fine for most rabbits.
- Use fresh grass hay on top (see Chapter 9) and an absorbent bedding on the bottom of the litter box.
- Do not use cat litter or pine or cedar shavings in the litter box because they can harm your rabbit.
- Hay should be as fresh as possible, because many rabbits will not eat dried, old hay.
- A rabbit will eat where he poops and pees, and this is normal.
- You should very rarely, if ever, see cecotropes in your rabbit's litter box or lying around if he is healthy and eating properly.
- The hard, round bunny poops that do not smell have been through your bunny's digestive system twice.
- Change the bedding in your rabbit's litter box every day, especially if he is a larger bun.
- Fresh hay should be given every day in the litter box, whether the bedding is changed or not.
- Always store your rabbit's hay in a cool, dry container.
- Moldy hay can be toxic for your rabbit.
- Completely empty your rabbit's litter box of hay when you clean it.
- Never use household cleaners in your rabbit's litter box or living area.
- Using a grate in between the layer of bedding and the hay is a useful trick.
- Yellow feet are a sign of contact with urine.
- Never use a wire-bottomed cage to solve your litter-box issues.
- The lye-like qualities of rabbit urine can quickly stain or discolor things, so use a 1:1 white vinegar/water solution on the area to remove the stain and the odor.
- If your rabbit is peeing in a specific corner or area, then either move his box there or put a second box in that location.
- Litter-box training is only effective on spayed and neutered rabbits.
- The longer your rabbit has gone without being litter-box trained, the longer it can take to train him to use the litter box.

Chapter 14:
Run Time, Playing with Your Rabbit, and Toys

Exercise and Run Time

Your bunny needs daily exercise, or "run time," as rabbit people call it. Rabbits are very active pets, and even the most sedentary buns require time in a space large enough for them to run, jump, and play for several hours each day.

If your bunny is spending many hours a day contained in an X-pen or rabbit abode while you are at work or gone for the day, you will need to arrange for him to spend some time outside of this enclosed environment. This needs to be done in an area large enough for your rabbit to burn off energy by running, hopping, jumping and, if he is contented, some big bunny binkies. "Binkies" are the silly dances bunnies do when they are happy. I promise you will know one when you see one. I tell people all the time that they have not lived until they have seen a bunny dance (binky).

Your bun should get at least three hours a day of run time, preferably in the early morning or late afternoon/early evening. Rabbits are crepuscular, meaning they tend to be most active just after dawn and a few hours around twilight. Most rabbits will sleep a lot during the middle of the day, typically from about late morning till late afternoon.

That said, most rabbits I know will accept their run time at any hour, if they are "locked up" for any length of time. See **Chapter 10** for tips on housing your rabbit, and "run space" needs to be more like a room-sized space in order to accommodate some fast running and jumping—and serious binky-ing.

With their high activity levels comes the desire for bunnies to do what bunnies do: Hopping, running, dancing, and playing are all a big part of what happy bunnies like to do each day. A cage-bound or penned bunny will quickly become grumpy and unsociable if he's kept inside too long without sufficient exercise time. Getting your bunny out for exercise is a critical part of keeping your pet bunny healthy and happy.

Even large rabbits like to play and do "binkies."

I have found that rabbits who are not getting out of their containment are also not getting human interaction, which they crave. Your rabbit's run time should also include some quality personal interaction with you. Your bunny will be anxious to show off for you, and may attempt to communicate to you that he wants to be petted or groomed by running up to you and placing his head on the floor in front of you.

You will also see him playing all kinds of fun games for your benefit. Bunnies love to make their people laugh, and if you chuckle at or praise one of your rabbit's antics, he will most likely do it again. Often, when first let out to play, your bunny will show his satisfaction with you having chosen to release him by circling quickly around your feet or right in front of you.

If you have kept him in too long, however, you are likely to get a thump or have your bun run off to a corner to "show you the rump" (a sign that you have really upset your bunny; see **Chapter 15: Bunny Communication**, to learn more about what your rabbit is saying to you).

Chelsea loves doing binkies during her "run time."

Of course, you are going to have no idea what your bunny is feeling or doing if you are not there to interact and see his antics. You may think

Binkies are a universal sign of happiness in your rabbit.

it is the same if you let your rabbit out to run in a hallway or bathroom without you present, but your rabbit yearns for socializing with you. The longer he is alone by himself, the lonelier he is when he does get to see you. It the rabbit world, it is a snub to enter another rabbit's presence and not acknowledge him.

People who want to bond and develop trust with their rabbits will need to include time every day for this important interaction. Even a friendly pat on the head when walking by is considered proper rabbit protocol that will go a long way towards developing a relationship with your lagomorph companion.

If at all possible, your rabbit's run space should be in a place where you hang out the most so that your bunny becomes part of the family. It is critical that you bunny-proof this space (see **Chapter 12: Making Your Home Safe for Your Bunny, aka Bunny-Proofing**) beforehand and supervise him when he's out to run and play, no matter what part of your home you select for his run space.

Indoor run time is always preferable to outdoors, and outdoor playtime should only be done under your very close supervision and using some kind of containment or restraint. After my years of working at the shelter, you would not believe how many people tell me that their bunnies were in the yard one minute and gone the next. The recovery rate for stray rabbits is basically zero. Another common thing I hear is that someone's rabbit played in the backyard for years and then he suddenly disappeared. That just goes to prove that, given enough time, a rabbit will either find a way to get out or a predator will find a way to get in.

As I mentioned in **Chapter 12**, many people choose easy-to-bunny-proof areas such as hallways, bathrooms, and kitchens for their bunnies' run spaces because there are not usually a lot of electrical outlets with things plugged into them and not much furniture that can be chewed. The only problem with doing this is, how much time do you plan on spending in your hallway or bathroom? A kitchen can work, but remember that your bunny will be underfoot and running circles around your feet, trying to get your attention while you are cooking. Would you want to risk tripping over your bunny while carrying a pot of boiling water?

Back bedrooms can only be a good choice if you spend many hours there each day. If you only go into your bedroom to change clothes and sleep, then when will your bunny get that quality time he craves—and needs—with you?

Thus, your bunny should have his playtime in the area where you and the family hang out. If your family spends most of its time in the living room, then your rabbit should be spending his time there, too.

Do not ever attempt to punish your bunny by hitting him. He will not understand and will quickly grow to mistrust you. As I've said before, rabbits have very good memories and are very slow to forgive if you scare them. You can simply tell your bunny "no" firmly and move him away from what he is doing, but most of the time he will return in minutes if not seconds. Remember, rabbits are just like three-year-old kids.

Interacting with Your Bunny During Playtime

Your rabbit will often ask you to interact or play with him. It can be something as small as hopping by for you to acknowledge or pet him, or it may be a more blatant demand, such as a nudge to your ankles or legs to get your attention. The proper response from you is pats on the head.

Failing to acknowledge, walking away, or turning your back on a rabbit when he has requested your attention is an insult in bunny language.

Dwarf rabbits are usually very active and need lots of playtime.

The best way to interact with your bunny during playtime is to get down low, at his level, and watch his body language. Find out what your bunny's saying in **Chapter 15**.

Doing any activity on the floor will usually result in several visits by your bun to "supervise" and see what you are doing. As for lounging on the couch or in a chair, it can take a while for rabbits to feel comfortable enough with their humans to jump up there with you. You can try calling your bunny and enticing him with a treat, but do not expect your bunny to hop up next to you right away.

Bunnies love to run and play in tubes.

105

If your rabbit is shy and not sure of you, try getting on the floor and acting disinterested in your bunny. Lying there and just watching TV or reading a book will often result in your bunny coming over to check you out and perhaps even asking for some attention and pets.

Explore petting slowly and carefully in the beginning with your bun (especially if he's on the shy side). He will tell you quickly what he does and does not like, and the more you play and interact with your rabbit each day, the more quickly you will bond and learn about each other. The hours your bunny gets to spend running and playing every day will soon become his favorite part of the day, and probably yours, too.

Toys

You can find dozens of toys for rabbits at pet stores and online, and you will also find that most of them are a waste of money. You can invest a small fortune in rabbit toys, only to discover that they are promptly ignored when left in your

rabbit's area. All of my rabbits' favorite toys have been simple, everyday items that I haven't needed to buy.

These homemade toys are simple and fun. You can see that they get chewed a lot, so they must be replaced every so often.

Toys that are fun for most rabbits are newspaper, pages out of old phone books (some people give their bunnies whole phone books to tear up), empty toilet-paper and paper-towel tubes, and chunks of wood from fruit trees with the bark still on. I have even heard of folks giving their junk mail to their rabbits to "properly" dispose of. Most commercial printing inks used now are vegetable based and non-toxic to your rabbit, but avoid shiny or slick paper, such as the newspaper inserts, since they have coatings on them.

Toys that make noise and can be tossed are also favorites of many bunnies. Solid-plastic teething rings for babies (not the gel-filled kind) are fun for your bunny to carry and throw around. A plastic shower-curtain ring with some of the outer rings from Mason jars looped together make lots of noise and are irresistible for rabbits.

Some bunnies like to nudge, push, and throw balls around to play, and I've even seen a few rabbits who like to play with baby rattles—but then I have also seen a couple who chomp

These are examples of some of the toys my rabbits like to play with. Notice that they are simple and inexpensive.

down on them and destroy them immediately. Always be careful when giving your rabbit toys that can be broken or cracked when they chew on them. Most of the time, a rabbit will not swallow the pieces that they chew off a toy, but they can. If you see him chomping chunks of plastic off a toy, take it from him right away. You do not want to have to send your bun into emergency surgery to remove a piece of a toy that was accidentally swallowed.

Ideal toys for your rabbit include unpainted wood or cardboard toys that do not have anything metal such as staples holding them together. Otherwise, be sure to opt for toys that use non-toxic vegetable dyes—they will specifically say this on the packaging.

With a dozen store-bought toys and chews lying around and hanging in their condos, my rabbits prefer simple stuff like a toilet-paper or paper-towel tube stuffed with fresh hay. They spend hours eating the hay and chewing the paper to get more. Each of my rabbits devours two of these "hay burritos" each day.

Anything made of willow is entertaining for your bunny. Natural willow balls, rings, baskets, and many other shapes are available in a multitude of sizes, and bunnies like to eat them as much as they enjoy tossing them around. You can purchase these anywhere from pet shops to websites to craft stores; just be certain that the willow is not painted or coated with varnish.

Sometimes rabbits make toys out of unusual things.

Toys made from dried fruitwood twigs, such as applewood, are also amusing for most rabbits. Be sure to select ones that are constructed from wood that hasn't been sprayed with pesticides. One important note: Never give your bunny bamboo; bamboo is not good for rabbits. The fibers in it can harm their insides.

One of my bunny's favorite toys is a toilet paper tube stuffed with hay. We call these "hay burritos."

Both willow and fruitwood toys are safe for your rabbit to consume, as is cardboard (surprisingly), because each contains lots of fiber, which is good for his digestive system. If your bunny's choppers are healthy, his grinding back teeth will literally pulverize everything he eats to a pulp.

Large cardboard tubes are great for rabbits to race through and even lounge inside. The same goes for cardboard boxes with holes cut into the sides. There are some multi-story cardboard boxes you can find online specifically for rabbits to play in, and this is one of the few toys worth buying rather than making yourself. Other kinds of tubes and mazes can also be purchased online, and I have found that most rabbits love exploring and playing in these things.

My rabbits like it when I rearrange their assorted boxes, ramps, and tube toys every morning. They spend an hour entertaining me by exploring and running through them, showing their glee with spontaneous bursts of speed and hops. Some rabbit lovers exploit their rabbits' curious natures by making or buying a big maze for them to play in and explore. They intrigue their rabbits by changing the configuration of the paths inside.

There are some commercially available cardboard "hidey boxes" like this three-story model that my bunnies love.

Similarly, there are many toys made for cats that rabbits love, such as cat play structures and cubes, especially the multi-level ones that can be hopped on and climbed all over. You can create your own from wooden and cardboard boxes with a few cut-out holes for entrances. Rabbits enjoy the security of being cozy inside and will take long snoozes in them; these types of structures are colloquially known as "hidey boxes" in the rabbit-loving community, because it's so common to find our lagomorphs lounging for hours at a time in them, completely hidden from view. My rabbits

all like to chew on their hidey boxes, causing them to constantly be changing shape. I call this "bunstruction." Naturally, you will need to replace your bunny's hidey boxes when they will no longer do the job they were "built" to do.

One thing to keep in mind when placing hidey boxes and tunnels in your rabbit's area: Boxes are like burrows or tunnels to your rabbit and being in them seems to trigger the natural instinct to dig, so you will want to put carpet remnants or sample squares underneath them to protect your floors. Between the chewing on and the digging in the hidey-box toys, your good carpeting, expensive rug, or nice flooring can take a real beating if you don't.

Another great, easy-to-make bunny toy is to put some of his hay inside a small paper bag and tie it with some natural fiber twine. (Do not use plastic twine, plastic zip ties, or paper/metal twist ties.) Sometimes, I will put a single treat inside the bag as well for them to find. My rabbits love tearing the bag apart to be rewarded with the hay inside. I only use the treat inside for special occasions, because I carefully control how many treats our rabbits get.

Uncoated willow baskets are great toys.

Never use foil-lined boxes or bags when you make this type of toy: Your rabbit cannot digest the foil lining and it could cause an obstruction or, worse, a toxic reaction, since many foil linings have lead in them. No type of metal is ever safe to give to your rabbit to chew on that he can ingest.

Boxes are favorite toys of most all rabbits.

Further, never give your bunny a balloon or anything rubber to play with. Plastic toys filled with any kind of gel or fluid are also off-limits.

When considering whether a toy is safe for your bunny, imagine it being chewed on and what that result would be. Are pieces going to come off? Is fluid or something else in the item going to leak out? Is some kind of stuffing going to be ingested by your rabbit? Are there very small pieces that, if broken/chewed off, could be swallowed? If so, then this is not a good toy for your bun. Remember, think three-year-old child,

except this three-year-old can chew through solid wood and plastic, and he cannot regurgitate anything that gets stuck in his throat. Then evaluate the toy again, and decide if it's safe to let your bunny play with it.

It is best to have a bunch of toys inside your bunny's abode when he is there by himself to give him something to do while he spends time alone. Bunnies get bored easily, especially when they are confined, and a bored rabbit is usually a grumpy (and more destructive) one.

When you spend time with your bunny during his playtime, pay attention to which toys are his favorites, and offer him different toys to play with to see what captures his attention. These are the toys you want to leave in his abode area when you are not there to keep him entertained.

Some cat toys make great bunny toys.

Summary

- Your bunny needs daily exercise or "run time."

- Your bun should get at least three hours a day of run time.

- Your rabbit's exercise time should include some quality personal interaction with you.

- You are going to have no idea what your bunny is feeling or doing if you are not there to interact with him and see his antics.

- To bond and develop trust with your rabbit, you will need to include time every day for interaction.

- Your rabbit's run space should be in a place where you hang out the most so that your bunny becomes part of the family.

- Indoor run time is always preferable to outdoors.

- Outdoor playtime should only be done under your very close supervision and using some kind of containment or restraint.

- Do not ever attempt to punish your bunny by hitting him.

- Your rabbit will often ask you to interact or play with him.

- Doing any activity on the floor will usually result in several visits by your bun to see what you are doing.

- Explore petting slowly and carefully in the beginning with your bun.

- Most toys for rabbits at pet stores and online are a waste of money.

- My rabbits' favorite toys have been simple, everyday items that I haven't needed to buy.

- Newspaper, old phone books, empty toilet-paper tubes, and chunks of wood from fruit trees are examples of great rabbit toys.

- Toys that make noise and can be tossed are also favorites.

- Some bunnies like to nudge, push, and throw balls around to play.

- Be careful when giving your rabbit toys that can be broken or cracked when he chews on them.

- Anything made of natural, unpainted willow is entertaining for your bunny and good for his digestive system.

- Never give your bunny bamboo; bamboo is not good for rabbits.

- Large cardboard tubes are great for rabbits to race through and even lounge inside.

- Cardboard boxes with holes cut into the sides are fun "hidey" toys.

- There are many toys made for cats that rabbits love, such as cat play structures and cubes.

- Boxes are like burrows or tunnels to your rabbit, and being in them seems to trigger the natural instinct to dig.

- Another great, easy-to-make bunny toy is to put some of his hay inside a small paper bag.

- Never use foil-lined boxes or bags.

- Never give your bunny a balloon or anything rubber to play with.

- Putting toys inside your bunny's abode gives him something to do while he spends time alone.

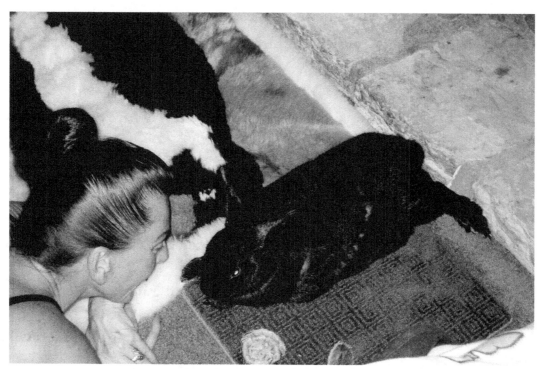

You must be able to understand your rabbit's signals in order to communicate with him.

It helps when interacting with your rabbit if you get down on his level.

Chapter 15:
Bunny Communication

In order to socialize better with your bunny and to have more meaningful interactions with him, it is very helpful if you understand "bunny talk." Rabbits speak a language all their own that is made up of signals, body language, and even sounds that originally were meant to send messages to other rabbits in their social group. Unfortunately, most people who have pet rabbits have no idea what their bunnies mean when they are "speaking" to them.

If you want to communicate with your rabbit, you must think like one and not try to comprehend his messages in terms of how other kinds of pets like cats and dogs relate to us. Rabbits operate on a totally different type of social hierarchy than these other kinds of animals. Dogs are dogs and rabbits are rabbits, so spending some time learning rabbit language will certainly build a better relationship between you and your bunny.

Rabbits are, in fact, intelligent creatures (despite the "dumb bunny" misnomer) and will learn your habits and behaviors fairly quickly. They can easily learn simple commands, especially for any kind of food or treat. **Chapter 18**, which is about training your rabbit, will discuss this in detail, but understanding your bunny and the signals he's sending you first will make training him a lot easier.

Imagine if, every time you tried to tell people something, they either ignored you or gave you a totally inappropriate answer that showed you know that they did not understand what you had just said. It would quickly get very frustrating and you might even shy away from trying to communicate with them any further.

Most rabbit communication is based on simple signals and protocols about dominance and territory; this is especially true if you are just meeting a bunny for the first time. The more you understand what your bunny is saying to you, the better you will be able to react properly and follow the proper etiquette (from your bunny's point of view), thereby opening the door to better communication. It also builds up your rabbit's self-esteem and confidence, because he knows there is "order" in his house. Do not underestimate the importance of this in your rabbit's eyes.

In rabbit society, the "top" rabbit wants respect at all times and others must show proper submissiveness by grooming him (or her) whenever it is asked of them. In the bunny world, asking for respect is actually more of a demand and not really just a polite request. Ignoring an appeal for grooming equates an insult, and can result in annoyance and frustration. An aggressive or very dominant rabbit will usually respond with biting or nipping to show his displeasure for the breach of protocol by the rabbit who is of lower rank. This is why some rabbits will give you that little nip when you stop petting them for a short period. In lagomorph language, it is how they say, "Don't stop petting (grooming) me!" The ironic thing is that most people will interpret this as their rabbits telling them to stop when it really means the exact opposite.

Bunny grooming is mainly focused on the top of the head and, for many rabbits, petting anywhere else is not acceptable. When rabbits are angry at each other, they will nip each other on the rump, so petting there for most rabbits will result in them hopping away or nipping you to tell you that they do not like being touched there. Unlike dogs, who often love having their hind ends rubbed, rabbits usually interpret this as an insult or bad behavior on your part and do not appreciate the sentiment, no matter how well-meaning it may be.

Of course, I am generalizing with all of these descriptions, because there will always be exceptions, but most rabbits all speak the same language and will relate to these signals similarly by instinct. Since many of these signals have multiple meanings, you will want to put them into context when trying to assign a meaning to them. Once you take the whole body posture, attitude, and other cues into consideration, you will usually be able to discern a fairly accurate meaning of what your rabbit is trying to say to you.

In the bunny world, a normal rabbit interaction would go is like this:

One rabbit is sitting in his territory and another one hops up and stops a small distance away in front of the sitting bunny. The first bunny will perk up his ears and face the second bunny head on with his nose twitching and ears focused on the second bunny, if he is interested in interacting.

When a rabbit puts his head down, it is a demand for grooming.
The rabbit who is being groomed is expressing dominance.

If the first bunny is not sure about this new rabbit entering his territory, he may turn sideways or, if he is really upset about the encroachment, turn his back and show his rear end to the second bunny. The sideways signal is saying, "I am uneasy about you, and may not want you here." The showing of the rear end is a complete snub meaning, "I do not want anything to do with you."

Or, the first rabbit may take a step or two forward and put his head down on the ground. This is not a sign of submission, but rather a demand for submission from the second bunny. The rabbit with his head down wants to be groomed on top of his head. If the second bunny submits to this demand and grooms the first bunny, the whole interaction has been successfully settled between the two rabbits.

Depending on whether the visiting rabbit is a dominant or submissive bunny will determine what signals he sends back in return and vice-versa. It is a simply choreographed exchange that plays out over and over in the rabbit world of communication.

Learning how to react and communicate by understanding and interpreting your bunny's signals is not terribly complicated, but many of the signals have different meanings in different contexts. If your rabbit is giving you a signal by thumping because you disturbed his abode, it may not mean the same thing if he is thumping because he hears the neighbor's cat outside and is warning everyone of danger.

Most of your rabbit's signals are silent, but he may make some sounds and noises, too. Grunting and growling are usually extreme warnings saying, "I am about to attack if you do not back off!" You might even see him box or jump up with his front paws when making these sounds—this is an angry bunny who is doing his best to tell you to stay away and leave him alone.

I have heard some bunnies make softer growling noises while eating, and these are obviously happy sounds of enjoying their food. I have heard other buns who will grunt when they are excited or nervous, especially when they're being picked up. Each of these sounds has different meanings in the context in which they are made.

One of my current rabbits, Star, likes to make a sharp sigh when she is disappointed about something, but then she has a softer one that she makes when she is contented. She has even recently started making a low grumbling noise when she cuddles with me, signifying extreme satisfaction. I have heard of other rabbits who vocalize their emotions as well. Getting close and learning about your bunny will get you in tune to his favorite ways of telling you things.

Once you learn the basics of your rabbit's language, all of the things your rabbit is doing will suddenly make a lot more sense. There are many different kinds of personalities in rabbits and so they all interact differently, but their language is pretty universal once you speak it.

Rabbits become more trusting and socialize with their families better when they can be understood. It also becomes much easier to diagnose problems and issues when you have a better understanding of what messages your bun is sending you. When he suddenly starts chewing on your favorite book or leaving big piles of poop in a new location, it may be because you have been ignoring some message being clearly given to you in your bunny's mind.

By learning your rabbit's signals and reacting properly to his messages, you will find that he is more interested in socializing with you instead of shying away. Some of the more obvious signals such as body posture are easy to recognize; so are ear positions. Putting them into the proper context and responding back with an appropriate signal creates a gratifying "conversation," during which more trusting interactions can develop, such as playing.

More subtle signals, like nose wiggling and body shudders, can also give you a big insight into exactly what your bunny is thinking at the moment.

Basic Signals

Forward-Facing Body Postures

There are several forward-facing postures, and each has slightly different meanings. These are some of your rabbit's most important gestures, and you will want to learn to distinguish between them, since their meanings vary widely.

When your rabbit faces you head on and is leaning forward slightly with his ears facing forward as far as they will go towards you, it means curiousness. This will often be accompanied by frenzied nose wiggling, and it will appear as if he is trying to focus in closely on you

Saul's posture says he is not sure he wants contact.

115

with his ears. It is a relaxed and interested posture. Sometimes you will notice that your bunny's ears are independently trying to tune in to what is going on in two different directions at one time: This is another sign of being curious about something. The key here is the leaning forward, which expresses being aware and open to his surroundings, and is a sign of a secure rabbit who is not feeling afraid.

If the ears are facing more sideways than forward, it can mean that your bunny is aware of you there, but has not decided if he wants to approach you or let you approach him. This signal is subtle and may mean that your rabbit is less than sure about being approached.

Ears laying down and facing backwards while the body is positioned facing toward or slightly sideways to you is a sign of mild unhappiness, whereas having the ears down while showing you his backside is a sign that you are truly in the doghouse and have one very upset rabbit.

Blueberry is showing interest or curiosity.

Notice that, with all of these forward-facing postures, ear position and body angle are important.

Sideways-Facing Body Postures

Being turned slightly away from you has a few meanings. First, it is a sign of uncertainty: By being slightly turned, your rabbit is in a position to flee if he sees something that he does not like.

By turning sideways, Groucho can easily escape if he wants to.

It can also mean that he does not want to be approached right now and will scamper away if you get too pushy or try to pet or pick him up. When you approach your rabbit and he turns sideways to you, it is best to do the same. Do not continue rushing in headlong to be closer. By mirroring your bunny and turning sideways, you are saying that you understand his desire to be standoffish at the moment. When you remain facing forward and move closer to a bunny who has told you to "back off," he will usually run away unless he is a very aggressive bunny, at which point he might actually charge you to make you stay back.

"Showing the Rump"

One of the ultimate insults in the bunny world is being "shown the rump," topped only by the ears totally back in conjunction with showing of the said rump. When a rabbit shows you his posterior, he is saying, "I am ignoring you, and you are not there." He is clearly stating, "Leave me alone or else. I will not deal with you until I am done being mad at you!"

Head Extended and Down Flat

This is a demand for grooming or petting. The ears are usually laid back a bit. The more flat to the back the ears are when putting his head down, the more aggressive the demand for the grooming. In bunny language, it is an insult to not pet or "groom" a rabbit who has demanded it in this way. Expect some annoyance if you ignore this command, and perhaps even a nip if you persist in remaining oblivious.

This is a semi-aggressive stance, with ears back and ready to lunge.

Boxing, Lunging, Grunting, and Other Aggressive Behavior

Rabbits have many ways of showing aggression, and some feisty bunnies do not hesitate to display it, either. There are so many reasons why a bunny can become what people think of as "mean." Understanding why your rabbit is giving you these ultra-aggressive signals will go a long way towards ending the behavior.

"Boxing" is when a bunny lifts his front paws off the ground and tries to scratch or "box" you by quickly working his front feet while they are off the ground. This is usually accompanied by lunging. When a rabbit is displaying these behaviors, a bite cannot be very far behind if you

Getting "shown the rump."

do not pay attention. The rabbit is warning you in his most stern language to back off and leave him alone.

Vocal sounds such as grunting and/ or growling are obvious warning signals to you: Short, deep, grunting noises—often accompanying boxing, lunging, or showing the rump—are further indicators that the bunny wants to be left alone. You will often see this type of behavior when entering the abode of a bunny who is "cage protective."

In order to make your rabbit cease his aggressiveness, you should take your hand and come from over the top of his head and put your hand firmly on top of his head and neck. Never approach a rabbit who is displaying aggression from down low under his head or chin. This gesture by you is adding insult to injury: You're now demanding that he groom you. This will mostly likely result in a nip or bite for the outrage.

Even the most aggressive or feisty rabbits will usually calm down with the firm but gentle pressure of your hand on top of the backs of their heads. It is a natural signal that wild rabbits use when wanting to exhibit control over others. Of course, be prepared for the bunny to immediately become aggressive again when you remove your hand.

Ears

A rabbit's ears are his most expressive feature, and you can really see clearly what he's feeling by watching the position of his ears. Lop-ear rabbits can also use their ears to express themselves; they just cannot move them quite as fully as an "up-ear" bunny.

Ears forward: amount of interest is determined by how far forward the ears are.
Ears straight up: neutral attitude.
Ears cocked or tuned in different directions: tuning in, interested in what's happening.

A rabbit's ears are his most expressive feature.

Ears back halfway: possible aggression pending or aloofness, depending upon body posture.
Ears flat back: anger, disgust, or discontent, depending upon body posture.

Tail

Tail position is another very apparent indicator of what your bunny's feeling at the moment, though not used as much as ears for signaling. Aggressive behavior is usually accompanied by a tail that is sticking straight up or out. When you see that tail in the air like a flagpole, you know that you have a bunny who means business. Sometimes, tail position can help you distinguish between aggressive postures and more friendly ones.

Sounds

Bunnies do make sounds—vocal and otherwise—to communicate. Here are the different sounds they can make, and what those sounds usually mean:

Thumping

Thumping is done with a rabbit's powerful hind legs, and there is no mistaking this sound since it will resound on even the most solid floors. It has a couple of meanings, the first being a warning to others of some possible danger. This could be a large bird or cat that the bunny hears or some other noise that is not recognized, and is therefore possibly a danger.

The other reason rabbits often thump is to show dissatisfaction or displeasure. If you just moved a favorite toy or did not give your bunny the treat he was expecting, you could get a thump expressing unhappiness with your actions. This kind of thumping is usually accompanied by a "showing of the rump" to further impress his displeasure with you.

Grunting

Rabbits usually grunt during aggressive displays. Rabbit grunts sound a lot like pig grunts, and you will recognize it when you hear it. Often, grunting goes along with lunging and boxing at a person or another rabbit. Making grunting sounds means that your rabbit is willing to fight and he is telling you so. A hard bite may not be far behind. Not all rabbits will bite after they have displayed this kind of aggression, but is should be a red flag to you that you could get bitten if you proceed without due caution.

Growling

Growling differs from grunting in that it is more breathy and not as sharp and forceful. Growling does not always mean anger in some rabbits. I have run across a couple of rabbits who growl while they eat. It is kind of like us saying "Mmm." I have heard other buns who growled when they got stressed, such as when I picked them up and they did not like it. So growling can mean both anger and displeasure, and can sometimes mean "Yummy!" Again, context is an important thing to consider when trying to decipher the meaning of a signal.

Sighing

Not all rabbits will make sighing noises, and the one rabbit I have who does make these sounds actually has a couple of different sighs that meant different things. Her short, sharp sigh—which is almost a high-pitched grunt—is usually given to me to let me know she is not very pleased with something. It is kind of like a human saying "tsk-tsk" in disgust.

The other kind of sigh that she will make is a lower, softer sigh that signifies contentment. I have heard a few other bunnies make this sound too, but it is not a universal one made by all buns. Some rabbits are simply more vocal than others.

Screaming

This sound is like the very loud crying of an infant child. There is no mistaking this sound and, once you have heard it, you hope you never hear it again. It means that your bunny is either in extreme pain or is extremely afraid. Rabbits will normally only scream when being attacked by a predator or in so much pain that they cannot stand it. Often, it is the last sound a bunny makes before he dies.

Tooth Grinding/Purring, or Bruxing

Tooth grinding or purring, called "bruxing," is when a rabbit grinds his back teeth in such a way that it creates vibrations that can be heard if you get close enough or that you can feel if you are petting his head. The noise resembles a "crunch-crunch-crunch," and is a sign of contentment and happiness. It is similar to a cat purring, which is why it's sometimes called "tooth purring." I like to play little games with my buns when they are making this sound. I will give them a "kiss-kiss-kiss" on top of their heads and then put my ear there. Often they will mimic the grooming motions of my kissing with bruxing. When your bunny is sitting next to you and making this sound, he is showing you that he loves your company.

Tooth Clicking

The difference between tooth grinding (bruxing) and tooth clicking is that the bruxing is soft and can usually only be heard up close or felt by putting your hand on the bunny's head. Tooth clicking is more of a chattering sound, and much louder—you can often hear it several feet away. This behavior indicates pain, and a rabbit should always be thoroughly checked out by his vet if he is sitting hunched over (another sign of pain) and clicking his teeth.

Nose Wiggling

One of the more subtle signals you can receive from your rabbit comes from his nose. I think a rabbit's nose is hardwired directly to his brain, because the surest sign that your bunny is thinking hard about something is his wiggling nose. It seems like the faster his nose wiggles, the more intensely he's pondering something.

Nose wiggling also shows awareness and being in tune with what's going on around him. When a rabbit is totally relaxed and not thinking about much of anything, his nose will be relatively still. Yet as soon as he becomes aware of or something catches his attention, that nose will start going a hundred miles an hour.

Edward's interest can be seen by his forward-facing ears and quickly wiggling nose.

Nose wiggling combined with ear and body position can further signify what is on your bunny's mind. Mild interest is a slow-moving nose; intense interest would cause some serious nose twitching.

Other Signals To Note

Breathing Hard

Breathing hard can mean that your rabbit is feeling very stressed, but that's not always the case. Because rabbits smell spatially (which means they can smell where you are and how far away) and do not see very well up close, your bunny could just be trying to discern what is around him by taking in more air to smell.

Rabbits can smell who and where you are, and it is very highly tuned sense. Not only do they smell that you are off to the right or left of them, but exactly how far away you are, as well. When your bunny appears to be breathing hard, he could just be trying to survey more of his surroundings.

Shuddering

A shudder is when your bunny hops up slightly with his front feet and then shakes his head and ears while lightly coming back down on all fours. This is a sign of happiness, and your bunny is telling you about it. Think of that classic James Brown song, "I Feel Good," and the part where Mr. Brown lets out that ear-splitting "WOW!" This is the same thing that your rabbit is saying to you.

Asking for Grooming

Your bunny is asking to be groomed when he lays his head down flat in front of you (or another bunny). His nose will be forward of his front paws and his ears slightly back. This is actually aggressive behavior and, when done to another rabbit, is a command to "lick my head or else!"

While it may appear to the uninformed to be a submissive posture, it is purely dominant behavior in the rabbit world. When rabbits are together, they ignore this demand at their own peril. You may also experience some serious disgust from your bunny if you do not comply with your bunny's demand for grooming. He may show you his rump or even thump. Many buns will give you a small nip to say "Hey, pay attention! I want some grooming!" if you ignore their request, which is what they would do to another bunny.

Bathing

Rabbits are bathing all the time, which is why they are such clean indoor pets. Many times when a rabbit is bathing it means nothing, but if you come into a rabbit's realm and he starts bathing in front of you without looking at you, then he could be trying to be aloof. He is basically saying, "Don't bother me; I am busy."

Bathing can also be a snub between two rabbits, and you may see one rabbit mirror this action when he sees another rabbit bathing. He is saying back, "Yeah, I have no worries, either." Mirroring a rabbit's behavior back to him is soothing when he's feeling threatened, and is a non-aggressive signal that one rabbit tells another that both of them are having the same thoughts. You can often tell your rabbit that you are both on the same page by mirroring his signals to you. It is kind of like repeating back a message to someone so that they know you got it right.

Begging

Rabbits are supreme and expert beggars. They will usually beg for a treat or snack by sitting upright on their hind legs. Since rabbits are very bottom heavy, this is not a stable position for them so try not to laugh when they wobble and sometimes almost fall over backwards.

It is very easy to train your rabbit to sit up for his treats, since he will likely do anything for his favorite foods. Be careful to not overdo it with the treats. Your bunny will quickly learn how to push your buttons to get those treats, and you will find him there in front of you begging over and over throughout the day if you give in easily.

Ricky is begging for a treat while Lucy takes a nap.

Eye Bulging

When your rabbit's eyes bulge out, it means that he is afraid. I have a big girl rabbit who hates to be picked up, and her eyes will bulge out really far every time I do it. It is a sure sign that your rabbit is stressed and afraid about something. Often, you will observe eye bulging in conjunction with your rabbit thumping out a warning.

Licking You and Your Things, and Bunny Kisses

Some rabbits who are too shy to actually lick or groom you will groom the things around you or your clothing.

The most special gift that your rabbit can give you is a bunny kiss. In rabbit language, this is actually grooming. Since our rabbits think of us as big bunnies, this is a very highly regarded message from your bunny. Some rabbits will expect a mutual sign in return, such as a rub of their ears or on top of their head in reciprocation. Not all rabbits will groom a human, so you are lucky if you have a rabbit who likes to tell you how much he loves you by giving you kisses. One of my rabbits actually knows what the word "kisses" means, and if I hold her to my face and ask for one, she will usually give it to me. I have never seen another bunny do this, so you should not expect this behavior from your rabbit. If you ever get kisses from your rabbit, it is a good sign that he really cares about you, because kisses are never given out lightly.

Kisses from bunnies are to be treasured.

Nose Bonks and Nudging

Bumping you with his nose is a loving way of trying to get your attention. Many times, you will feel your bunny nudging your ankles or legs, usually twice quickly in succession. This is him trying to get your attention, usually meaning some grooming or petting is in order.

It is considered a very loving and affectionate signal. Angry or disapproving rabbits will not come near you, and so by actually touching you that way, they are saying "I like you, so how about us getting together for some quality time?"

Circling Your Feet

This is a sign of excitement. It is often done by unaltered males who are sexually frustrated, but if your spayed or neutered bunny does this, then he is very happy and excited by your presence.

Chinning

When your rabbit rubs his chin on something, he is transferring his scent from glands under his chin to the object. This is a way of marking territory and objects as "his." This is more common behavior with unaltered rabbits, but all bunnies can do this. It is harmless, since we cannot smell the scent that they are leaving behind and it's not destructive to objects.

Pee or Poop Outside the Litter Box

If your rabbit is litter-box trained and he is leaving pee or poop in places other than his litter box, then he could be marking territory. This behavior is dramatically reduced after spaying or neutering, but if a rabbit feels that his territory is being violated, he can suddenly start engaging in this type of behavior. This often occurs when another rabbit is introduced into the home and each is trying to claim his own territory.

Groucho is "flopped over," denoted by his feet sticking out to the side. This means that your rabbit is very relaxed and has no fears.

If the poop is spread all around instead of in a neat pile, then it is definitely marking behavior. To get this to stop, you can try putting a litter box in the specific area that is being marked, but if the bunny is scattering it everywhere, then that may not be possible.

Sometimes, this behavior can mean that you have violated your bunny's territory by moving or removing some of his belongings. Once your rabbit feels that the threat to his territory is gone, he will usually stop this kind of marking.

If you have really made your bunny angry, the ultimate expression may be leaving you pee or poop "presents" to ensure you know of his fury. In the bunny world, this is the utmost insult.

Flopping

When a rabbit is really relaxed and happy, he will flop over on his side. Sometimes he will lead with his head, turning his head nearly upside down, or he'll flop over with his whole body, resulting in kind of a full-body collapse onto his side. When blissfully relaxed, this flop may continue over until the rabbit is completely on his back. Only very happy and contented bunnies will show this behavior: A bunny lying down with his feet out to the side or behind him is in no position to run or flee, so he must feel very safe in order to let himself relax like that.

"Pancaking" or Sprawling, and Superman

As prey animals, rabbits will rarely relax completely in any place they do not feel 100-percent secure. They keep their feet underneath them in case they have to suddenly sprint away from danger. Only when your bunny is feeling very safe and relaxed will he lie with his front and/or back legs extended out. The further out he extends his legs, the more relaxed he is.

When some rabbits get really sprawled out, they will appear to be a huge bunny puddle on the floor, with their bodies flattened out and both front and hind legs stretched out as far as they will go—a sure sign that a rabbit is happy and feeling good. This is also called the "Superman" pose, because your bunny will look like Superman when he is flying through the air.

When Lucy is relaxed she does her "pancake" imitation.

Bunny Dances, or "Binkies"

When a rabbit does a dance, he is telling the world that he is so happy he could do a jig—and what a jig he can do! I always tell folks that you have not lived until you have seen a bunny dance, also called a "binky." There are many

Ruby is doing her bunny dance, known as a "binky."

variations of the bunny binky, and I find that each bunny has his own personalized version (some have even perfected several varieties).

I will try and describe some of them to you, because one of the true joys of having a house rabbit is watching him enjoy himself by doing big binkies. One of my rabbits, Ricky, likes to hop straight up high into the air and turn around 180 degrees in mid-air, landing in the same spot that he started. He will usually look over at me to make sure I saw him do it. If I laugh or say his name, he will typically do it again. Sometimes Ricky will just be standing there and all of a sudden jump three feet sideways.

Ricky's girlfriend, Lucy, likes to race around really fast and then, mid-run, do very long or high hops into the air. Often while in mid-air she will flex her feet as if to say, "Wooo-hooo!" Sometimes she'll do a whole string of these hops that blend into a flying-dancing maneuver that is quite something to behold. I always laugh when she does this, and it seems to make her happy that I am enjoying it so much, so she will do it again. One of my favorite binkies that Lucy does is the "zig-zag" binky, where she is zigging and zagging while running at top speed.

I have also found that rabbits can actually learn new moves from other bunnies, so you may find one rabbit imitating his partner's dances one day. I take this as a sure sign of the intelligence of rabbits.

Foot Flicking

A bunny who is unhappy with you will often hop away from you, flicking out his hind legs at you as he leaves. This is a sign that he is mildly displeased. I sometimes get this behavior from a rabbit I have picked up when he did not want it. As soon as I set him down, he will quickly hop away, flicking his hind feet at me in disgust.

Tail Spinning

I have not seen this behavior in very many rabbits, but it means excitement. My one-eyed girl, Star, is a prolific tail spinner. Whenever she gets excited, her little tail will go around and around like a pinwheel. It is a happy kind of excitement, and she is usually getting ready to dance or binky when she does it.

Digging

Digging has three meanings: The first one is frustration. My bunny who sits in my lap will sometimes dig on my leg or chest when she feels I do not understand something she is trying to tell me.

Another meaning is nest-building behavior. Unspayed females will often do this, because they are always preparing to have babies. Sometimes, they will continue this behavior even after they are spayed, and it is more instinctual rather than a signal.

The third meaning of digging behavior is a bunny challenge. Rabbits will dig in front of another rabbit to signify a challenge over territory. When a rabbit does this in front of another, it's like throwing down the "territory gauntlet," and the usual response will be for the challenged rabbit to respond by digging as well. It is an aggressive behavior when done in this way. You may need to watch closely because a bunny fight may be about to happen.

The "Superman" pose denotes being relaxed and unafraid.

Summary

- To have more meaningful interactions with your rabbit, it is very important for you to understand "bunny talk."

- If you want to communicate with your rabbit, you must think like one.

- Rabbits are intelligent creatures and will learn your habits and behaviors fairly quickly.

- Most rabbit communication is based on simple signals and protocols about dominance and territory,

- In rabbit society, the "top" rabbit wants respect at all times.

- Bunny grooming (petting) is mainly focused on the top of the head.

- Many rabbit signals have different meanings in different contexts.

- Most of your rabbit's signals are silent, but he may make some sounds and noises, too.

- Rabbits become more trusting and socialize with their families better when they can be understood.

- More subtle signals, like nose wiggling and body shudders, can also give you a big insight into exactly what your bunny is thinking at the moment.

Amy's sideways posture means that she is not sure if she wants to be approached.

Lucy has flopped over and is sleeping in total bliss.

When your bunny lays his head down, he is "presenting" himself for grooming. We humans groom rabbits by petting them on the head.

Chapter 16:
Training Your Rabbit

Many people are very surprised to learn how intelligent and trainable pet rabbits are, and there is a myriad of behaviors and tricks that you can train your rabbit to do by using his favorite thing in the world: food.

A popular way to train rabbits is called "clicker training." There are books and videos available describing the process in detail, but you do not need to use a clicker to train your bun. Some of the simple things that you can try training your bunny to do are going back to his abode for a treat (as opposed to chasing him around the house five hundred times) or coming when he is called. I have trained rabbits to jump up into my lap for a treat or onto my belly when lying on my back on the floor.

More advanced training can be things like teaching your bunny to follow a feather or string that, over time, can be used to teach him to hop over obstacles or through tubes or hoops. I have seen fine demonstrations by bunny trainers who have taught rabbits to run quickly through an obstacle course or play fun games like "bunny bowling" or hoop jumping.

I have trained all three of my rabbits to take a treat from my lips. This is quite simple to do, because rabbits want to get a small treat from you and will quickly learn how to do it. All I do is put the treat in my mouth, put my mouth next to their heads, and before long, they always go looking for one there. This is very cute, because if I lie or sit on the floor, my rabbits are constantly coming up to me and "kissing" me on the lips to see if there is a treat there.

The keys here are that it is for food, it is something that they can easily do, and it is also something that they want to do. These are your guidelines for determining if a "trick" you are trying to teach your rabbit is something that can easily be done. Some similar "tricks" you can teach your bunny are going back to his abode, sitting up, jumping onto something, and running through a tunnel. With a little imagination, all kinds of feats such as these can be performed, if you work with your rabbit.

Not all rabbits can be trained to sit with you quietly the way that Star does.

Some people train their rabbits to a sound or voice command as their rabbit does a desired behavior, and then they give him a small treat.

127

Keep the treats extremely small, because a lot of training will result in your bunny getting too many treats. Some trainers use single rabbit food pellets as treats. I get small, flat cookies made for bunnies and break them into quarters or sixths so that the pieces are very small. Resist the urge to use fruit because rabbits will do anything for fruit, but you do not want your rabbit to get into the habit of only performing for sweet treats. Over time, this can result in obesity and a dramatically shortened lifespan for your rabbit.

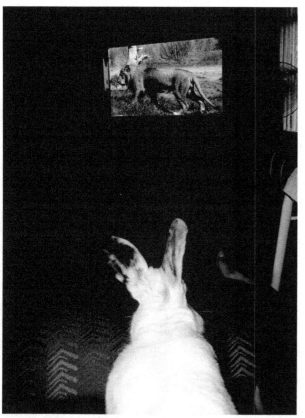

Star has been trained to sit and watch TV in my lap. She will actually tell me when she needs to use her litter box.

When my rabbits are being mischievous and getting into something and I want them to stop, I will sometimes give them a squirt with a water bottle. This is also a good way to break up two rabbits having a small argument. When bonding two or more rabbits, having a water squirt bottle handy is indispensable for breaking up squabbles and halting aggressive behavior. After that, its use should be rare and not deployed several times a day, or else something is wrong. Constant disciplining will lead to your rabbit becoming afraid or resenting you.

As I've stated before, never discipline a rabbit by hitting him. Being hurt in any way will teach your rabbit to not trust you and will destroy any kind of bond you may have had. Rabbits have extremely good memories, and he will associate you with being hurt.

My bunnies have become very well-trained to realize that, after a stern "no," if they do not cease and desist, a squirt from the water bottle will soon follow. Now, I only have to shake the water bottle and they know to start behaving. I have not actually had to squirt them in months, and only reserve that for when they are refusing to stop doing something like chewing on the furniture or carpet, which is rare.

The water bottle is the strongest negative reinforcement I will use on a rabbit. Usually, since all of my bunnies know their names, I can just call their names a little loudly and they know I am aware that they are getting into trouble. Of course, then it becomes a battle of wills, because the second I turn my back or leave the room, then they are back at whatever they know they are not supposed to be doing.

That is why, if your bunny is chewing on your shoes, rather than squirt him and yell at him to stop fifty times a day, it is much better to just remove them from his reach. This is always the easier and smarter alternative, because how many pairs of shoes are going to be destroyed before your bunny finally learns (if ever) that he should not chew them? Using this logic is important when living with a rabbit, because even the best-trained rabbits will only learn a few tricks. Do not think you are going to have the most socialized, polite bunny that there ever was, because that is just not realistic. For complete information on bunny-proofing, see **Chapter 12**.

Instead, focus on teaching your bunny a few simple things, such as coming when he is called or jumping on your lap or chest when you are on the floor. Another good one for your rabbit to know is how to go back to his abode when it is time for him to go inside. Why race around, stressing your rabbit out by trying to chase him back to his area when he is not ready to go? Instead, you can get him excited to go back if you have a small hay cube waiting for him. Hay cubes are small, healthful treats that most buns love. If your rabbit is not fond of hay cubes, then experiment with things like a sprig of fresh greens or three or four pellets of food. Just be careful to not use sweet treats so that your bunny is doesn't get too many calories from his training.

We have trained our rabbits to go back to their condos each evening with a bunny cookie. It used to be a fiasco, with us chasing our thumping rabbits all over the house every bedtime. Upon us making it a habit to give them each a cookie at bedtime, the bunnies now come and tell us that it is time for bed. They get so excited that they binky and dance all the way to their condos as soon as they know their special cookie is on the way. This is much better than them being angry with us for chasing them into their condos for the night.

To call my bunnies, I have a small plastic container with a few of their favorite treats in it. Every time I call them, I shake the container and the sound brings them running. For appearing, they each get a small treat. If they stick around wanting another, I then coax them to jump up into my lap for a second small one. I often have all three of them piled in my lap to get a treat. I remind you that all three are not bonded, but have learned that all treats cease if they have a spat. They never nip or get grumpy with each other when they are in my lap for those treats.

Do not be afraid to experiment with using small treats to teach your bunny new behaviors. He might really amaze you with the things that

he can learn to do. Your rabbit might even teach you a few things along the way! Just remember to keep your expectations at a reasonable level, because a rabbit most likely will never be taught to "fetch" or to "catch" objects like a dog.

Star is used to going places with the family inside her pet carrier.

I always remember how my little girl bunny Pamela used to hop down and nibble on my toes when I would be lying on the floor watching TV. That meant she wanted to snuggle under the blanket with me, and so I was required to lift the edge of the blanket so she could be covered over with it.

If you are in tune with your bun and spend time learning his language, you might be surprised at the things you will learn together. Some rabbits can be trained with just a little petting as a reward, but I find those buns to be rare. Almost every rabbit I have ever met will practically do back flips for a treat, and so positive reinforcement with small, wholesome treats is the recommended way to train most rabbits.

Consider, when training your bunny, whether what you are attempting to train him to do is something that a rabbit would want to do and if he can do it naturally. If your rabbit is terrified of water, then why would you want to teach him to play in a kiddie pool? Now, if your bunny looks for any excuse to get out to run and hop in the rain, then maybe he might enjoy some supervised pool time when it gets hot during the summer. The key word there is *supervised*.

Training your rabbit to hop around on a harness and leash is just not possible with a lot of rabbits. If your rabbit panics and screams with a harness on, then it is probably better not to stress him so much just so you can experience a leash-trained rabbit. It is all about common sense.

I am not saying that if your rabbit does not immediately like or learn something that you should give up, but if he is showing extreme stress and panic, then you need to be a good parent and consider his nature and personality. You should not try to make him conform to your vision of what a "great pet bunny" should be. Once again, common sense goes a long way here.

As with most creatures, as rabbits get older they tend to become smarter and learn things faster. I have also found that rabbits living with other rabbits actually learn from each other. My girl rabbit Star likes to ride inside her litter box from the living room to her condo at night. The other two rabbits watched her do it for a few months and decided that they also wanted to ride to their condo as well when it was time for them to go to bed. First Lucy demanded a ride at night because she had seen Star do it, and then Ricky decided that he was not going to be left out. This is a perfect example of how rabbits can learn from just watching each other.

Training your rabbit should be a fun and enjoyable experience for him; this is truly the only way you will ever succeed in doing it. Commands and discipline will not work. You will have to find something that your rabbit loves, and then use it to reinforce the behavior you are trying to get him to do. And that's really rabbit training in a nutshell.

By training your rabbit to tolerate a leash, you can include your bunny in fun famiy outings like going to the beach or park.

Summary

- Many people are very surprised to learn how intelligent and trainable pet rabbits are.

- A popular way to train rabbits is called "clicker training."

- The guidelines to training are: Reward with healthy food, it is something that he can easily do, and it is also something that he wants to do.

- Some people train their rabbits to a sound or voice command.

- Keep the treats extremely small.

- Never discipline a rabbit by hitting him.

- The squirt water bottle is the strongest negative reinforcement I will use on a rabbit.

- If your bunny is chewing on something, it is much better to just remove it from his reach.

- Hay cubes are small, healthful treats that most buns love.

- Do not use sweet treats (fruit included) so that your bunny does not get too many calories from his training.

- Some rabbits can be trained with just a little petting as a reward, but most cannot.

- Training your rabbit to hop around on a harness and leash is sometimes just not possible.

- You should not try to make him conform to your vision of what a "great pet bunny" should be.

- As rabbits get older, they tend to become smarter and learn things faster.

- Find something that your rabbit loves, and then use it to reinforce the behavior you are trying to get him to do.

It is impossible to train a rabbit not to chew on interesting things, and just because he hasn't chewed it yet does not mean he never will.

This is the kind of comb I prefer because it seems to work on most rabbits. Care must be taken to use it gently, though.

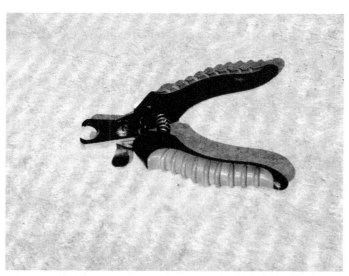

I prefer this type of nail clipper because it is very accurate and it is easy to see where you are cutting.

Chapter 17:
Grooming Your Rabbit

As I've said before, grooming is one of the best ways to bond and spend quality time with your rabbit, but it also serves the useful purpose of helping him get rid of excess fur and keeping his toenails trimmed. Best of all, it gives you the opportunity to check your bunny over for possible health problems you might not otherwise catch.

Fur and Shedding

All rabbits shed, or molt, three to four times a year, and part of having a house rabbit is learning how to deal with this. Rabbits shed in a couple of different ways: Some lose their fur all at once, and it seems to just be coming out in clumps anywhere you touch it. Others shed from one end to the other in a kind of progression; it will appear as if they have a "shelf" of the longer, old fur where it meets the shorter, new fur.

Typically, rabbits will have one major shed per year and then the other ones will be much lighter. How long a molt, or shed, lasts depends a little bit on the breed and genes, but also the weather. Molts leading into a hot summer tend to be the largest—and longest ones.

During heavy periods of shedding, a rabbit's energy level can become quite low. I notice my bunnies also have increased appetites when they molt. When a rabbit gets too much fur inside his intestines a blockage can occur, so ensuring that your rabbit eats lots of high-fiber hay each day is particularly important during molting times.

Combing

Remember that rabbits are smart, so you should put your bunny's grooming supplies, e.g., toenail clippers and comb, where he can't see them before you go get him for his grooming so he doesn't always associate your approach with grooming if he's not a fan of it.

Have your tools and a wastebasket in easy reach beforehand so that you aren't struggling to reach things with your rabbit on your lap. I put the bunny on all fours on a towel on my lap while I am sitting in a chair in an area that's easy to clean of any "flyaway fur."

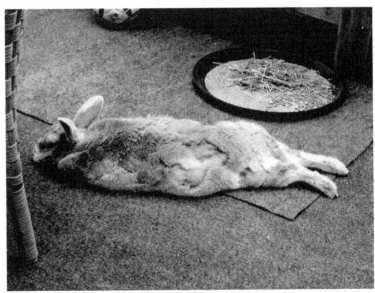

Mister Bunners in a heavy molt or shed.

Once you have your rabbit on all fours on your lap, you must keep control of him at all times. Some bunnies sit calmly while being groomed, but most will test you to see if they can just hop down and get away. Aggressive rabbits may even try to nip or scratch you.

Keep your free hand on top of an aggressive rabbit's head to ensure that he does not nip you. Placing a towel on your lap will help prevent scratches on your legs from their freshly trimmed toenails, which can be sharp. It also protects you from any nips on the legs.

Start combing at the head and work your way down his back. Use your other hand on top of your rabbit's head to control him.

A little trick is to lift your bunny's hind end so that his legs hang down, allowing your to comb the fur there.

First, a few words about combs themselves: I have combed and brushed hundreds of rabbits, and they can get hurt from even the softest combs and brushes. Even the kind with

rounded ends on the tines can puncture the very thin skin of a bunny if it hits at the wrong angle hard enough. I once had a bunny kick while I was using one of these combs with rounded tips, and the force made it pierce my lip. Worse, I have caught a bunny's tail on this type of rounded-tip comb, and it caused a small laceration to the bunny, so be aware that all bunny combs and brushes can hurt a rabbit if used too hard or incorrectly. And, never use a dog or cat brush—especially the type with wire tines—on your rabbit! Here's why:

Several years ago, I was using a wire-tined cat brush on my little girl bun in the middle of her big molt. I was being too aggressive, and caught her hind end with the tines, tearing off a piece of fur and skin the size of a golf ball. Not only was I horrified, I now had a rabbit emergency on a Sunday. It took my bunny's rabbit vet nine staples applied under anesthesia to repair the damage. I learned a very hard lesson at the expense of my poor bunny, and have never used one of these wire brushes again on a bun. Mind you, I had brushed literally hundreds of rabbits with this kind of brush before during my shelter work and never had a problem. But you just can't take a chance.

It's a good idea to place a towel on your lap the first several times you groom your bunny, until you know that he is not going to nip or scratch you hard on the leg so that he can escape. If your rabbit is attempting to nip you, use the "hand-on-top-of-the-head" trick to stop this while you comb him.

Be sure to be gentle, as rough combing can pull out whole chunks of fur and still scratch the skin. If you feel resistance from the fur or encounter any mats when combing, ease off and work gently through it. Combing should feel good and not hurt in order for your bunny to learn to accept his grooming.

I recommend the combs that have rubber strips woven between the tines, because they're excellent at getting even the finest of bunny dander, which is so much finer than most other pet hairs. (Rabbit dander seems to float forever once it's in the air; it is the stuff that makes a big puff cloud when you touch your bunny during a molt.)

Starting at the neck, work the comb carefully through the fur, watching closely to see if it catches at all. If you feel the comb catching on some fur, do not pull through it, because you can actually pull out a complete patch. Instead, back off and work your way very gently through those areas. The fur that is ready to come out will just allow itself to be combed out easily. If you are too forceful, you will be removing fur that is not shedding, which is not only painful but can cause skin lesions and sores.

During a molt, small bald patches are normal and will regrow fur within about a week, so do not be alarmed. If you see broken or sore skin, then you have removed too much fur and have damaged your bunny's skin. If this happens, watch this spot closely for any signs of redness, pus, or infection; any of these signs will require a trip to your exotics vet for evaluation.

Care must also be taken to avoid hitting bones with the comb. I find that, when a bunny is sitting on your lap, his legs are underneath him, and so his shoulders and feet are exposed to the comb as you move it through the fur on his sides. It hurts to hit a joint or bone with the comb, just like it hurts you to hit your "funny bone" on something.

For better access to the upper thighs and rear end, I like to take one hand and cradle it underneath the hindquarters, slightly lifting the back legs up while leaving the front legs resting on my lap. Again, be mindful of the hip and leg bones when using this method.

I suggest combing your rabbit once a week during non-shedding periods, and every day or two during molts to minimize the amount of hair he ingests to reduce the chance of intestinal blockages.

You should also regularly check your rabbit's ears while grooming him to look for any redness or crusty deposits inside, which could mean ear mites. If you find any evidence of them, or he seems to be scratching or shaking his ears frequently, take him to your exotics vet to have this checked out.

Trimming Toenails

While you're combing your bunny, check a couple of his toenails to see if they need trimming. When a rabbit's toenails get too long, they get snagged on things, and then the whole nail can easily be pulled out, which is not only very painful but can allow serious infection to set in. I have seen a rabbit have to have his leg amputated because he pulled out a toenail, which then became infected. Regular "pedicures" every four to six weeks can help prevent this.

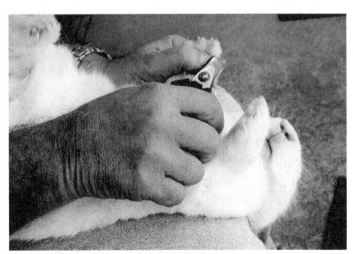

Once you have turned your rabbit over, it makes it easier to see where to safely cut the nail. ***Chapter 8*** *illustrates how do turn your bunny over.*

135

There are different kinds of toenail clippers you can choose for this task, and some seem to work better than others, from my experience. The "guillotine" style has a sharp blade that slides down like a guillotine; I do not like this style myself because I find it harder to see exactly where I am cutting. I prefer the nail cutters that look like a pair of pliers or rosebush trimmers because I can get a better view of what I'm doing. Do not get the small scissor type that look like a pair of sewing scissors: These are intended for cutting small bird nails and will not work well on thick rabbit toenails.

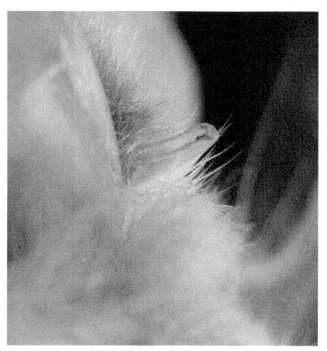

The reason you turn your rabbit over to cut his toenails is to see the groove at the bottom of his hail. Notice the groove stops where the quick starts.

Also have styptic powder (available at most pet stores) on hand to stop any bleeding that may occur, should you accidentally cut a nail too short. If you do not have styptic powder, then plain baking flour can be put on the bleeding toenail. The flour clots up with the blood and will help stop the bleeding. A bleeding toenail should be healed by the next day; if not, call your rabbit veterinarian.

The easiest way to trim your rabbit's nails is to do it while he is on his lying on his back, upside down. To turn your rabbit onto his back, first hug him up to your chest with his back feet still on your lap and his head facing toward you. Bend forward at the waist until your bunny's back is touching the top of your legs. Then, when you sit up, your bunny should be laying on his back in the crack between your legs. Most rabbits will not stay like this very long unless they are restrained in some way.

I like to gently pin the ears between my knees to keep the rabbit from squirming; you do not have to pin them really hard, since just the sensation that they are restrained keeps most bunnies still. If a rabbit is not staying still with just his ears pinned, then I will drop his head a little bit in between my knees and pin his whole head. Again, this does not have to be very hard or firm, as just the feeling that he is pinned should keep him pretty quiet.

You may have to stop several times with some rabbits to readjust their position to make sure that they are held in place securely while you're trimming the toenails. Take your time and remain very calm. It helps your bunny to be calmer when you yourself are relaxed. Over-stressing your rabbit can have dire consequences. If he is completely freaking out, stop this procedure and have it done by his vet.

You will need to push the fur out of the way so you can clearly see the nail.

136

Some people also take a towel and place it over the bunny's stomach while he is upside down—they feel this helps keep the bunny calmer and from squirming too much. If you find you are having trouble keeping your bunny still with your legs, then try the towel method.

Another technique is to put a towel on your lap and then let it sag between your legs a bit to form a nice little trough into which your rabbit's body will rest. With this method, his whole body falls a little bit into the "cradle" created with the towel between your legs.

The reason I like to trim a rabbit's nails while he is upside down is that there is a groove that runs on the underside of the nails when they are long. Where that groove ends is usually where the quick starts, so for rabbits with black nails, this little trick is pretty handy (with white toenails, the blood vessels and quick are easy to see). Some people shine a penlight through the black nails in order to see the quick, but if you learn to see the concave groove in the nail, you will always have a handy guide right on the toenail itself. I have run across three or four rabbits out of the hundreds whose nails I have trimmed who do not have this groove, but that is rare. In this case, it is better to under-trim the nails than to make a mistake and go too short.

Do not trim too close and always try and trim above the quick area 1/16 to 1/8 of an inch. Closer than that will result in hurting your bunny. Trust me, he will tell you when you do because he will kick and flinch. When you do it correctly, your bunny will not flinch or move while cutting a nail.

When you're cutting a toenail, make your cut decisive and quick. Do not hesitate when cutting, right or wrong. It is better to cut too close and deal with a little bleeding than to latch the cutter onto a half-cut nail, because when your bunny kicks or squirms from the pain, the nail

ends up being pulled completely out of the toe. Your safest bet is to always look twice and make very certain exactly where you want to cut—again, it is better to leave the nail a little long than to go too short.

Some rabbit experts I know use a "tap-tap-cut" method. This means that when they have determined where they want to cut, they tap a couple times lightly with the cutter. Not enough to partially cut the nail, but your rabbit can feel it when you cut too close. If your rabbit flinches when you go "tap-tap" with the cutter, then you are trying to cut too close. STOP!

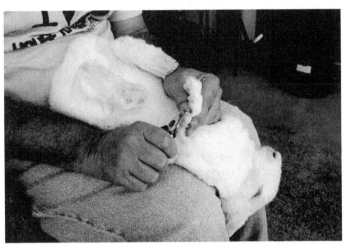

See how Lucy's head is pinned between my knees and my free hand holds her paw and nail firmly.

If a toenail is pulled out, do not panic. Applying styptic powder will help stop any bleeding and then watch the injured toe for the next week or so. These nails usually never grow back in straight, but do they grow back in a month or two. A sideways or crooked toenail is probably one that has grown back after being previously pulled out.

For those who just cannot bring themselves to trim their bunnies' nails or whose rabbits just will not allow them to do it, rabbit vets will do it for you for a small fee (usually around $10-$15).

Summary

- Grooming is one of the best ways to bond and spend quality time with your rabbit.

- Grooming gives you the opportunity to check your bunny over for possible health problems.

- All rabbits shed, or molt, three to four times a year.

- Typically, rabbits will have one major shed per year and then the other ones will be much lighter.

- During heavy periods of shedding, a rabbit's energy level can become quite low.

- Have your grooming tools and a wastebasket in easy reach beforehand.

- Rabbits can still get hurt from even the softest combs and brushes.

- Be sure to be gentle, as rough combing can pull out whole chunks of fur and scratch the skin.

- Care must also be taken to avoid hitting bones with the comb.

- You should also regularly check your rabbit's ears for ear mites while grooming him.

- When rabbit's toenails get too long, they get snagged on things.

- Have styptic powder (available at most pet stores) on hand to stop any bleeding that may occur from trimming a nail too short.

- The easiest way to trim your rabbit's nails is to do it while he is on his lying on his back.

- It helps your bunny to be calmer when you yourself are relaxed.

- Some people also take a towel and place it over the bunny's stomach while he is upside down.

- There is a groove that runs on the underside of the nails when they are long.

- Do not trim too close and always try to trim above the quick area.

- When you're cutting a toenail, make your cut decisive and quick.

- Some rabbit experts I know use a "tap-tap-cut" method.

- If a toenail is pulled out, do not panic.

- If you do not want to trim your rabbit's toenails, rabbit vets will do it for you for a small fee.

Chapter 18:
Bonding Rabbits

Rabbits are very territorial and they will not get along with other bunnies unless they are bonded together. Bonding rabbits consists of socializing them to accept each other as living partners. There are some good benefits to bonding a pair of rabbits, since bunnies are very social creatures and they tend to get lonely when you are away from your house for long periods. If you have a lifestyle where there is not often someone home, having another bunny to keep your rabbit company will help keep him happy.

If you have ever seen a bonded pair of rabbits, they do everything together. They will spend a lot of time cuddling and grooming each other. It is so sweet to see two buns kissing each other and then flopping over, leaning on one another for comfort. The only negative about having two bonded buns is that a single rabbit gives 100 percent of his attention to his family, while a bonded pair gives 80 percent of their attention to each other, and so their human friends do not get as much. If you want your bunny to be totally devoted to you, then you probably do not want to bond him with another bunny.

Because rabbits are so territorial, you cannot put two bunnies together without bonding them first. Siblings in a litter of buns are naturally bonded until they reach sexual maturity; then you may notice dominant behaviors occurring, which can result in fighting. Two rabbits who are not related absolutely must be bonded first before allowing them to live together.

Bonding rabbits is not a science, but rather a series of procedures that can be tried until the right ones that work are found. What works for one set of rabbits may not work at all for another. Persistence and consistency works the best. Irregular bonding sessions do not work as well as several regular sessions each day.

To bond two rabbits together, you must start with a "date," or initial meeting. It is best to begin with two rabbits who show promising signs of being able to be bonded. It helps if they already somewhat like each other and have not already been fighting. With their good memories, rabbits will remember the vicious bite on the hind end that another rabbit once gave them.

Ricky and Lucy are my two bonded rabbits. It took me six weeks to get them both together.

The most important thing to remember when bonding is that open space is your enemy. The smaller the space the rabbits meet in, the better. Large areas create stress for a rabbit because, in his mind, that is more territory for him to have to defend or decide who is dominant over. Small is best, and I suggest using an area no bigger than 4' x 4'; 3' x 3' is even better.

During the initial introduction, observe both rabbits' body language, and have a squirt bottle of water set to a stream to squirt at them if they become aggressive in any way. Do not wait for them to bite and fight with each other: squirt them at the first aggressive signal, such as ears laid back flat and tails straight up in the air. Discourage circling and chasing, which are also aggressive signals.

What you are doing initially is watching the bunnies' behavior and body language to see if they like or dislike each other. Rabbits who immediately like one another are obviously a lot easier to bond than two who do not.

Grooming is a good sign when bonding two rabbits.

It is not a good sign if both rabbits completely ignore one another. In bunny language that is an insult. Better that they look at each other and acknowledge the other's presence. One bunny mounting or humping the other rabbit is not necessarily a bad thing. It is an aggressive behavior, but if the submissive bunny does not fight it or nip when mounted, then it is actually a good thing. It means that he will accept being submissive to the other rabbit. If a small tiff occurs when one bunny tries to mount the other, then there is an argument going on about who is going to be the dominant bun.

It does not mean that they cannot be bonded, but there will need to be some work done to make it happen. Rabbits will sort out amongst themselves who is the dominant one. The problem with letting them sort it out themselves is that fights are usually involved in doing it that way. Serious injuries can occur when two rabbits fight. Death can even happen from a bad ear bite, so you do not want to let your rabbits fight it out. Grudges can be held for a very long time between two rabbits who have had a bad fight. It's much better to not ever let a fight develop in the first place—that way, you can avoid a huge vet bill or permanent injury, as well as a much more difficult bonding.

Once you have decided to try to bond two bunnies together, you must start off with them living nearby each other. I like to use a bonding cage, which is a large cage that is separated down the middle. Mine has fine chicken wire that I put inside an extra-large rabbit cage. The bunnies lived in opposite sides and I switched the sides every day to get them used to living in each other's spaces. I only let one out at a time for run time and all sessions together were closely supervised.

You must not put the two rabbits together in any area that either one will consider his own territory. A fight is sure to develop if one rabbit is going to claim his territory and challenge the other. Always put them together in neutral territory where neither rabbit has been, such as on your bed or in your bathtub. Some people like to use the top of their washing machine while it is on a spin cycle (more on why later). An X-pen set up in a place your rabbits never usually go, such as a grassy spot in the yard or a shady spot on the patio, are also good choices.

Two rabbits who are totally bonded for a long time can still start to fight with one another when they are put into a large space that they are not familiar with. When rabbits are put into a new area, they both must reassert who is the boss over this new area, and if the new area is a large one, the stress of so much space can cause two very well-bonded rabbits to argue.

This is proof that the psychology of rabbits dictates that they continually behave in their dominant and submissive roles when in a pair. Just because a rabbit is content to be submissive to a dominant bun in his cage or X-pen does not mean that he will automatically be that way in a new area. That must be mutually agreed upon by both rabbits, using normal signals and rabbit protocol. So when rabbits enter a new space, they will go through a set of signals with each other to assert their positions in the hierarchy. Sometimes, one bunny just does not feel like being dominated that day and a fight will break out between two buns who have spent months together in a pen without ever having a tiff.

When rabbits are having bonding sessions, it is best to not only keep the space small but also to keep both rabbits a bit off-guard. You do not want one of them getting very brave and trying to assert his dominance too strongly. You want them both to be slightly unsure of what is going on. In a scary, stressful situation, rabbits will band together by instinct. By creating an atmosphere of uncertainty, rabbits are much less likely to start picking on the other bunny, and vice-versa.

What finally worked for me was taking both buns and putting them into a small pet carrier. Then I put them into the back seat of the car and drove around with them inside. The scariness of the car ride and the small space had both buns huddled together. They forgot all about their past squabbles and differences. Trips away from the home are great for bonding, since being in a strange new place is conducive to not fighting.

The reason some people have bonding sessions on top of the washing machine is that,

when it is running and vibrating during the spin cycle, the rabbits are slightly afraid and forget to argue about who is boss. You can be inventive when trying these scenarios. Locations to have bonding sessions are unlimited.

I recommend at least one bonding session per day until bonding is complete. The more the better, and you cannot do it too much. I have had as many as five or six sessions per day with two rabbits. Each session should last around 15-20 minutes at first. You can extend the sessions as you have some success. Never leave two rabbits alone during the bonding process, or a huge fight could result.

An excellent way to control rabbits who are meeting each other is to use a leash so you can quickly separate them.

Rabbit fights are very quick, and within fifteen or twenty seconds they can be completely over, leaving one or both rabbits severely injured. You need to stop two bunnies from ever reaching the brawling stage by giving them a squirt from a water bottle if they start showing aggression. Once two rabbits are fighting, you must reach in and pull them apart as soon as possible.

Rabbits who are fighting are in a rage: They lash out and bite anything that comes close, so you may end up with a fierce bite yourself while separating your buns. Some people wear gloves when bonding for that reason. A frenzied fight almost always leaves one or both buns with some wounds. Wounds are usually not able to be seen, unless they are bleeding heavily. It is not until the next day, when the scabs form on the skin, that you will be able to feel the wounds on your bunny. I have searched fruitlessly for wounds after a fight, only to find a huge sore the following day. Your bunny's thick fur makes it very difficult to find fresh wounds.

My bonded pair spend most of their time cheek-to-cheek.

If you suspect that your rabbit has sustained a bad injury, such as a gaping wound or he is bleeding, take him to your rabbit vet immediately. The wound may require attention such as stitches or staples to close it and to reduce the chance of infection.

Another important thing to remember is that, if the two bunnies you are trying to bond get into any kind of fight, you must not take them away from each other immediately. Stop the fight and then put them close together, side by side, and pet them both. Do not allow them to learn that if they fight, it will result in them being separated. Otherwise, you may find them always fighting so that one of them will get taken away.

Teach them that a fight does not result in the other being removed. Make sure that they do

not continue to fight while you are holding them down together. If you must keep your hand on top of both of their heads to make them remain calm, then do so. Anything to keep them from going on to fight again is good. After five or ten minutes of them being forced to be together quietly, then you can separate them and end the bonding session.

It is very important to always remember this step. You do not want your rabbits to associate fighting with being removed from the other. Always end your bonding session on a calm "together moment" and never with an argument or fight.

Bonding sometimes can happen in as few as a couple of days; on the other hand, I have seen rabbits spend two years in bonding sessions and still not be completely bonded. Bonding two bunnies is a lot of work. I have found myself questioning whether it was worth the trouble when it has been a month of several sessions a day and I seemed to be getting nowhere. I have heard of two rabbits taking over a year to become bonded.

This is when you need to keep trying different things and don't continue using the same methods over and over that are not working. The rabbits will often become comfortable with a certain bonding location or method, and so you will need to change things up so that they do not know what to expect. It is that uncertainty that makes the rabbits forget about fighting and finally decide to be together.

If one location results in immediate fighting and aggression, then do not use that location again. Find another place to do your bonding sessions. Car rides are one of the most popular ways to get two rabbits to bond quickly, since most rabbits are usually afraid of them. It is best if you have two people when doing car-ride bonding sessions, because you do not want a fight breaking out while you are trying to drive, causing you to get into an accident. Have someone else drive while you sit in the back seat with the buns to stop any fighting that may occur. Rabbits will not usually fight in a moving car, but there are always exceptions. You have to plan as if they were going to fight in order to prevent an all-out war while you are unable to stop it, which would be the case if you were alone in the car with the bunnies.

Multiple rabbits can be bonded, and I have seen up to six bonded bunnies before. I will tell you that it is much more difficult to bond unrelated threesomes than a pair. If you are trying to turn a twosome into a trio, it can sometimes unbond your previously bonded pair, which is something that must always be considered when adding another bunny to a bond. It is a risk that you take when you attempt bonding more than just two rabbits.

Siblings can remain bonded long after sexual maturity, if they are spayed/neutered early. The easiest bonds to achieve are boy-girl bonds. Two boys can be bonded, but two girls are the most difficult to bond together. Females have territory issues because of their mothering instincts, and female rabbits are known to kill the babies of other mothers; therefore, females tend not to want other females around if they have powerful maternal instincts.

Despite this, many different bonded combinations are possible. I have seen one boy with a "harem" of five girls. I have seen males and females mixed in a large group. These large groups tend to bond off into pairs or smaller groups, with each of the rabbits preferring the company of certain rabbits over other ones. Small arguments may occur in order for disputes to be settled, but this behavior is normal as long as there are no all-out brawls.

There are some people who just put rabbits together and let them work things out, but I contend that this bonding method has huge—

and unacceptable—risks to it: You surely do not want any of your pets getting hurt, and severe bites leave scars and can be disfiguring. I have known many rabbits with nicked ears and missing lips from bad fights.

There are tons of different methods and complete websites on how to bond two rabbits. If you are looking for new ideas and locations to have bonding sessions, search online for more ideas. You may just happen to stumble upon the right one that really works for you. And again, if something isn't working, do not give up: Keep trying new locations and methods until you notice your rabbits grooming each other and not getting aggressive with each other.

Mounting is dominant behavior and means "you belong to me." It can lead to fighting, if the bunny does not want to submit.

And, once you find the method that works, keep doing it. You'll know you've found the right tactic when you see lots of kisses being given to the dominant bun from the submissive one. Once you feel that you are mostly there with the bonding, do not make the mistake of suddenly giving your buns too much space. Gradually increase their amount of space over the course of several weeks: Let them have one small space for three or four days and then give them another foot of space. Then let them get used to that slightly bigger space for a few days before giving them another foot of space.

Since a fight can start and then be over in seconds, I suggest that you never leave the two buns alone together for at least the first couple weeks. I slept on my living room floor the first week with my two freshly bonded buns, just to make sure they did not suddenly start fighting in the middle of the night.

Head mounting is another aggressive, dominant behavior.

It took me six weeks to bond my last pair, but most of the real bonding happened in the last two weeks. I kept trying different areas and methods until I found the car-ride method and learned about not giving them too much space. If you really want to bond your buns, you cannot easily give up.

One good trick I have learned is to put both rabbits into a harness and attach each one to a leash. This way the rabbits can be easily separated if they start to fight. You might prefer this to the other method of wearing heavy gloves. Of course, you must remain very attentive when using any method because of how quickly a fight can develop.

Another good technique is to obtain a small pet stroller and to put both rabbits into it and take them for a walk around the block. This works especially well if neither rabbit has ever been in a bunny stroller before. It is better to use a stroller that did not previously belong to one of the rabbits that you are trying to bond, in case he might think that it is already his territory.

One friend of mine put a small X-pen on top of her coffee table and bonded her rabbits there. Her apartment was small and there were not many places that her first rabbit had not already claimed for himself. With a little creativity, you can come up with your own ideas and tricks to make your bonding process a success. Just follow the simple rules of not using a place either rabbit thinks is his and keep the space very small. A little fear or uncertainty is also good to keep the buns from trying to be too dominant and a little off-balance. This goes a long way to preventing fights.

Some experts say that any two rabbits can be bonded, but I am not so sure about that. Consider if there was someone that you absolutely loathed; would it be possible to make you like that person? I think that, in bonding, rabbit personalities really do come into play and it is always easiest to start out with two buns who already have a liking for each other. This does not mean bonding will come easily, but why make it harder than it already is?

Ricky and Lucy in their bonding cage before they were bonded.

Sitting side by side and any kissing or grooming are very good signs. In order to promote good, positive behavior, I have used small fruit treats smeared onto the head of one or both of the bunnies. Banana is a good choice for this, but it is sticky and hard to get out of the fur later. Applesauce also works well. By putting the treat on the head of the buns, the bunny getting it licked off is fooled into thinking he is being groomed. He does not care it is because there is fruit smeared on his head.

Be careful to not get carried away with giving too many of these treats during bonding sessions. It is only to get the buns grooming each other and healthier rewards should be used at the end of a session if a treat is given. I liked to give my bunnies a small piece of a healthy rabbit cookie at the end of each session to get them looking forward to the next one. Since I had five or more bonding sessions a day, treats can quickly add up, so keep them very small and not of the sugary sort, i.e., fruit or carrots. I only used fruit to put on top of the rabbits' heads to encourage them to groom each another.

Bonding rabbits is a very rewarding thing to do, but it should not be undertaken lightly because it is a lot of hard work and it does not always work out. You may end up with two rabbits who do not get along rather than just your original one. If this happens, then you may find yourself having to provide two completely separate living spaces because your bonding was not successful.

However, once successfully bonded, your rabbits will share everything from their litter box to their food bowl and living area. If one rabbit goes to the vet, then both must go. They must never be separated or you risk unbonding them. If a rabbit goes out of the house, such as to the vet and then returns home with the smell of other animals on him, it could result in a fight and them becoming no longer bonded.

To prevent this from happening, your bonded pair needs to always be together and never apart. Some rabbits will actually pine for their partners when separated. I saw one bonded pair where one bunny got sick and had to be in isolation. Her partner completely stopped eating and did not start eating until she was rejoined with her partner. If part of a bonded pair suddenly dies, you may have to find a replacement for the partner right away. Some rabbits become so despondent and unhappy over this that they will soon pass away themselves, out of loneliness.

Daizey and Widget are bonded sisters.

My girl bunny who was bonded with my kitty became very bonded with me after she lost her feline friend. She became very clingy and turned into a lap rabbit who always wanted to be with me. Bonded rabbits who lose their partners will often need to replace them in order to remain happy. Rabbits grieve just like people do over the loss of a loved one. Give them some time to mourn and then get them a new friend as soon as you can.

Summary

- Rabbits are very territorial and they will not get along with other bunnies unless they are bonded.

- A bonded pair of rabbits does everything together.

- Siblings in a litter of buns are naturally bonded until they reach sexual maturity.

- Bonding is a series of procedures that can be tried until the right ones that work are found.

- To bond two rabbits together, you must start with a "date," or initial meeting.

- The most important thing to remember when bonding is that open space is your enemy.

- Rabbits who immediately like one another are obviously a lot easier to bond than two who do not.

- It is not a good sign if both rabbits completely ignore one another.

- One bunny mounting or humping the other rabbit is not necessarily a bad thing.

- Serious injuries can occur when two rabbits fight.

- Start off with the rabbits living nearby each other.

- You must not put the two rabbits together in any area that either one will consider his own territory.

- When rabbits are put into a new area, they both must reassert who is the boss over this new area.

- When rabbits are having bonding sessions, it is best to not only keep the space small but also to keep both rabbits a bit off-guard.

- I recommend at least one bonding session per day until bonding is complete.

- Trips away from the home are great for bonding.

- A frenzied fight almost always leaves one or both buns with some wounds.

- If you suspect that your rabbit has sustained a bad injury, take him to your rabbit vet immediately.

- Teach them that a fight does not result in the other being removed.

- Always end your bonding session on a calm "together moment" and never with an argument or fight.

- Bonding two bunnies is a lot of work.

- Keep trying different things and don't continue using the same methods over and over that are not working.

- Car rides are one of the most popular ways to get two rabbits to bond quickly.

- Multiple rabbits can be bonded, and I have seen up to six bonded bunnies before.

- Once you find the method that works, keep doing it.

- Never leave the two buns alone together for at least the first couple of weeks after bonding.

- If you really want to bond your buns, you cannot easily give up.

- A little fear or uncertainty is also good to keep the buns a little off-balance and from trying to be too dominant.

- Sitting side by side and any kissing or grooming are very good signs.

- Bonding should not be undertaken lightly, because it is a lot of hard work and it does not always work out.

- Bonded rabbits will share everything from their litter box to their food bowl and living area.

- If one rabbit in a bonded pair goes to the vet, then both must go.

- If part of a bonded pair suddenly dies, you may have to find a replacement for the partner right away.

In order for siblings to remain bonded, they both must be spayed or neutered at about thrre or four months old.

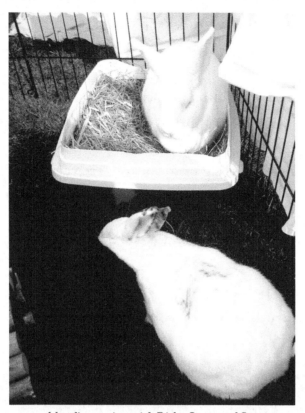

A bonding session with Ricky, Lucy, and Star.

This 3'X3' x-pen is the perfect size for these two rabbits' bonding sessions.

Chapter 19:
Rabbit Health and Wellness: Issues from Common To Critical

I am not going to go into a lot of detail in describing many of the rabbit maladies that you may encounter along your journey into being a rabbit lover. This is because I do not want to give any kind of impression that you can diagnose or treat these ailments without the help of a good rabbit-savvy veterinarian.

Even rabbit experts realize that, for many common bunny health problems, the only appropriate thing to do is to take your bun to the vet. This is why you must seek out an exotics vet as soon as you decide to adopt a bunny. A good relationship with an exotics vet who has a lot of experience treating rabbits is critically important to successfully helping your rabbit to live a long, happy—and healthy—life. Please do not underestimate the importance of this.

The best rule of thumb is if you suspect a problem in any way, it is time to visit your vet. Experienced bunny parents are always on the lookout for changes and subtle hints that their rabbits may not be feeling well or are having any problems. Once it's determined that a problem exists, the first thing they will do is call their vets. Hopefully, you will have already taken your bunny in for a wellness checkup and your vet will know your rabbit; this goes a long way toward making the diagnosis and treatment of any subsequent ailment easier and more timely for your rabbit when he needs it the most.

Rabbit, or "Exotics," Veterinarians

One of the things that comes with having a companion pet is making certain that, if he needs medical attention, he immediately gets

it. Finding a good rabbit vet—also known as "exotics" vets—in some parts of the United States can be challenging, and some folks have to travel some distance to reach a good one. This does not mean that you should just forget about doing this.

If you were to have an emergency with your bunny, you need to know where you would rush your rabbit to try to save him. Certainly, you would not be willing to just throw up your hands and watch your pet die (if you would, then it goes without saying that a house rabbit is certainly not the right pet for you). I feel that one of the most important things (although expensive) that we do for our pets is making sure they have healthy, pain-free lives. Doing this includes visits to the right veterinarian.

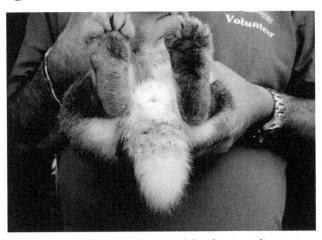

This rabbit has badly stained feet from standing in his urine. It breaks down the fur and eventually his skin. Bad cases require your rabbit to see his vet.

The House Rabbit Society website is a good place to start in your search for your bunny's doctor. You can find your local HRS chapter or the chapter closest to you, which will have a vet list for you to use. This is an invaluable resource, because it makes it unnecessary for you to check out what could be dozens of exotics vets yourself.

Once you have found the ones who are the closest, do your homework to see which one is the best for you and your bunny. Remember that the best ones are rarely the least expensive, so cost should not be your determining factor.

You can also check out your local vets by asking other rabbit people you might know about their opinions and experiences with their rabbit specialists. If you do not know any other rabbit people, then search online for rabbit-forum sites where vet advice and comments are made. There are quite a few, and you should not have too much trouble finding several of them.

Before you visit a vet, you can call and ask for some info such as if he or she is an Exotics Specialist Trained Veterinarian. Ask how many rabbits he or she treats a month to try to gauge the experience level of the vet you are considering. Personally, I believe that the more experience a vet has with bunnies, the better off you will be. You do not want your rabbit to be the first case of head tilt or GI stasis that vet has ever seen.

One of the things that many good rabbit veterinary specialists suggest is a wellness check while the rabbit is healthy. Rabbit test results can vary dramatically from rabbit to rabbit, and diagnosing problems from a blood test becomes extra difficult when there isn't a normal baseline test to compare results to. By having a blood panel performed at a wellness checkup, tons of money and precious diagnosis time can be saved in the future should a sudden or critical health issue occur. My rabbits' vet suggests that these baseline tests be run every year; I think that you should do them at least every two years for the results to be useful in an emergency.

A good, trusting relationship with your rabbit's vet is also important to have, so do not wait until you desperately need one to start your search. I personally know the guilt that comes from making the wrong veterinarian choice

and having a negative outcome for your rabbit, and I guarantee you do not want to carry that burden. Being prepared for any possible rabbit emergency—and even common illnesses that require veterinary treatment—is an important part of being a good bunny parent.

For more information about exotics veterinarians and veterinary costs related to rabbits, see **Chapter 4: How Much Does Having a Bunny Really Cost?**

Common Rabbit Health Issues

As I've mentioned in previous chapters, it is difficult to tell if your rabbit is sick or not feeling well because, as a prey animal, he instinctively will not allow others to know when he is ill.

All too often, the first time many rabbit owners realize their bunnies are hurting or sick is after the situation has been going on for several days. This is a big reason why rabbits need to live indoors right next to their owners. If you are not closely associating with your bunny and in tune with his everyday demeanor, you will never know that your rabbit is ill until he simply stops eating and passes away.

The first sign that a rabbit is in pain is that he sits a bit upright and hunched over. He may appear to be panting or be loudly grinding or clicking his teeth. If you notice your rabbit appears to be in pain, try giving him some of his favorite salad greens to see if he will eat them. A rabbit who looks to be in pain and is not eating his favorite foods is in trouble.

There could be many reasons for this and I do not want to try to teach you to diagnose these problems through this book. It is better to let an expert see your rabbit and find out what is wrong. Rabbit-savvy vets are lifesavers for many common conditions and you should never delay taking your bunny to see one, because just one day can be the difference between life and death. It only takes a rabbit one day of not eating and pooping to suddenly die.

GI Stasis and Bloat

Two of the most common rabbit ailments are gastrointestinal (GI) stasis and bloat (gas). I've discussed this at length in previous chapters of this book, but am going to cover it thoroughly again here so that this particular chapter can be used as a stand-alone reference.

GI stasis can sometimes be rectified if caught and treated soon enough, which is why it is very important to monitor your rabbit's litter box daily to make sure he is peeing and pooping. You should also watch his food and water intake on a daily basis. Any change in his normal eating, drinking, peeing, or pooping habits needs to be closely monitored for further evidence of a problem. Your rabbit needs to do all of these things several times a day to be healthy.

Rabbits are fermenters, and so they must constantly eat and poop to be healthy. They can get too much gas in their intestinal tracts, which can cause them pain and their intestines to stop working properly. When their guts stop moving and they cease eating and pooping, this is called "gastrointestinal stasis," or GI stasis for short. GI stasis is a deadly condition that is very common in rabbits, and many things can cause it, including fur blockage, fatty liver disease, and numerous other intestinal conditions. Because it can quickly be fatal, it is not something you want to take a "wait-and-see" approach to; a rabbit with any of the symptoms of GI stasis needs immediate veterinary care.

If you find no poops in your bunny's litter box—which is likely to be your first sign of GI stasis—you do not need to panic and take him

directly to the vet, but you will want to watch his box very closely to see if he is putting anything in there from that point on. If another few hours go by and no poops appear, this is definitely cause for concern: Contact your rabbit's vet and plan to take him in immediately. Do not wait through a day or two of no poops before acting.

Finding cecotropes in your rabbit's litter box regularly means your rabbit may be suffering from over-feeding or intestinal distress.

Symptoms include being in pain along with not eating or pooping. Offer your bunny his favorite treat or salad greens to see if he will eat. If he just eats a couple bites and then turns away and you know this is not normal, you should be very concerned. At this point, watch him for a few hours to see if he comes out of it and suddenly passes his gas or gets a desire to eat. Also watch to see if he leaves a bunch of normal-looking poops in his litter box. If any of these occur within two to four hours, you may be out of the woods this time, so sigh with relief, but keep a close eye on your bunny for the next couple of days.

Another important symptom to recognize is your rabbit's stomach being bloated or distended. Rabbits will often look as if they have been blown up like a balloon when they get bloat or GI stasis. When you feel your bunny's tummy between his pelvis and ribs, it should normally be soft and squishy. If it feels hard or solid, that is a serious problem—see your vet right away.

Hours can literally be the difference between life and death.

If poops do appear in the litter box but are not normal in appearance (either abnormally large or misshapen), then something is still wrong with your bunny. If he leaves a bunch of cecal pellets (cecotropes) around, which are the small, mushy poops rabbits usually eat, this is also a sign that your rabbit is not feeling normal. Learn more and see photos of cecal pellets in [**Chapter 13**: Hay in Your Bunny's Litter Box and Litter Box Training]. If there are several signs like this and it has been three to four hours with no improvement, take your bunny to the vet immediately. If it is after

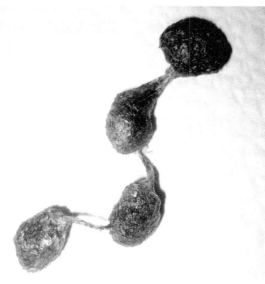

Ingesting too much fur when bathing can result in a "string of pearls" when your bunny poops. Fur can cause serious blockages, which is why grooming is so important.

your regular rabbit vet's office hours, go to the nearest emergency veterinary hospital.

GI stasis and bloat are so dangerous because, once the GI tract shuts down, toxins quickly build up and can cause liver or heart failure. This can occur in a matter of hours; I have known rabbits to be happily hopping around one night and dead by the next afternoon. These related conditions also cause your bunny a lot of pain, which is another reason to rush to the vet as

soon as you become aware of or suspect that your rabbit is suffering from GI stasis and/or bloat.

Dental Issues

Dental problems are another common rabbit health issue. Many dental problems are a result of bad genes or breeding. In our local area, there was a woman who used to breed (rather carelessly) lop-eared bunnies and then sell them from a laundry basket in a local park because of the public's love for them. Whenever this woman would have a baby bunny with teeth issues, she could not sell it because it was obviously not OK, so it would become part of her breeding stock. Popular rabbit breeds encourage breeders to try to make money by overbreeding and selling them with no thought of the potential health consequences to the animals.

This one woman unknowingly concentrated the bad-teeth genes in her rabbits and is now responsible for many hundreds of hereditary cases of a dental condition called malocclusion in rabbits in our area. Rabbits' teeth grow up to nine inches a year, so they must constantly chew on fibrous food to wear them down. When the teeth do not meet together properly (malocclusion), the teeth cannot grind themselves down, which results in the teeth growing so long that they must be trimmed regularly by a veterinarian or they will actually grow right out of the mouth.

I have seen really bad cases of malocclusion where the bunny looked as if he had tusks from this condition. There are many ways to deal with it, most of which entail having the teeth regularly trimmed down. Years ago, maloccluded teeth were simply cut off using wire cutters, but that results in "crazing," or cracking, of the tooth enamel, and infections and abscesses can occur from this. Now, vets no longer use that method and will grind them down instead to avoid complications.

As veterinary medicine and dentistry have progressed, newer methods have been developed to completely remove maloccluded front teeth in rabbits so they no longer have to be trimmed all the time. This is a relatively new procedure, but it can be well worth the expense, because regular tooth trimmings get rather costly over time. Surprisingly, rabbits do not need their front teeth to eat and be healthy.

These genetic malocclusions will usually present themselves by the time a rabbit is six to eight months old. After that, it is rare for a rabbit to have this genetic condition, if it has not been present before. Then rabbits tend to not have dental issues until they get much older, usually over six years old.

Dental issues are one of the three most-common reasons a rabbit must visit a vet, especially for senior buns over age six. One of the first signs of a dental problem is weepy eyes or a runny nose. This does not necessarily mean that the problem is his teeth, as these symptoms can also indicate a respiratory or eye infection. Overly wet or dripping eyes are definitely a reason for your bunny to see a veterinarian. Only a rabbit vet can tell if it is teeth or another problem causing this.

A dental issue can sometimes be detected if your rabbit's eating habits suddenly change: If he suddenly stops eating hay when he used to be a big hay eater, teeth can be a suspect. If he suddenly stops eating his little bit of pellets each day, then the hard, crunchy pellets may be causing him pain because his teeth are giving him problems.

Rabbits typically do not need to see a vet very often, but when they do have a problem, it almost always requires immediate attention. Rabbit vets can be up to three times more expensive than dog and cat vets, so it is prudent to use a good diet and healthy living conditions to prevent any unnecessary visits. See **Chapter 4: How Much Does a Bunny Really Cost?** for more information on this subject.

Obesity

Like I discussed in **Chapter 9: Your Rabbit's Diet**, a really common rabbit issue is obesity or being overweight, which can be a serious problem for a bunny, because rabbits tend to get fatty liver disease when they're overfed. Fatty liver disease eventually reduces liver function until the body suddenly goes into GI stasis. Once a rabbit has reached this point, it is very difficult to save him. The best way to prevent this problem is to not overfeed your rabbit in the first place, and to never give him sugary or fatty foods. A rabbit who eats mostly hay with a small daily salad is the healthiest. Rabbits who get lots of fruit and treats and/or too many densely nutritious pellets tend to have lots of GI stasis, cardiovascular issues, and liver problems, all of which can be fatal.

Looking back at pictures, my Mr. Bunners was obese.

Bladder Sludge

Another common rabbit malady is bladder sludge or stones. Calcium can build up in some rabbits and result in their bladders becoming full of "sludge," or material that cannot be excreted. It used to be thought that these rabbits were being fed diets too high in calcium, but we now

153

know that it is a disease instead because, when all the calcium was removed from these rabbits' diets, their bodies would leach calcium from their bones and the bladder sludge would still continue. Veterinarians now have new options for treatment of this issue.

The main symptom of bladder sludge is urine that appears very thick and gritty. Rabbit urine can normally be orange or red in color with a slightly "heavy" consistency. However, if the urine becomes overly thick or viscous and takes on a gritty appearance—as if there are particles suspended in it—that may indicate a sludge problem. Only a vet can tell for sure.

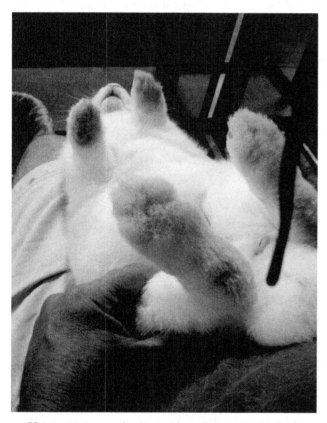

Urine staining can lead to scalding. Prevent feet stains by using a grate in your bunny's litter box with lots of hay.

Other symptoms of a bladder problem are urine scalding or staining around the rectal area. Rabbits can become incontinent or leak urine when these problems become evident. Seeing a lot of yellow staining between your bunny's hind legs should be cause for concern and is a signal to have him checked out by his vet. It might be nothing, but it is best to have it looked at.

E. Cuniculi

The last condition I want to make you aware of is head tilt, thought to be caused by a parasitic protozoa called Encephalitazoon cuniculi—E. cuniculi for short. Almost all rabbits have this parasite in their bodies when tested, but it is thought if a rabbit becomes very stressed, toxins released by the unchecked overgrowth of this protozoa cause extreme, debilitating outward symptoms such as blindness, paralysis, and head tilt.

E. cuniculi can be fatal, but rabbits can, and do, recover from it if they receive immediate veterinary treatment. Therefore, it is imperative that your bunny see an exotics vet right away if he shows any signs of this disease, which include cataracts or whitening in the eyes, inability to keep his balance (called "rolling"), falling over on his sides repeatedly, or sudden inability to hold his head upright (called "head tilt"). Some rabbits with head tilt can actually get eye damage from their heads tilting so far over that their eyes are dragged on the floor.

Special antibiotics and other medicines can be used to control and sometimes reverse this disease, and veterinary research is ongoing to learn more about this problem. The common precursor to this syndrome is some highly stressful event to the rabbit, such as too much heat, becoming stray, or being left alone for several days.

Rabbit Emergencies

There are numerous things that are to be considered "rabbit emergencies," including:

- Injuries such as broken bones and wounds
- Ingestion of foreign objects

- Poisoning
- Head tilt or difficulty keeping balance
- Respiratory illnesses or distress
- GI stasis/bloat
- Any signs/symptoms of pain
- Paralysis,
- Bad falls
- Dental emergencies

Every one of these problems warrant an immediate visit to your rabbit's exotics vet. I will try to describe some first aid for you for some of these issues, but this is only so that you can quickly get your rabbit to his vet. However, each one of these problems is life threatening and will need medical care right away.

The first and most obvious one is an injury from an errant interaction with another animal or a child. Rabbits have hollow bones like birds, which makes them very vulnerable to breaking bones. Their skin is also quite fragile and can easily be torn, sometimes in large pieces. If a large piece of skin is hanging loose, do your best to hold it down in place and rush to the vet. You may need to hold your bunny in your lap, if he is too injured for a pet carrier.

If there is bleeding, firm pressure with a clean cloth or towel will help. Keep pressure on the wound until you reach the vet. This will most likely require two people, one to drive and one to handle the bunny. Time is of the essence in rabbit emergencies. Do not wait to go to the vet.

Another rabbit emergency is if he suddenly stops eating or pooping. You must check these two things every day to make sure your rabbit is healthy and normal. It should be a big red flag for you if either of these habits suddenly changes. Either of these symptoms in conjunction with lethargy or abnormal lack of energy should be a real cause for alarm. This should alert you to monitor him even more closely, and if your rabbit goes half a day without pooping and refuses his favorite treats or greens, then you must take him to the vet. A rabbit can die by going as few as 24 hours without eating, drinking water, or pooping. This condition is known as GI stasis and it is very serious. An experienced rabbit vet will have dealt with this problem many times.

This is Star when she was first brought in to the sheloter wounded from an animal attack. I still find it hard to look at these pictures.

In some cases, GI stasis indicates an even more severe underlying problem such as liver or cardiovascular disease. Sometimes, it is caused by another condition that is relatively easy to remedy, like a dental problem or respiratory infection. Good rabbit vets will have seen all of these issues multiple times and should have no problem discerning the difference between them all.

Another rabbit problem that mimics GI stasis is bloat. This is a buildup of gas in your rabbit's intestinal tract that can kill as quickly as stasis. This is due to toxins being released that actually cause cardiac failure rather quickly. Your rabbit's stomach will often look distended as if it were a blown-up balloon, hence the name "bloat." I am not going to try to help you diagnose the difference between GI stasis and bloat, because both are dire and often fatal. If you even suspect either of these conditions, your rabbit needs to get to his vet ASAP.

One final emergency that often goes unnoticed until it is too late is your bunny chewing and swallowing something harmful. It is not good for him to swallow plastic or foils because those materials cannot be digested. Rabbits chew things into very small pieces and their throat is not very large, so they usually cannot swallow large pieces of indigestible stuff. The problem usually arises when they swallow a large amount of these things or the thing that they eat is toxic to them. Also remember that rabbits are unable to vomit, so anything they swallow cannot be regurgitated and must go through the entire digestive tract.

Star after her first surgery to remove her infected eye.

This is why bunny-proofing is so crucial, along with supervision at all times when your rabbit is outside the safety of his usual area. Bunny-proofing is also a lot of preparation, so I think the key to handling and weathering rabbit emergencies is being as prepared and proactive as possible for whatever might happen. If you assume the worst and prepare for it, then you will always be one step ahead of the game should a crisis situation arise.

Giving Medications To Your Bunny

Once you have seen the vet and he or she sends you home with your rabbit's prescriptions, you will need to know how to administer them to your bun. Always have the staff at your bunny's vet demonstrate how to give every single medicine prescribed before you leave the office. Otherwise, you are going to get home and have questions that cannot be easily answered. Still, do not hesitate to call your vet back with your questions, because it's always better to ask a "stupid" question than to make a terrible mistake.

If you are required to give your rabbit oral medication, ask your vet to put some sweet flavoring into it to make giving it to your rabbit easier. Over the years, I have been to many rabbit vets, and the good ones will put fruit-flavored syrup into medicines such as Baytril and Medicam, which inherently have terrible tastes. The fruit flavoring definitely makes it more palatable to the patient and your job as "nurse" much easier. If your vet does not have a syrup flavoring for your medicine, then you should ask him or her to please start carrying it, because adding it to the medication makes your job of administering it so much easier. In larger cities, you can also have the prescription filled at special "compounding" pharmacies—your vet can call the medicine into one for you—that always have these fruit-flavored syrups on hand. Note that compounding pharmacies are significantly more expensive, but the additional cost might be worth it to you.

Giving oral medication is a little tricky and best done on a tabletop so the bunny cannot scamper away. I like to put a towel down so that he does not slip around on the smooth, slick surface, making him more comfortable.

Prepare the dose(s) beforehand and, once your bunny is in place, hold him with his rear end facing you. Cradle him while putting the syringe to his mouth. If the medicine has been flavored, most rabbits will lap it up as you slowly push the plunger on the syringe. Be careful to measure the correct amount of medicine and give it the exact number of times per day that is recommended. This is important.

If your rabbit does not take the medicine willingly, you will need to hold him steady while you put the syringe into his mouth. If he resists, then work the syringe around to the side of his mouth, between his cheek and teeth, and slowly feed it to him. Do not give it to him too fast or he can inhale (aspirate) the medication into his lungs and choke. Give your bunny time to swallow it by going slowly. If your rabbit is spitting out the medicine, then you need to confer with your vet to determine a better way to give it. If he is spitting it out, then you do not know how much he is really getting during your attempts.

Sometimes your vet will ask you to give your bunny subcutaneous fluids, which is basically an injection of water with some minerals in it that you inject under your rabbit's skin with a needle. This is to give him the much-needed fluids directly into his system, bypassing his stomach.

It may sound and look like a scary procedure, but it is no more difficult than syringing his medicine into his mouth. Ask your vet to demonstrate how to do it; the hardest part of the whole thing is that you may need a third hand to steady your bunny while holding his skin up to put in the needle. It does not hurt the bunny if the needle is sharp and fresh. You can use these needles several times before they become dull.

Another option for getting meds into your bunny is to take him to his vet's office for each dose of medication, especially if it involves subcutaneous fluids or other kinds of shots and you're uncomfortable giving them. While this may be time consuming and involve a lot of driving, it might be worth it to you. That way, your bunny is home with you, but his medicine is being professionally delivered. Many vets will not charge for this, but be sure to check with yours first if you elect to take this route.

In the worst cases, it is sometimes better to have your rabbit just stay at his vet's office so that the medications can be closely monitored and professionally given. This is expensive, and you probably want to give it several tries yourself before you use this option as a last resort. Your rabbit would much rather be with you while he is sick, instead of in some strange doctor's office.

Never give your rabbit medicine that is for another animal and/or is not prescribed by your rabbit's vet. Many drugs that are safe for dogs and cats will kill your rabbit.

Putting a towel down when feeding your sick rabbit Critical Care® helps a lot, because it's messy.

Another very common thing you may be asked to give your rabbit if he has GI stasis is a liquid food called Critical Care®. It is basically rabbit pellets dissolved in water. It looks like green gruel, and most rabbits are not fond of it. Follow my previous instructions on how to syringe medication into your rabbit's mouth.

When feeding Critical Care®, I find holding the bunny still to administer the syringes full of the liquid food is the hardest part. If you have someone who can help hold your rabbit on the towel-covered tabletop, it makes it a lot easier. You will especially need a towel in place to catch the drops of food that your rabbit spits out or that do not make it into his mouth. It can be a messy process, but it can be a lifesaving procedure when your rabbit is sick. You will likely be told by your vet to do this several times a day. Following his or her instructions to the letter is very important, because this is usually the only thing that will help keep your rabbit's digestive system functioning. Once it completely shuts down, it is very hard to get it restarted again.

Never skip or forget medications and treatments that have been prescribed. If you have to work late or cannot be there to give them to your rabbit when they need to be, then arrangements must be made for someone to do it for you. When you are giving these treatments to your rabbit, it is because his life is in danger. Failure to follow your veterinarian's recommendations can have very bad—even fatal— consequences.

Never use cedar or pine shavings in your rabbit's litter box. They can cause liver disease in your bunny. Use paper pulp products or just newspaper with lots of fresh hay on top.

Do not be afraid to call your vet and ask for advice or assistance. Better to ask what you may think is a dumb question and maybe learn something than to just let it go. You are your rabbit's lifeline in these situations, and he is counting on you to take care of him.

Toxic To Your Rabbit!

In this section are the things that I know to be poisonous or toxic to your rabbit. Should your rabbit ingest or come in contact with any of these things, it will almost always qualify as an emergency, and you should take your bunny to the vet immediately for treatment.

There are literally thousands of products, plants, and substances that are harmful to your rabbit, due to his sensitivity to them. The ones I am going to mention here are the most common ones; this list is by no means complete.

Wood Shavings and Cat Litter

First, I want to advise you to never use pine or cedar shavings in your rabbit's litter box. I have seen big bags of pine shavings at our local pet stores with pictures of rabbits on the front. This should be criminal, in my opinion, because a rabbit who has prolonged exposure to these types of shavings can have sudden liver failure, causing death. Let me say this again: [*Never use these products anywhere near your rabbit.*] Aspen shavings are OK to use; just be sure that they are not mixed with pine or cedar.

The same thing goes for cat litter. Cat litter will kill your rabbit when he inhales the small particles, which are usually some kind of clay. These clay particles will build up in your rabbit's lungs and cause respiratory failure. [*Never use any type of cat litter, clumping or non-clumping, around your rabbit.*]

Due to rabbit anatomy and the way their noses are so close to the ground, they naturally inhale a lot of stuff from their litter boxes and areas they hop in. Rabbits also have very sensitive respiratory systems. This is why pesticides and chemicals, especially aerosols and sprays, are dangerous for them and should never be used in an area that your rabbit will visit. These poisons are designed to stick around a long time in order to be considered effective. Even the leftover residue from these products that lingers days—sometimes months—after application is dangerous to your bunny when he's exposed to it.

Pesticides and Mousetraps

Many of us live in areas where ants and other bugs can be an issue inside the house. You must refrain from applying bug killers or any kind of poison in an area near your rabbit. I suggest to people that a regimen of keeping the kitchen clean (no dirty dishes in the sink), keeping anything sugary sealed and in the refrigerator, removing trash to the outside bin as soon as possible, and only applying insecticide outside the perimeter of the house to prevent the little critters from getting in are the best courses of action. I have heard of some people using sprays up high in areas that their rabbits cannot reach, but never down on the ground level. I personally do not use any insecticides indoors and prefer instead the methods I described above.

When using mousetraps or commercial products for pests, never allow them to be where your rabbit can get close to them. This is a much more common problem than you might imagine, and I do not have to tell you what can happen. Also take caution when storing these items so that a mischievous rabbit cannot crawl into a cabinet and become exposed to them; this should be part of everyone's bunny-proofing of their homes.

Holiday Hazards

During the holiday season, a lot of decorations and objects that are not normally in your home will be displayed, especially at Christmas. Holiday tinsel and decorations with plastic parts that fall onto the floor can become curiosities for your bunny. Chewing on them is almost irresistible. If plastic or metal tinsel is swallowed, your rabbit could end up with a serious intestinal blockage that requires surgery to correct and from which the survival rate is not very good.

Wound care after surgery is very important, and you can't skip any of your rabbit's prescribed medications.

Extra bunny-proofing is necessary during the holidays: Keep your bunny from chewing on or eating holiday wrapping paper, which often has special coatings or is made of foil or cellophane, because it is undigestible. Ribbons and bows are also dangerous, as they are not only unable to be digested, but present a choking hazard (remember, rabbits don't have a "reverse gear" and can't vomit like cats). Don't allow your bunny to chew on your live Christmas tree or drink the water in the tree stand—both are toxic to him—and your artificial Christmas tree, which is made of undigestible fibers, fabric, and metal, is also a danger.

Many people also enjoy decorating for other holidays during the year, such as Halloween and Easter. Be sure to keep all decorations out of the reach of your bunny. Always keep in mind that he's nothing more than a long-eared, curious three-year-old who hops, and those jack o' lanterns, faux spiderwebs, candy bars, and plastic eggs you've put out are things to be investigated . . . and gnawed. You don't want to end up with a thousand-dollar emergency vet bill because your bunny ate a 99-cent plastic spider that got stuck in his throat, or have him pass away because he gobbled a chocolate bunny on Easter morning while you weren't looking.

Medications

The reason rabbits are so frequently used as lab animals is because they are hyper-sensitive to so many things. Medicines meant for cats or dogs cannot be given to rabbits without dire consequences, and antibiotics can be particularly deadly. There are only a few specific antibiotics

Dony was a rabbit who came to the shelter crippled, probably caused by someone carelessly stepping on his little foot.

that can safely be given to rabbits. Never give an antibiotic to your rabbit unless it has been prescribed by a veterinarian expressly for him.

Most antibiotics—even those regularly given to other kinds of animals—will start a downward spiral that will kill your rabbit in just a few days. I have heard some terribly sad stories about rabbits who got just a little bit of the wrong antibiotic and then there was nothing that could be done to save them afterward.

Let me say it again: [*Never give your bunny any medicine—especially antibiotics—unless prescribed by your rabbit's doctor.*]

Another medication that you absolutely cannot use on your rabbit is the anti-flea treatment Frontline®. Frontline® is highly toxic to your rabbit, causing fatal seizures, and he may not survive even a single application of this deadly medicine. I cannot stress this enough. Should your bunny need treatment with a topical anti-flea medicine, the only ones approved for use on rabbits by exotics veterinarians at this time are Advantage II for Cats® ("under 9 pounds" version) and Revolution®. It is imperative that you consult your bunny's vet prior to using even these products, so that you can ensure they are safe to use, based upon your particular rabbit's health status. Again, not to be repetitive, but I feel I must repeat this for your bunny's safety: [*Never use Frontline® on your rabbit.*]

Be sure to separate your bunnies from each other when treating them with Advantage II® or Revolution® for 12 hours after treatment so that they don't lick the medication off each other. Gastrointestinal distress has been reported in rabbits who have ingested the medication.

Flea collars are also toxic to most rabbits, since the medication contained in them is designed for cats and dogs, as is the amount of medicine contained in the collars.

Chocolate

Theobromine, a component of chocolate, is a toxic compound. Rabbits have difficulty metabolizing it. Dark and semi-sweet chocolate have more of this substance than does milk chocolate. Often, rabbits can eat a small amount of chocolate and not suffer any ill effects. The toxicity has to do with the amount of it that they eat in relation to their size and how much theobromine is present.

A tiny piece that is accidentally eaten should not hurt them, but the fat and sugar can instigate a bout of stasis or bloat by changing the flora inside their gut. For this reason alone, chocolate should never be given to rabbits. If your bunny ingests anything that he should not eat, it is best to keep a close eye on him and take him to the vet immediately if he stops eating or pooping for more than a couple hours, especially if he shows any signs of discomfort or pain.

Cocoa mulch is thought to be poisonous to rabbits because it is derived from cocoa bean hulls, so it is a good idea to not allow your rabbit to eat or chew on this stuff.

Plants and Flowers

Many household and landscaping plants and flowers are toxic to humans, dogs, cats and rabbits. Rather than try to separate all the toxic ones from the non-toxic ones, it is always a good idea to make all of your houseplants inaccessible to your buns. Even non-toxic plants can cause gastrointestinal distress in your rabbit.

One of the biggest problems for rabbits is that, after 500 years of domestication, they have lost their ability to discern good plants from bad ones like wild rabbits can. A domestic rabbit will readily eat a very poisonous plant in your house or yard simply because he doesn't know any better. Never assume that your rabbit knows the difference and will only eat what is safe for him; unfortunately, the exact opposite is true.

You can automatically assume that any plant that's toxic to humans or other pets is also toxic to your bunny. Here is a partial list of plants and flowers that are poisonous to your bunny and that should be kept completely away from him.

- Agave
- Almond
- Aloe
- Andromeda
- Anemone
- American Elder
- Apple seeds
- Arrowgrass
- Asian Lilly
- Asparagus Fern
- Azalea
- Begonia
- Bird of Paradise
- Black Locust
- Black-eyed Susan
- Boxwood
- Buttercup
- Calla Lily
- Castor bean
- Common milkweed
- Crown of Thorns
- Cyclamen
- Daffodil
- Daphne
- Delphinium
- Dumbcane (Dieffenbachia)
- Eggplant leaves
- Elderberry berries
- Elephant Ear
- Foxglove
- Geranium
- Holly berries
- Hyacinth
- Hydrangea
- Iris
- Ivy berries

- Jack-in-the-Pulpit
- Jimson weed
- Kelanchoe
- Lantana
- Larkspur
- Lily-of-the-Valley
- Lupine
- Mistletoe berries
- Morning Glory seeds
- Mountain laurel
- Narcissus bulbs
- Nightshade
- Oleander
- Oriental bittersweet
- Philodendron
- Poison Hemlock
- Poison Ivy
- Poison Oak
- Poison Sumac
- Potato
- Ranunculus
- Rhododendron
- Rhubarb
- Sago Palm
- Sweet Pea seeds
- Sweet Potato
- Skunk Cabbage
- Toadstools and mushrooms
- Tobacco leaves
- Tomato leaves
- Tulip bulbs
- Wisteria
- Yew

Clearly, this is a small list and by no means complete. You can find much more comprehensive lists by searching online, but I recommend that, unless you specifically know a plant is safe, it should never be kept near an area your bunny can get to. It is best to not even put them anywhere near your rabbit's space, because if a leaf or berry falls off the plant, he can ingest it before you can pick it up. As for your yard, don't let your bunny play near any plants or flowers with which you are unfamiliar or unsure of their toxicity to him.

Heat and Your Bunny

What many people do not realize is that heat can quickly be fatal for a rabbit, because a rabbit does not have the ability to perspire or regulate his body temperature in any way. A rabbit's natural internal body temperature is higher than a human's to begin with—around 100-103° F being normal for most.

Since a bunny's fluffy, dense fur is designed to retain heat during cold weather, obviously rabbits can tolerate more extreme cold temperatures than hot ones. And because heat cannot easily escape his body, combined with his naturally high internal temperature, once air temperatures reach about 80° F or more, it's time to take steps to help your rabbit stay cool and comfortable.

There are several ways to provide your bunny with ways to keep cool. The first is frozen water bottles: Simply fill a plastic bottle most of the way with water, freeze it, and then put it in your rabbit's X-pen or condo for him to lie against. I recommend putting a towel underneath the ice bottles, since the condensation will leave large puddles underneath as they melt. Just watch out that your bun does not shred the towel that you use, if he is that kind of bunny. Use carpet-sample squares under the bottles instead if he is one who likes to shred towels. And, do not underestimate your rabbit's intelligence; give him a chance to learn the benefits of something like an ice bottle. Just because he does not use it the first time or two, he'll figure it out soon enough.

A one-square-foot piece of tile is also nice and cool for your bunny to lie on. Place one or two in his area for him to stretch out on; thin pieces of stone or marble are also OK, but the cheapest tiles will work just as well. Some people refrigerate them before giving them to their bunnies to make them extra cold, but they are naturally cool to the touch without that.

It also helps to have floor fans for your bunny. He probably won't like the fans blowing directly on him, but circulating the air in his area will help keep him cooler. If the temperature inside your house is getting higher than 80° F, then you may want to consider some kind of air conditioning for your bunny's sake. In a heat emergency, where the temperature in your home is over 90° F for a sustained period of time (more than an hour, such as in a power outage and/or if your air conditioning goes out), gently rub a cool, wet cloth on your bunny's ears. I have even dipped my buns completely into cool water, and the three or so hours it takes for them to dry also helps cool them down. Dipping them into water should not be done outside, since it can attract flies and insects to lay eggs on your bunny (read about "flystrike" in **Chapter 3: Why Rabbits Need To Live Indoors**).

Heat is not something to take lightly, and many of those poor rabbits who live in backyard hutches die every year in hot-weather conditions. You do not ever want this to happen to your companion rabbit and so you must consider his comfort every time it gets warm. Think of it like this: If it feels hot to you, imagine yourself wearing a full-length fur coat, hat, and boots *and* having a fever—that's how your bunny feels in hot weather.

Caring for Senior Rabbits

Larger rabbits over six years old and smaller buns over eight are considered senior rabbits. Just like in dog breeds, the larger buns tend to live a few years less than the smaller ones. As with senior humans, special care must be taken in regard to, and you must be more alert for, possible medical issues that can arise with older rabbits. Seniors buns will probably end up seeing a vet more often than younger ones because many health issues, especially chronic ones, tend to appear as they age.

Well-kept rabbits can live ten to twelve years, but in order to achieve their full lifespans you must always be vigilant about their diets. Any sudden change in eating habits, weight, poops in their litter boxes, and/or general well-being must always be given attention. If your older bun starts losing weight, you may need to supply him with some alfalfa or other foods that will help him maintain his optimal weight. You should only do this on the advice of your rabbit's vet, though.

A frozen water bottle keeps bunnies cool on hot days.

Rabbits who are about to die can suddenly become anorexic and stop eating entirely. It may be due to pain from a tooth or intestinal problem, or it may be because they are so weak or sick that they do not feel like taking in any food. I hear it all the time from bunny parents that their rabbits just stopped eating and then quickly died.

If your rabbit suddenly stops eating for even twelve hours, that qualifies as an emergency. Senior rabbits have several common problems for which medical attention is appropriate. The top three are dental issues, cardiovascular issues, and gastrointestinal issues, followed by bladder and respiratory problems.

This is why senior buns should start seeing their vets at least once a year: An annual checkup will help catch any chronic or developing issues before they lead to other, more serious problems.

Older rabbits are usually less active and will sleep more. This is normal in many species. You must allow for that and give your senior rabbit more time to relax unstressed. Some senior rabbits do not do very well around boisterous kids and very playful pet dogs or cats. They often just do not have the energy to cope with them like they did when they were younger. Teaching your kids and pets to be respectful of your rabbit is even more important if your bunny is a senior citizen.

As you can see, Star has fully recovered from all her surgeries and is now a happy, well-adjusted bun.

With an observant bunny parent, proper feeding, and a comfortable environment, indoor rabbits are living longer and longer all the time. Exotics veterinary care has become dramatically better in the past decade, so rabbits are now receiving much-improved medical care, prolonging their lives—and even saving them— from diseases such as cancer. I have met rabbits who are almost 15 years old, which just a few years ago was unheard of. If you love your pets like I do, you will want them to spend as much time with you as possible, so this is wonderful news.

Pet Insurance

Providing veterinary care for your house rabbit can quickly get expensive, as I've said

before. I think there is nothing worse—and less excusable—than putting your bunny to sleep because you cannot afford the $2000+ veterinary bill it would cost to save your rabbit's life.

Until recently, there were no options for a person who did not have a credit card or savings account to tap into. In Europe, there have been pet-health insurance companies for years and many cater to the large population of people who have pet rabbits.

At the time of this writing, there is only one company in the US that is providing health insurance for exotic animals including rabbits. I have researched their policies and find that they are a great solution for those on whom a large vet bill would be a hardship.

It works like this: After you apply for and purchase one of these insurance policy plans, you pay a monthly premium. If you incur a covered vet bill, you are reimbursed a percentage of the bill. Some things are not covered, such as pre-existing conditions or elective procedures, so it is important to read each plan's coverage and limits carefully before you sign up.

I have heard very good things from the people who have used one of these plans. They said that they got reimbursements promptly, as long as it was for things that their particular policies covered. The insurance has allowed them to afford huge vet bills that would have been impossible without it.

These insurance plans run between $150-400 a year, and I recommend not getting the cheapest policy. The more comprehensive the plan, the more things that are covered, and so the extra $200 in premium costs a year could be the difference between a $2200 procedure being covered or not. Just make sure you know what you are signing up for and carefully read the exemptions and non-covered procedures in the policy. This way you will clearly understand what the plan you've selected does—and does not—cover.

A large percentage of vet procedures will be covered on most policies, so this could be the answer for a person who does not have the means to absorb a $1000 vet bill and wants to protect his or her pet by providing the best medical care possible. This is especially true if you have multiple pets or rabbits, since there is a discount for carrying "multi-pet" policies.

I hope that other companies, who currently only cover dogs and cats, see that rabbit lovers want (and need) pet-insurance policies too and will start offering them. This is important, so that there is competition and better coverage options for us rabbit lovers. I personally know how quickly the vet bills can mount up when your rabbit is sick. If you are like me, you will want to do everything possible to help your bunny, but that is hard when you know the bill is running into the thousands of dollars.

Having a pet-health insurance policy gives you peace of mind during a stressful time, when money should not be your main concern. Of course, this requires planning ahead and not waiting until the last minute. The time to think about and act on this is when your rabbit does not need healthcare, not when it is a matter of life and death, because then it will be too late.

Another option is a pet-care line of credit available from several companies. Your vet should have the information about at least one for you to look over. These work like credit cards and charge interest for loaning you the money for emergency vet services. I suggest if you need something like this to apply before you actually need it so that there is no chance of your credit being turned down when you need it the most.

These are just a couple of ways of dealing with the expense of your rabbit's veterinary care if you do not have the financial resources to afford some necessary but expensive care.

Avoid letting your rabbit become overweight for optimal health, especially for Rex rabbits like Mr. Bunners.

Another bunny who is overweight.

Summary

- For many common bunny health problems, the only appropriate thing to do is to take your bun to the vet.

- The best rule of thumb is, if you suspect a problem in any way, it is time to visit your vet.

- It is difficult to tell if your rabbit is sick or not feeling well.

- Part of having a companion pet is making sure that, if he needs medical attention, he immediately gets it.

- Do your homework beforehand to see which exotics veterinarian is the best for you and your bunny.

- You can check out your local vets by asking other rabbit people.

- I believe that the more experience a vet has with bunnies, the better off you will be.

- Good rabbit veterinary specialists suggest a wellness check while your rabbit is healthy.

- A good, trusting relationship with your rabbit's vet is also important to have.

- Rabbit-savvy vets are lifesavers for many common conditions.

- One of the most common rabbit ailments is gastrointestinal (GI) stasis, or bloat (gas).

- Finding no poops in your bunny's litter box is likely to be your first sign of GI stasis.

- If you suspect GI stasis or think that your rabbit is in pain, contact his vet and take him in immediately.

- One of the first signs of a dental problem is weepy eyes or a runny nose.

- For many common bunny health problems, the only appropriate thing to do is to take your bun to the vet.

- The best rule of thumb is, if you suspect a problem in any way, it is time to visit your vet.

- It is difficult to tell if your rabbit is sick or not feeling well.

- Part of having a companion pet is making sure that, if he needs medical attention, he immediately gets it.

- Do your homework beforehand to see which exotics veterinarian is the best for you and your bunny.

- You can check out your local vets by asking other rabbit people.

- I believe that the more experience a vet has with bunnies, the better off you will be.

- Good rabbit veterinary specialists suggest a wellness check while your rabbit is healthy.

- A good, trusting relationship with your rabbit's vet is also important to have.

- Rabbit-savvy vets are lifesavers for many common conditions.

- Two of the most common rabbit ailments are gastrointestinal (GI) stasis and bloat (gas).

- Finding no poops in your bunny's litter box is likely to be your first sign of GI stasis.

- If you suspect GI stasis or think that your rabbit is in pain, contact his vet and take him in immediately.

- One of the first signs of a dental problem is weepy eyes or a runny nose.

- A dental issue can sometimes be detected if your rabbit's eating habits suddenly change.

- A really common rabbit issue is obesity or being overweight, which can shorten his life by half.

- Another common rabbit malady is bladder sludge or stones.

- Head tilt, thought to be caused by a parasitic protozoa called Encephalitazoon cuniculi—E. cuniculi for short—is usually preceded by a stressful event.

- E. cuniculi can be fatal if immediate veterinary treatment is not administered.

- Rabbits have hollow bones like birds, which makes them very vulnerable to fractures.

- Rabbits' skin is also quite fragile and can easily be torn, sometimes in large pieces.

- You must check that your rabbit poops and eats every day to make sure he is healthy and normal.

- Bloat (gas buildup) can kill as quickly as GI stasis.

- An emergency that often goes unnoticed until it is too late is your bunny chewing and swallowing something harmful.

- Always have the staff at your bunny's vet demonstrate how to give every single medicine prescribed before you leave the office.

- Never skip or forget medications and treatments that have been prescribed.

- There are literally thousands of products, plants, and substances that are harmful to your rabbit.

- Never use pine or cedar shavings in your rabbit's litter box.

- Cat litter will kill your rabbit when he inhales the small particles.

- Rabbits also have very sensitive respiratory systems.

- You must refrain from applying bug killers or any kind of poison in an area near your rabbit.

- Mousetraps or commercial products for pest control should never be allowed where your rabbit can get close to them.

- Extra bunny-proofing is necessary during holidays.

- Many medicines meant for cats or dogs cannot be given to rabbits without fatal consequences.

- Never give your bunny any medicine—especially antibiotics—unless prescribed by your rabbit's doctor.

- Frontline® is highly toxic to your rabbit, causing fatal seizures.

- Theobromine, a compound found in chocolate, is toxic to rabbits.

- Many household and landscaping plants and flowers are toxic to humans, rabbits, and other pets.

- A domestic rabbit will readily eat a very poisonous plant in your house or yard simply because he does not know any better.

- Heat is not something to take lightly, because heat can be fatal for a rabbit.

- Seniors buns will probably end up seeing their vets more often than younger ones do.

- Any sudden change in eating habits, weight, poops in their litter boxes, and/or general well-being must always be given attention.

- If your rabbit suddenly stops eating for even twelve hours, that qualifies as an emergency.

- I suggest that senior buns start seeing their vets at least once a year

- Having a pet-health insurance policy can help give you peace of mind during a stressful time.

- Pet-care lines of credit are available from several companies.

Three Mini-lop brothers riding together
in their stroller.

Chapter 20:
Traveling with Your Rabbit

When going on vacation or to visit family in another town, you may decide to travel with your rabbit. This is something that can be done, if a little planning is done and a slower pace is taken. Flying with a rabbit is basically out of the question, since at the time I am writing this, there are only two airlines that will even consider allowing a rabbit on board an aircraft, and one of those is considering banning them.

Travel with a bunny is extremely stressful for you and for him, especially air travel, so unless you absolutely have to, I would strongly recommend that you not attempt flying with your pet. A long car ride is possible, but you will probably not cover nearly as many miles daily as you would without your bunny along.

Rabbits usually will not eat or drink while in a moving car. Some will not even pee or poop. We all know how harmful it is for them to go any period of time without doing those things (see the "Rabbit Emergencies" section of **Chapter 19**). When traveling long distances with your bunny, you will need to stop every couple of hours to let your bunny have a chance to eat some hay and drink some water. A little hopping in an X-pen would also be advisable, to stimulate his intestines so that he can poop a bit, too.

If you cannot take the extra time and effort to do this for your rabbit, then it is probably better if you board your rabbit at a bunny bed-and-breakfast for the time you are gone. Travel is very stressful for your pet, so a holiday at a rabbit hotel may make him a lot happier than 10 or 20 hours in the car. Check your local House Rabbit

Society website or contact to see what rabbit-sitting services are available in your area. Often, people who are real rabbit lovers make extra money on the side by babysitting other people's bunnies.

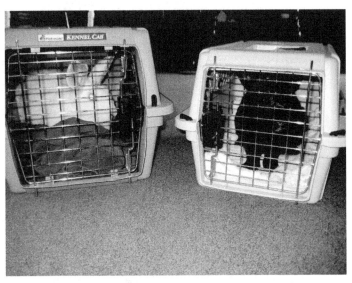

Before they were bonded, Ricky and Lucy rode in separate pet carriers for their car rides.

If you decide to take your bunny on a road trip, you will need to set up an area for him to be comfortable during the ride. It is too small and hot to ride for extended periods in a small pet carrier. They are good for short rides across town, but if you are planning on driving over an hour or so, then you may want to set up a nest-like area in the back seat for your bunny that includes his litter box and some hay to eat. You will want to create barriers inside your car so that he cannot suddenly hop up into the front seat and cause you to become distracted or have an accident.

You will need to carry an X-pen to set up at rest areas when you stop to let your bunny stretch his legs. Since your bunny will almost never drink water while moving, be sure to give him some cold, fresh water. Give him 20-30 minutes to move around and do his business before continuing on the road. This will dramatically slow your travel time, but it makes it much safer for your rabbit.

When taking your bunny on a trip, you run a real risk of him getting sick from the travel and stress. If your rabbit does not eat or poop for half a day or more, he could enter into a GI stasis condition, which would require immediate vet attention. This is why you should investigate and have available the contact info for a rabbit vet in the area you are going, just in case.

Groucho is looking out of the window on a train trip.

I cannot impress upon you enough that you run a definite risk of stressing your rabbit into a stasis situation. Traveling with your bunny must not be undertaken lightly. Having your bunny get

sick in a strange town without the support of your usual vet would be a scary situation.

In order to prepare for a trip, you will need to acclimate your rabbit to car rides. Start out with short 20-30 minute trips and progress up to rides that last over an hour. You do not want your bunny in a panic while you are speeding at 70 m.p.h. down the highway. Some rabbits take to car rides better than others, and you will have to determine if you think your bun could tolerate an extensive trip.

Part of preparing for a road trip with your rabbit is doing some homework and finding qualified rabbit vets in the places you will be going. Hopefully, you will not need them, but if you should, you want to have the information available.

I have heard about some bunnies who "travel in style" in a motor home or RV. This also solves the complicated problem of where you are going to sleep on your trip, since many motels and hotels will not allow bunnies in their rooms. Nothing is more embarrassing than getting caught sneaking a pet carrier into a room that does not allow pets or, worse, having your bunny chew a big hole in their carpeting that you must now explain (or ending up with a big, surprise charge on your credit card later, after the damage is discovered). It is always best to call the hotel directly and ask them point blank if they will allow your rabbit to stay there. Better to know in advance than to be driving around after a long day on the road looking for a sympathetic motel operator.

RV travel makes a lot of sense with rabbits, but you must be very careful to not allow them to escape. I know of some bunnies who go on vacation every summer with their families in an RV and they love it.

X-pens are used inside the RV to create safe spaces and barriers, and the rabbits seem to do very well traveling this way. Still, you must be very careful not to leave your rabbits closed up inside during the day when it is hot. Temperatures can easily climb above what is tolerable for a bunny. The same thing goes for leaving your rabbit inside of your car, especially during summer months. Temperatures in a closed car—even with the windows cracked—can reach over 140° F in a matter of minutes on a hot summer day. This can quickly be fatal to a rabbit, so extreme caution must be used to not let your rabbit sit alone inside a closed vehicle during the heat. Take him in his carrier inside with you, even if you're just "running inside for a second."

My rabbits like to travel inside a large pet carrier during car rides. I find it makes it a lot more comfortable for them if I put a big carpet-sample square inside to give them something to grip with their toes and prevent them from slipping and sliding around inside the carrier when I make turns or stop the car; otherwise, they can have trouble remaining safe and secure inside.

China is attached to her stroller with a leash in case she suddenly decides to hop out.

Summary

- **Traveling with your rabbit is something that can be done, if a little planning is done and a slower pace is taken.**

- **Traveling with a bunny is extremely stressful for you and for him.**

- **Rabbits usually will not eat or drink while in a moving car; some will not even pee or poop.**

- **A holiday at a rabbit hotel may make him a lot happier than 10 or 20 hours in the car.**

- **You will need to set up an area in your vehicle for him to be comfortable during the ride.**

- **You will need to carry an X-pen to set up at rest areas when you stop.**

- **Traveling with your bunny must not be undertaken lightly.**

- **During travel, you run a definite risk of stressing your rabbit into a stasis situation.**

- **To prepare for a trip, you will need to acclimate your rabbit to car rides.**

- **Some bunnies "travel in style" in a motor home or RV.**

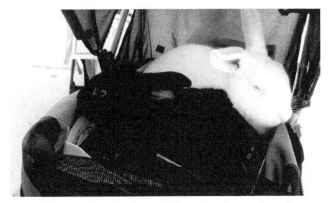

Ricky and Lucy in their stroller, going for a train ride.

171

When out and about with your bunny, be sure to provide shade because rabbits do not tolerate direct sun very well. Do not forget your ice-water bottle!

A group of bunny lovers meet each month at the beach. We call ourselves the "Beach Bunnies."

Chapter 21:
Coping with the Loss of a Bunny

Anyone who has a house rabbit will have to deal with this issue at some time or another. I know that, personally, it gets harder for me each time one of my bunnies passes away because I have become so much closer to my pet rabbits over the years.

When you live with a bunny for ten or more years and have developed a strong bond with him, losing him can be devastating. In my family, we have cried and grieved pretty hard over each one, especially the last couple we had. I think what makes it the most difficult is that, often, rabbits will get sick and pass away very suddenly—they're fine, hopping around and acting totally normal one day, and then very sick and at the vet the next . . . and then gone.

Since so many rabbit ailments can become deadly within just a day or two, I feel these are the losses that are hardest to take, since you cannot prepare yourself for them. When your bunny is sick for a long time and you are in and out of the vet's office, you can mentally begin to prepare yourself for the possibility of your bunny dying.

It is truly a terribly sad day when your rabbit leaves this world, and many people grieve just as much over the death of a pet as they do over the loss of a dear friend or family member. This is normal; we tend to bond very closely with our pets, and I have been inconsolable over losing a bunny in the past.

There is no escaping the grieving process, but I have found a couple of things that have helped me through the grieving process. After a short time, I found that, by volunteering at a local shelter or rescue, I could transfer my bereavement into productive, positive work helping other bunnies.

The tendency for many people is to go out and get another bunny right away. I have found this to be a very good thing to do for me. For several months after losing a rabbit, I usually do not feel like I am ready for another one, but I have also found that, the sooner I push myself through this feeling and adopt another rabbit, I can actually start the healing process and feel better more quickly.

A week after this photo was taken, Benjamin Bunny suddenly passed away.

Helping other rabbits at a shelter is a great way to find a new rabbit to adopt. By working and interacting with many bunnies at a rescue or shelter, you can easily find one (or more!) who you feel will be a good match for your family. I did this before adopting my current bonded pair, Ricky and Lucy. I waited three months before actually adopting them, but the funny thing is that I knew the first day I met them, they were the ones I had connected with and wanted. Funny how that worked out.

Giving love and time to shelter bunnies really does go a long way to healing your sorrow over losing your own rabbit, and every shelter needs committed rabbit people to not only work with the rabbits, but to help teach the public and even the shelter staff about bunnies. That was probably the most important thing I did, working at the shelters. Just because it's a shelter does not mean that the staff there knows very much about proper rabbit care, and it will do your heart a lot of good to make such a big difference in so many rabbits' lives.

The one thing I want to state very emphatically is that, whatever you do, please do not go out and *buy* a new rabbit. Adopting rabbits is so important because there are thousands and thousands of beautiful, sweet rabbits languishing in shelters and rescues all across this country, just waiting for a loving home. Every time someone purchases a bunny instead of adopting one, it not only takes a home away from a bunny in a shelter who is desperately waiting for one, it supports breeders—some of whom are unethical in their breeding methods, such as the one who has created such a problem in my local area with malocclusions in lops due to her inappropriate breeding—who make a living off of habitually and constantly producing unneeded rabbits for the pet population.

Summary

- **When you live with a bunny for ten or more years and have developed a strong bond with him, losing him can be devastating.**

- **Many people grieve just as much over the death of a pet as they do over the loss of a dear friend or family member.**

- **I found that, by volunteering at a local shelter or rescue, I could transfer my bereavement into productive, positive work helping other bunnies.**

- **The tendency for many people is to go out and get another bunny right away.**

- **Helping other rabbits at a shelter is a great way to find a new rabbit to adopt.**

- **Giving love and time to shelter bunnies really does go a long way to healing your sorrow over losing your own rabbit.**

- **Do not go out and *buy* a new rabbit.**

Our sudden loss of Pammy was extremely hard to take. It is what got me to start volunteering at the shelter and for the House Rabbit Society.

Chapter 22:
Volunteering To Help Rabbits

I hope that, after reading this book, some of you will want to join other rabbit devotees in helping homeless bunnies and/or educating the public about house rabbits. In just the county in which Denise and I live alone, there are hundreds of rabbits in the shelters. While the numbers vary a bit by the season, almost every shelter that has bunnies finds itself with several dozen or more rabbits in its care by summer each year—many of them abandoned after having been Easter gifts.

If you want to make a difference for house rabbits, there are many things that you can do, from spreading the knowledge that you've learned in this book (if you've found it helpful, please buy a copy for someone else, and ask them to do the same, and so on, and so on), to becoming a member of your local House Rabbit Society, to volunteering at your local animal shelter or Humane Society. Just donating a small amount of money—even an amount as little as $5 a month—can help tremendously, especially for local House Rabbit Society chapters, and it's usually tax deductible. Helping out as a volunteer at a shelter or Humane Society a few hours one day a week does so much good and affects so many lives. You can see that it doesn't require a lot of time or effort to make a positive difference for rabbits.

Volunteering at Shelters, Rescues, and Humane Societies

When it comes to rabbits, some shelters just do not "get it," and so you may end up being a voice for the bunnies when working there. Do not let that hold you back: Someone has to step up to the plate and try to educate not only the public,

but sometimes even the shelters themselves, who often will put all of their resources toward cats and dogs. The lagomorphs are frequently afterthoughts who get the smallest piece of the pie, so you may find yourself being the proverbial "squeaky wheel" attempting to get more oil for the buns at your shelter or Humane Society.

If you do elect to volunteer at a shelter, keeping a good rapport with the organization's management team can go a long way when you need to make a plea for the cause of the buns there. I often try to put the situation in a different light by gently asking, "What if it were a cat or a dog?" This may help the administrators to better understand your point of view.

This is how rabbits typically live at a shelter.

Volunteering at a shelter or rescue is one of the hardest jobs you will ever fall in love with. I always go through a sort of "separation anxiety" with each rabbit who gets adopted, but in the end, I am overjoyed that a bunny finally gets a loving "fur-ever home."

When my wife and I used to volunteer at our local shelter, we would bring home the job and spend all evening talking about the situations that arose that day while we were working. We came to a point where everything, even our conversations with other people, revolved around our shelter work. This became tiresome and too much for most people. I recommend having some other hobbies, and taking time out to do some things each week that have nothing to do with shelter work or rabbits. It will help keep your perspective in the long run, as well as help you avoid what's known as "compassion fatigue," or "burnout," which is quite common among truly dedicated volunteers. Burnout comes from the constantly high level of empathy and the emotional attachment volunteers often have for bunnies who spend a long time at a shelter or Humane Society.

Until our local House Rabbit Society chapter bought this shed, the bunnies at this shelter lived outside.

Some people find that, because of the corporate-like structure of some shelters and Humane Societies and their management/administrations, those organizations are not the ideal places that they want to donate their time, energy, or money. These folks will often elect instead to volunteer with private rescue groups, where they feel that they have more control over

the total welfare and final adoption of a bunny. You can look online to locate organizations of this nature in your area, or check out the national House Rabbit Society's website (www.rabbits.org) to find ones near you.

Volunteering for Your Local House Rabbit Society Chapter

A lot of rabbit lovers enjoy volunteering for their local House Rabbit Society (HRS) chapters; you can find yours by visiting HRS's website, where there is a listing by state of all local chapters that have been sanctioned.

If you discover that there is not a local House Rabbit Society chapter in your area, there's also information available on the HRS website about how to start one. It only takes a few people to start making a huge difference in a local community.

When you volunteer for your local HRS chapter, there is a multitude of ways you can help, depending upon your particular skill set and interests. Contact your local chapter and ask how you can help out—I can guarantee they won't turn you down. I credit my local House Rabbit Society chapter in San Diego with helping me start my long journey to becoming a rabbit teacher; it was through volunteering and handling hundreds of bunnies while working at the shelter that I got many of my hands-on rabbit experiences, and through attending San Diego House Rabbit Society classes given by rabbit experts, I really widened my knowledge base on rabbits. My local HRS chapter has been invaluable to me and to my rabbits.

Other Ways to Assist Rabbits

Adopting, loving, and learning about your first rabbit is just the beginning of your journey. Once you realize how special and unique each one is, you too may decide to become an advocate who educates people about what misunderstood creatures bunnies really are. You may just want to help out one day a week at a shelter, giving love to homeless bunnies or cleaning their cages. Or you might want to get involved with your local HRS chapter, furthering the cause of promoting the health and welfare of house rabbits. For each of us, the experience is personal and individualized, so whether you hear a calling to become a hands-on advocate or just a casual volunteer for rabbits everywhere, I want to thank you for any work that you do.

Star at an educational event for the HRS.

If you do not have the time or ability to help out at a shelter, rescue, or HRS chapter, of course a financial donation is another great way of helping the cause of rabbits. Every shelter, rescue, and HRS chapter is always in need of funding, and you can request that your donation be used in a certain way—most non-profit organizations will accommodate your wishes, and in almost all cases, your donations are tax deductible.

A Better Future for Bunnies

We have come a long way in the past 25 years for bunnies, but we still have an even longer way to go. Almost everyone is aware of what dog abuse is and, in many areas, it is no longer legal to tie a dog to a tree in the backyard and leave him there. But there are not so many protective laws for rabbits and in most states they are still considered livestock, which affords them no protection at all from abuse.

Hopefully, after thousands and then millions of people learn that the only appropriate and humane way to house and care for a pet rabbit is inside the home and not forgotten in a backyard hutch will the majority of pet rabbits start to live in better conditions. As a rabbit educator, I talk to thousands of people a year about their pet rabbits, and fully 80 percent—four out of five—are not keeping their rabbits in good living conditions. About the same percentage of bunnies are also doomed to a shortened lifespan by being fed an improper diet. Some of these people have had rabbits for decades and still they still don't know the proper way to care for them.

Educating the public is the only way we will ever change things for all rabbits.

These statistics do vary by different parts of the United States, and they are the worst in farm-oriented communities in the Midwest and South. With luck and enormous effort, perhaps someday these areas will think differently about how to treat rabbits, but let me tell you, those days are a long way off, considering where we stand today.

A couple of decades ago, virtually no rabbits lived indoors, and now about one in five of them does, so clearly we have made some progress in this area. Like I said at the beginning of this book, at one time I was guilty of doing all the wrong things with my own bunnies, so I never condemn or belittle a person for being unaware of the mistakes he or she is making. I feel that, if these people hear what they should be doing from enough reputable sources, then maybe they will decide to reevaluate the way they care for their pets and make positive changes.

Sadly, many people will never change, but some will. I am counting on the fact that, with a few more decades of education and work, an even a larger percentage of the rabbits out there will find themselves in happier, more comfortable living arrangements. It has been proven that these better conditions lead to the doubling of a rabbit's lifespan, so clearly there are benefits in the living-inside-the-house method of keeping rabbits.

Further, common sense would indicate that there must be something to these new ways of living with rabbits if the bunnies are living so much longer. On top of that, your rabbits are so much happier that way, too (witness a few big binkies from your bunny and you'll agree!). I invite you to help us lagomorph lovers spread the word and become a House Rabbit Society member and volunteer, and to consider volunteering at your local animal shelter or Humane Society (if they have rabbits). If your local shelter does not take in rabbits, then there is a task for you: Contact the director or president of the organization and find out why not.

Rabbits are the third most-popular—and the third most-euthanized—animal in the United States at shelters. If your community is not providing a way for stray or unwanted rabbits to be adopted out to new forever homes, then it should be. It only takes a few active voices to make a big difference. You can help change the rabbit world. We need ambitious, dedicated people who want to carry the house-rabbit banner. The world is waiting to hear from us, only they just don't know it yet.

If you don't have the time to volunteer, maybe you can donate money to help.

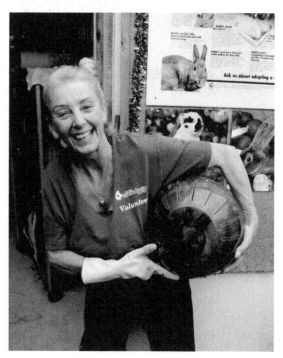

Volunteering to help rabbits is the hardest job you will ever love.

Summary

- You may want to join other rabbit devotees in helping homeless bunnies and/or educating the public about house rabbits.

- If you want to make a difference for house rabbits, there are many things that you can do.

- Volunteering at a shelter or rescue is one of the hardest jobs you will ever fall in love with.

- A lot of rabbit lovers enjoy volunteering for their local House Rabbit Society (HRS) chapters.

- When you volunteer for your local HRS chapter, there are a multitude of ways you can help.

- If you do not have the time or ability to help out at a shelter, rescue, or HRS chapter, of course a financial donation is another great way of helping the cause of rabbits.

- We have come a long way in the past 25 years for bunnies, but we still have an even longer way to go.

- A couple of decades ago, virtually no rabbits lived indoors, and now about one in five of them do.

- If your community is not providing a way for stray or unwanted rabbits to be adopted out to new forever homes, then it should be.

- We need ambitious, dedicated people who want to carry the house-rabbit banner to continue to improve the lives of rabbits everywhere.

- Rabbits rule!

Another HRS educational event at a pet store.

Resources

rabbit.org

This is the website for the national headquarters of the House Rabbit Society. This is a very useful link to locate an HRS chapter near your location. They also maintain a list of qualified rabbit (exotics) veterinarians for your area. For a more comprehensive vet list, use this site to find the HRS chapter website nearest you.

sandiegorabbits.org

This website belonging to the San Diego chapter is a nice example of a regional HRS chapter's web presence. Use the national HRS website (rabbit.org) to find your local chapter's site.

thebunnyguy.com

This is where to visit "The Bunny Guy" on the web. Tons of useful links, products, and latest information about house rabbits.

luckybunnyrabbitrescue.com

This is my favorite rescue and they desperately need your donations. They are a no-kill shelter for rabbits in the Riverside County area of Southern California, and are an affiliate of the San Diego House Rabbit Society.

myhouserabbit.com

Lots of great photos and ideas for rabbit abodes for your indoor bunny companion.

fuzzy-rabbit.com

This site has a very active forum about house rabbits. They also have some useful information on rabbit care and behavior.

http://homepage.mac.com/mattocks/morfz/rabrefs.html

The most comprehensive list of links to rabbit health and behavior webpages I have seen yet. While this information is extremely useful, please do not try to be the veterinarian for your rabbit if he is sick by trying to diagnose his problems yourself. Take him to see his vet, if you suspect that he is sick.

cramptonarts.com/rabbits/r_feedback.html

This site has good basic rabbit information including some good tips for bunny-proofing.

bunspace.com

This fun site is like Myspace for rabbits. There is a huge free component, but a membership will allow unlimited use of all the entertaining interesting features including hundreds of forums and message boards. Trade gifts and communicate with rabbit lovers all over the world.

Glossary

abode/condo: indoor house for your rabbit, preferably without a wire bottom

Angora: a long-haired breed of rabbit whose fur is used for creating soft yarn

backyard bunnies: rabbits who live outdoors in a hutch, or worse outdoors with no hutch at all

binky: crazy bunny dance that means your rabbit is happy; each rabbit has his own style

bladder sludge: calcium buildup in the bladder

bonded rabbits: two or more rabbits who live together and share their things

bonding:- the process of getting rabbits to live together without fighting

boxing: an aggressive behavior in which an angry rabbit sits up on his back feet while quickly working his front feet in a scratching/"boxing" motion

bruxing: also known as tooth purring, it is the grinding of teeth to express contentment, similar to a cat purring

bunny-proof: the act of making an area safe for a rabbit by removing, covering, or creating a barrier to the unsafe objects or places

cage protectiveness: a behavior in which a rabbit will attack anyone who tries to reach or come inside his cage

cecotropes: rabbits eat all of their food twice; when it has gone through them only once, it comes out as soft, smelly cecal pellets or cecotropes, which resemble a small, dark bunch of tiny grapes

cecal pellets: cecotropes

chinning: a form of scent marking using scent glands under the chin to mark territory

cord protector: a covering for any kind of cord that will help discourage your rabbit from chewing it

dewlap: the fold of skin under a female's chin from which she pulls fur to make a nest for her babies

E. cuniculi: protazoan parasite that can cause head tilt, blindness, paralysis, and other problems; usually brought on by stress of some kind

euthanize: medical termination of an animal's life

exotics vet: a veterinarian who has had additional training and specializes in treating small animals including rabbits

Flemish Giant: a very large breed of rabbit

flop: a way that rabbits throw themselves over on their sides, signifying utter relaxation and happiness

foster: taking an animal into your home and caring for him until he gets adopted

free-run bunny: a rabbit who does not live in a cage or pen

Havana: a small breed of rabbit that is black in color

hidey box: a cardboard or wooden box for rabbits to take naps and play in

Hotot: a breed of rabbit who looks like he has heavy eyeliner around his eyes

House Rabbit Society (HRS): a international organization that promotes the proper care and housing of pet rabbits and their welfare

hutch: a rabbit abode usually associated with backyard rabbits and breeders

lagomorph: the zoological order to which all rabbits and hares belong

lap rabbit: the very rare bunny who will sit quietly with you to be petted

litter box: a container made for cats that is used to hold your rabbit's hay and for him to pee and poop in

litter-box train: the act of teaching your rabbit to use his litter box to pee and poop

lop-eared rabbit: a breed of rabbit whose ears hang down instead of pointing upward

malocclusion: a dental condition where the teeth do not meet properly, causing them to grow out of control because they do not naturally grind themselves down

molt: a seasonal shedding of fur that typically occurs three or four times a year

mounting: getting on top of another rabbit and simulating sex to express dominance

myxomatosis or myxo: a fatal blood-born disease spread by mosquitoes, ticks, and fleas that have bitten another previously infected rabbit

New Zealand: a large white or black breed

nose bonks: when a bunny nudges you with his nose

Palomino: a medium-size rabbit breed that is usually light tan in color

pancaking: when a very relaxed rabbit sprawls out with his legs extended and gets very flat, denoting comfort and happiness

prey animal: animals that are sought out by predators as food

predator: animals that hunt and kill other animals for food

rex: a breed of rabbit known for his extra soft fur and gaining weight quickly

run time: the time that your rabbit gets out of his pen or abode for exercise

socialize: the act of getting your rabbit used to social situations to make him a better companion and pet

spay/neuter: a surgical procedure to sterilize your rabbit (spay for females and neuter for males)

spokesbunny: a rabbit who goes to educational events to teach the public about house rabbits

tooth purring: the grinding together of the teeth that creates a soft grinding sound, meaning that your rabbit is contented (also called bruxing)

urine scald: when caustic urine comes in contact with a rabbit's fur and skin, it creates a type of "diaper rash" that breaks them down

wellness check: having an exotics vet examine your rabbit when he is healthy to provide an important baseline of his health for use in any future health emergency

X-pen: pet exercise pen made from thin metal bars that can contain your rabbit and keep him safe

Index

Disclaimer

All the suggestions and advice I give in this book have been learned from my own experiences with rabbits over the years, supplemented by my educational studies. Be advised that my recommendations are not a warranty or guarantee of any kind and that none is implied.

I promote the House Rabbit Society as a worthy organization for your support, but they have not given permission or authority for me to speak on their behalf. The House Rabbit Society has not reviewed this book nor approved its contents.

The procedures described in this book are my own personal methods. I wrote this book to share my tips and solutions for common rabbit issues, but how they are applied is your personal responsibility. Different methods may be used by other rabbit experts.

This book and its contents are no substitute for the advice and care of your exotics veterinarian (rabbit specialist). Do not change or replace any part of your rabbit's diet, care, and/or housing without first consulting with your rabbit's vet on the subject. He/she should be the one to ultimately tell you whether or not you can change or replace foods, care, and/or housing arrangements for your pet rabbit.

Made in the USA
Columbia, SC
04 June 2019